RUSSIAN FICTION
and SOVIET IDEOLOGY

RUSSIAN FICTION

and SOVIET IDEOLOGY

INTRODUCTION TO

Fedin, Leonov, and Sholokhov

By ERNEST J. SIMMONS

MORNINGSIDE HEIGHTS, NEW YORK

COLUMBIA UNIVERSITY PRESS 1958

To My Columbia Students

Prefatory Note

Without forcing comparison too far, it may be said that the novelists Konstantin Fedin, Leonid Leonov, and Mikhail Sholokhov are respectively the Steinbeck, Faulkner, and Hemingway of the Soviet Union. In their relative reputations in their own country and in the strikingly contrasting artistic flavor of their works, they bear a curious resemblance to the American authors. But the comparison should go no further. In the content of their fiction the Soviet writers are utterly different from the Americans.

As the foremost living Soviet novelists, Fedin, Leonov, and Sholokhov have been widely publicized in the Soviet Union. The present study is an effort to introduce these three authors in greater detail than has previously been accorded them in English. The concentration is on their development as Soviet writers of fiction, which compels a constant reference to political, social, and ideological factors that would otherwise be regarded as impedimenta in the exercise of literary criticism. With minor exceptions, the non-fiction works of these writers are not considered here.

Though most of the novels of Leonov and Sholokhov were translated into English some years ago, a deliberate effort is made in this study to convey, in the course of analysis and criticism, the substance of the fiction of all three authors in the belief that these works are not generally known to the English-speaking world. Further, a knowledge of the substance is peculiarly essential to an understanding of the various ideological shifts of the authors.

Quotations are made from English translations whenever available, but they have been checked against the originals and in a few cases altered when alteration seemed advisable. Acknowledgment for permission to quote is due A. A. Wyn Inc. (formerly L. B. Fischer) for Norbert Guterman's translation of *Road to the Ocean,* to Harcourt, Brace and Company for Alec Brown's translation of *Skutarevsky,* to Alfred A. Knopf for Stephen Garry's translations of *The Silent Don* and *Seeds of Tomorrow* (*Virgin Soil Upturned*), and to Dial Press for the translation by Ivor Montagu and Sergei Nolbandov of *Sot.* The spellings of Russian names in the English translations are retained, which accounts for some variations in transliteration. A list of the works discussed, their Russian titles and dates of publication, and available English translations may be found at the end of the study.

The author wishes to acknowledge with gratitude the help and inspiration which have come from his Columbia seminar students who, under his direction, have studied various special aspects of the works of these and other Soviet writers. Particularly helpful have been the following unpublished Master's theses deposited in the Columbia University libraries: Charles B. McLane, "Sholokhov and the Soviet Critics (1925–1947)," 1948; Alexander J. Rolick, "Fedin and Soviet Criticism (1919–1926)," 1950; David H. Stewart, "Sholokhov and the Soviet Critics Since 1947," 1954; Nathan Rosen, "Leonid Leonov: the Reforging of a Fellow-Traveler (1922–1935)," 1956. To Miss Elizabeth Moss of Columbia University Press I am indebted for a number of editorial suggestions.

Columbia University   E. J. S.
in the City of New York
October, 1957

Contents

RUSSIAN FICTION
and SOVIET IDEOLOGY

Introduction

In nineteenth-century Russia, literature was the conscience of the nation; in the Soviet Union literature seems to have become the guilty conscience. The outpouring of fiction, poetry, and drama over the last forty years stands as the record, faithful or unfaithful, of the incredible achievements of men and women subjected to a process of prolonged and violent social change, but the vast tragedy of their lives has been muted by an optimism officially decreed as the prevailing atmosphere of literary creation. Perhaps for the first time in the history of literature art has utterly repudiated the subjective and the sensual and minimized the element of enjoyment, and the artist has been forced to kill within himself the desire to convey a personal vision of humanity in his work. The primary purpose of literature in the Soviet Union is to instruct, and the obligation of the writer is to employ his medium to instruct in conformity with the spirit and letter of the latest ideological position of the Communist Party. Thus literature and politics become identical in a controlled state.

As a great elemental human experience the 1917 Revolution released the minds and emotions of writers and turned them to a fresh dedication of their creative powers, to an emancipation of the spirit of man from the confining influences of the past. Even the leaders of the Party at that time, largely conservative in literature and still filled with nineteenth-century revolutionary enthusiasm for the author's right to express himself freely, hoped that writers would treat the new life in old forms but in a context of values inspired by devotion to Marxian socialism. And for a few short years after 1917 writers experienced the freedom and creative *élan* of the only revolutionary period in Soviet literature. It was a period of literary excitement, of many contending movements with their strident manifestoes, of blatant nonsense and brilliant theorizing. And the literature produced, the poetry in particular, reflected with uncommon vigor the determination of writers to preserve their individual values in a world in revolt.

No precise date marks the end of this early revolutionary period of Soviet literature. The demands of Marxian dogma are sometimes credited with initiating the erosion. But Marxism had very little to do with it. The Communist Party realized soon after 1917 that creative literature, properly directed and controlled, could be employed as an extremely important propaganda weapon. So step by step, as the power of the Party grew stronger, it progressively deprived writers of their freedom of expression, until by 1934, with the formation of the single Union of Soviet Writers under Party auspices and direction, the Party's control of literature became absolute.

Since then the Party, in the case of a calling traditionally regarded as one of the most individualistic, has been denying authors the right to create as they saw fit while trying to convince them that they have this freedom. For the Party is aware that you cannot regiment creative artists like soldiers and achieve satisfactory results; yet it would like to achieve such results. Accordingly, the Party has been practicing on the literary profession an elaborate deception which takes many forms. All the devices of persuasion and propaganda have been employed to win writers to the cause of Communism on the logical assumption that what they create out of the depths of their faith will both conform to the official ideology and take on the enduring qualities of genuine art.

Further, the Party has organized the literary profession on a comprehensive national scale, surrounded it with a lofty social status, and provided generously for the material wants of the successful and the conforming. A complex and subtle system of pressures—Party, non-Party, social, organizational, and material—has been devised to inspire beginners and to whip recalcitrant writers back into the happiness of submission to the Party line. Censorship, government regulation of all the economic means of publication, and disciplined Communist control of writers' organizations, review sheets, and the editorial boards of literary journals and publishing houses further limit the possibility that any aberrant manuscript might find its way into print. And if one does, by some mistake or other, the terrible power of public denunciation in the Party press may well end the writer's career. In times of internal crises and Party purges even a worse fate may be visited upon a nonconforming author; this has been openly confirmed by the recently decreed pious "rehabilitations" of writers who have been executed or died in prisons or labor camps. The propagandized substance of belles-lettres at any given time, whether it be the five-year plans, industrialization, agricultural collectivization, Stakhanovism, or the condemned cult of personality, is of course never represented as a mandate to the writers from the Party, but as something which they have elected to write about in response to a felt need of the masses of readers. Finally, the Party has thrust upon all writers the art credo of socialist realism, which requires an author to present reality not as he sees it but as he understands it; and he is expected to understand it in terms of *partiinost'*, that is, the way the Party understands it.

What kind of literature is produced under these extraordinary circumstances among a people who in the past demonstrated a remarkable national genius in the creative arts of fiction and verse? The bulk of Soviet literature, especially the fiction, takes on the aspects of mass art, though

the increment of that art is feeble and the primary motivation—ideological, practical, and moral instruction—is different
from that of any mass art literature of the West. The unfailing ingredients are a plot that involves some form of labor
competition or struggle between the good of Soviet forces and
the evils of bourgeois survivals, a two-dimensional superman
or superwoman as hero or heroine, and the local Party secretary as the *deus ex machina* who sets all things right at the
end. And the inevitable moral is: "The Communist Party
knows best." Love, when it is allowed to rear its Soviet head,
is nearly always subordinated to getting on with the job or
to the dominant claims of the collective. Love, curiously, seems
to be an irrelevant aspect of reality, and it manifests itself
at odd moments amidst eager discussions about crop rota-
tion or the peculiar virtues of a Bessemer converter in steel
processing. In fact, so swiftly do things change in the Soviet
Union that sex in fiction has already moved from the Renais-
sance bawdry of early revolutionary literature to the pronounced conservatism of the present Victorian age in Soviet
fiction. One wonders what Pushkin, Lermontov, Tolstoy, Dostoevsky, Turgenev, and Chekhov would think of this wooden-
soldier parade of books from the Soviet press. Perhaps the
only feasible answer is in terms of the statistics: the most
celebrated works of these great writers of the nineteenth century are more popular in the Soviet Union than the works of
contemporary authors.

Literary criticism might have helped to neutralize if not prevent this debacle, for in the freer twenties brilliant movements
in criticism developed, of which one (Formalism) anticipated our own New Criticism in some respects. A scientism
characterized many of these critics, but their dogmas were
aesthetic and not political. Even the best of the early Marxian
critics could see in the world of art a vision of humanity not
dominated by the dialectic and attributes of artistic form not
related to the superstructure. However, the literary taste that

might have been cultivated under these auspices was soon sacrificed to political necessity. Soviet criticism is now as much an arm of the Party as is literature itself. The function of the critic is not to maintain standards, to deepen sensibility, or to invoke a climate stimulating to creative writing, but simply to evaluate a work in terms of its ideological conformity. Thus both literature and the criticism of it combine in a unity of purpose designed to promote, not the aims of art, but the aims of Communism. As a consequence the Soviet Union, in the forty years of its existence, has not produced a significant national literature. Though created by writers of peasant, proletarian, or new intelligentsia derivation and though peculiarly Soviet in content, its literary product has no claims to inclusion in the treasury of world art. This failure among so talented a people must be charged solely to the determination of the Communist Party to fetter the free creative spirit of the literary artist and bend it to its own will.

One may anticipate condemnation of this view by Soviet critics, who never weary of insisting that literature in a state striving to achieve Communism must serve the needs of the state and especially of its vanguard the Party. They will even insist that the people demand such a literature. But this has nothing to do with creative art or the free functioning of the artist, who can serve no purpose other than that of art.

What a challenging world for the creative writer was the post-1917 scene in Russia! Two centuries of struggle for freedom had ended in a tremendous explosion that shook every extremity of the vast country. Liberty, equality, and fraternity were on the lips of all. Even sleepy peasant Ivan had to get down off the stove and participate in the struggle. In the bloody violence of revolution and civil war and in the tragic turmoil of class struggle, events seemed stranger than fiction. And it was precisely fiction that eventually became the darling of the writers in their efforts to grasp the significance of the shattering social changes in Russian life. With the revolution-

ary fervor for innovation, there was a widespread demand for
new literary forms in which to cast the new social content of
fiction. Some interesting experiments were tried, but the
Party critics, who confused form with "bourgeois" formalism
and insisted upon lowering the level of literature to place it
within the comprehension of the masses, soon put an end to
such experimentation. It is thus a curious fact that the favorite
literary form in "revolutionary" Soviet Russia has become the
novel, the supreme art form of the nineteenth-century middle
class, and one about which some literary critics in capitalistic
countries today are beginning to wonder, perhaps prematurely,
whether it has not outlived its usefulness.

Indeed, the best of Soviet literature, which must be distinguished from the bulk of the production already mentioned,
may properly be considered an extension, in influence, in spirit,
and in form, of the great Russian novels of the nineteenth century.

Those few writers who have succeeded in contributing important artistic works have done so in spite of the Party but
not necessarily in final opposition to it. Often Communism
has been the central problem of their spiritual and creative
life, and the struggle between the will to believe and their
doubt and disillusion has been a powerful factor in the artistic
process of creation. But unlike well-known thinkers and writers
in the West who were at one time drawn to the Communist
dream, such as Gide, Malraux, Sartre, Koestler, and Silone,
they had no real freedom of choice, no ultimate escape. They
were part of a society to which some measure of submission
eventually became essential if they were to go on writing. If
out of sincere conviction they joined the Party, as a few of
them did, they were confronted with the tormenting difficulty
of how to preserve the integrity of their art while serving an
exacting ideology alien to the freedom of artistic expression.
In the spirit of the libertarian tradition of nineteenth-century
Russian writers, these exceptional Soviet authors have provided

the element of dissent, as far as that was possible, from the distortions and flagrant interference of the Party in literature. Sometimes they have won small concessions, but more often they have been brutally sacrificed to the demands for rigid conformity. A few have survived, perhaps because of their superior talents and their national and even international fame, but in the end they too, either because of weariness after years of struggle or because they have come to believe in the system under which they live, have drifted into conformity with obvious deleterious effects on their art.

In fiction, Tolstoy and Dostoevsky were the major influences on these writers but Gogol, Chekhov, and to some extent the ornamentalists in prose among the Symbolists at the end of the century played a part. Their contemplation of the present was caught up in the web of memory of a past which they had renounced but which still remained a source of enduring values and magnificent lost causes. In fact, the human problem that concerned them most profoundly, the central one in Soviet life for years, was the tragic struggle between the old and the new in the greatest social upheaval the world has ever known. In their fiction every phase and nuance of this cruel dilemma is psychologically analyzed in terms of the desperate choices that confronted men and women compelled to turn their backs on a past life which they often loved and to adjust to a new existence which seemed incomprehensible and filled with dangers. Some of these novels perhaps gained in realism and emotional impact from the fact that their authors were also undergoing the same agony of adjustment or alienation as their characters.

These are the authors who have contributed a modicum of artistic dignity to Soviet literature, and perhaps the best of them in fiction are Konstantin Fedin, Leonid Leonov, and Mikhail Sholokhov. Their works have sold in millions of copies, which is a tribute to their artistic effectiveness rather than to their ideological conformity. For their characters are

by and large living individuals, whatever their political allegiance, and the transcripts of Soviet life in these novels reveal a faithfulness to reality which, in the particular circumstances, only literary artists of high integrity and courage
would insist upon. Risking public condemnation as "bourgeois
deviators," they persisted in delving into the depths of human beings in their novels and in reflecting on man in general.
Each has his own conception of the novel and has experi-
mented with it as an art form, but all three draw their chief
inspiration from the great Russian classics of fiction in the
nineteenth century. And the dominating theme of their art is
the tragedy of those living in a world of sudden change where
the hard choices between the old and the new may be choices
between life and death.

Konstantin Alexandrovich Fedin, 1892-

Konstantin Fedin

In a little piece, "Chalk on an Overcoat," Fedin wrote that, like Gogol and Dostoevsky, "I am accustomed to believe that an artist should not only be able to arouse love, but must himself love." This is an unusual credo for a Soviet novelist; it is more suitable perhaps to Christian theology than to Marxism. For much of Soviet literature is dedicated to chronicling the endless struggle between socialist "good" and bourgeois "evil," in which human love is an incidental variable in a litany of hate for the "enemies of the people." Fedin's total experience with life, in which a sympathetic understanding of the Russian past and the European present has played a significant role, has neutralized the harsh encroachments of Soviet ideology. His fiction is a record of deep concern for contemporary man, of a search for truth in a world of anguished choices and sharp contradictions. His novels are saturated with thought, and unlike most Soviet writers who exude an atmosphere of official optimism, Fedin seems to have a keen awareness that the individual human condition is tragic, that the essence of it is loneliness and the end of it is death.

THE WASTELAND OF THE RUSSIAN PAST. Fedin is the oldest of the three novelists considered in this book. He was born in the Volga town of Saratov in 1892, and this fact has no doubt conditioned the quality of his mind and his artistic development which has departed considerably from the Soviet pattern. He was twenty-five when the 1917 Revolution came, and his literary inspiration and tastes had already been formed by his reading of the great Russian classics of the nineteenth century. A rather unhappy childhood in a lower-middle-class family, rebellious escapes from home, and education in the Moscow Commercial Institute were all unpleasant memories relieved only by youthful literary ambitions triumphantly capped by his first fugitive publication ("Trifles") in a Petersburg magazine in 1913.

In 1914 the First World War caught Fedin in Germany, where he had gone to perfect his knowledge of the language. Though he was interned as an enemy alien in Saxony and Silesia, he appears to have wandered over much of the country and to have observed with a penetrating eye the manners, customs, and mentality of the Germans. The impressions he stored up entered importantly into the substance of his first published novel, *Cities and Years.* Obliged to support himself, he worked at various jobs, such as playing the violin at peasant dances, giving lessons in Russian, singing in a chorus, acting in a theater; and he even took up painting. Nor did he neglect his writing at this time; he completed the manuscript of a novel which he later destroyed. Dostoevsky and Strindberg, and especially the German Expressionists, he admits, influenced him then. The tide of revolt that arose in Germany toward the end of the conflict stirred a favorable response in Fedin who sympathized with the antiwar protests of young adherents of the Spartacus movement. In fact, a latent pacifism, which eventually found expression in Fedin's fiction dates from this experience.

Meanwhile the Revolution in Russia had taken place and Fedin obtained a position as a translator in the first Soviet embassy in Berlin. But German officials, aware of his status as an internee, insisted on including him in a prisoner-of-war exchange. So in the fall of 1918 he arrived in Moscow after four years' absence and found a world he had never known, a world of revolutionary enthusiasm and changed values where the past was painfully dying and the future was unpredictable.

Like many young Russian intellectuals whose tender roots were in the past and whose soaring hopes were in the future, Fedin listened eagerly to the music of revolution during those chaotic days of 1918–19. A glorious new dawn for Russia seemed imminent. The fires of revolt would consume the social and political dross of the past, leaving behind the pure gold of Russian achievements, and the men of the present would build upon these a life of new spiritual and cultural values. At first Fedin plunged into the building of this new life with zeal. After some months of near-starvation in a position at the Commissariat of Education in Moscow, he went to the town of Syzran on the Volga. There he joined the Communist Party and undertook a staggering load of work. He edited the local newspaper, founded a literary journal, and served as a lecturer, teacher, agitator, and secretary of the executive committee of the town soviet. At the height of the Yudenich offensive in 1919, he was mobilized into the Red Army and sent to Petrograd. But most of his time in the army was spent in the political section as assistant to the editor of a military newspaper.

Here vivid experiences merged with journalism and Fedin wrote for the newspapers on a wide variety of themes and in a spirit sympathetic to the new regime. By the end of the civil war in 1921, he was in Leningrad. He wrote of this period in *Gorky Amongst Us* (1944): "I was absolutely alone in this immense city, tomorrow's capital, which did not suspect that another young man had appeared on her avenues with the dream of writing, with the hope of some sort of conquest or, perhaps, glory." In fact, he had already sent a story to the great Gorky, rather stuffily asking him for advice. It was the beginning of a long and valuable literary friendship for Fedin. Through Gorky he made the acquaintance, in 1921, of the Serapion Brothers, a madcap group of brilliant young Leningrad writers who were infected with the new revolutionary enthusiasm which, however, they translated into an artistic faith free from any Bolshevik banality. Fedin joined the Serapion Brothers, so named in honor of the Hermit Serapion in one of E. T. A. Hoffmann's tales. In their published manifesto, the Serapions demanded freedom from all regimentation, condemned political unanimity, sought literary inspiration in Russian and Western classics of the past, and professed belief in the one doctrine that "art is real and lives its own special life, independently of the source of its material." Under the influence of this brotherhood of bright spirits Fedin's muse flourished, and it is perhaps significant that at the same time (1921) he abandoned the Communist Party.

Certainly Fedin's first volume of short stories, *The Wasteland* (1923), is an artistic effort that draws its material almost entirely from the past. Thrilling contemporary events are studiously neglected and the Bolshevik emphasis on social significance is avoided. In these tales, Fedin writes to Gorky, his "feeling was attracted to the simple man, to the poor man living from day to day, whose labor is unnoticed—to the blameless drudge dragging the heavy cart of history from epoch to epoch." * Years later, looking back rather deprecatingly on the time when he wrote these stories, he called it his period of "literary measles." The "disease," however, strangely recurs in his later works.

The seven stories in the collection, written between 1919 and 1922, represent an escape into the "wasteland" of the Russian past, into a world of lonely, little people whose patient sufferings stir the compassion of the author. There are echoes of Gogol, Dostoevsky, Chekhov, and even of Bunin and Remizov in the selection of motifs, in descriptive passages, and in the psychological treatment of character—echoes which mingle and which confuse the reader, although the total effort bears the stamp of Fedin's originality.

* Quoted in B. Brainina, *Konstantin Fedin* (Moscow, 1951), p. 51.

"Anna Timofevna," the longest and most elaborately designed of the stories, is the study of a self-sacrificing, self-
effacing woman whose yearning to love and be loved is frustrated by a harsh provincial environment and the misfortunes
of life that fall to her lot. Anna's humiliations and beatings by
her drunken husband are only intensified after the birth of her
daughter because a girl could not continue the psalm-singing
tradition in his family. And then all Anna's fragile hopes of
happy parenthood vanish with the death of her husband and
little girl. Fate throws her another bone of hope—an aging,
decrepit first lover who is also a drunkard. His timid response
to her need for affection is gratefully rewarded by Anna's
humiliating efforts to support him and his wayward son by
peddling in the market place. Anna is a passive, meek, Dostoevskian character who earns her happiness through suffering, and the clearest symbol of her existence is the tormented
drudge of a horse in the story, which recalls vividly the symbolism of the horribly beaten horse in Raskolnikov's dream in
Crime and Punishment. But the latter part of the tale, in
which Anna's crushing burden is relieved by fugitive moments
of autumnal happiness, is cast in a simple Chekhovian vein,
especially the final scene where the dying Anna shyly, hesi-
tatingly asks her good-for-nothing second husband: "My dear
. . . how will you . . . without me?"

Close to "Anna Timofevna" in its realistic style, but entirely
different in motif, is "A Tale of One Morning." Fedin introduces his hero Savel Semenovich, a seemingly kind, gentle
man, by emphasizing his passion for birds. "He listened when
the birds sang and smiled with his mouth and perhaps with
his eyes, but this was never apparent." The religious Savel
never fails to thank God in his prayers for endowing him with
this love for birds. Then suddenly we are apprised of the fact
that this kindly lover of birds is by profession an expert hangman. As a convict long ago he had bought his freedom by
volunteering to execute a fellow prisoner. Fedin concludes

the story with a harrowing description of a hanging and the effect it produces on the tsar's officials and the anxious spectators. After his business with the noose is over, Savel pauses at the edge of the field to listen to the song of a titmouse. Fedin contrasts the moral ugliness of the spiritually deformed Savel with the beauties of nature which titillate his dormant soul: "Ah the autumn," thinks Savel, "when the maples suck up the gold from the earth and infuse it into the veins of their leaves; autumn, when the silk of the spider's web catches the sad rays of the sun; autumn, when the earth is grateful and weary, like a mistress—this is the autumn to be in the woods." Having lost all feeling for human beings, this hangman seeks compensation in a love of nature and birds, and in prayer. Fedin poses a difficult psychological problem here but fails to probe it deeply enough.

With one exception, the rest of the tales in *The Wasteland* —lesser efforts on the whole—also concentrate on pre-revolutionary themes in which love, self-denial, or self-sacrifice serve either to dignify or to debase the nature of the protagonist. The exception is "The Orchard" (1919), a carefully wrought story with a revolutionary setting, written before Fedin came under the influence of the Serapion Brothers. The tale opens with a lush description of the orchard in spring, when the blossoms are a riot of color and sweeten the air with their delicate fragrance. Every year at this time the refined old mistress of the manor would arrive from the city to sit for hours on the terrace silently enjoying the beauty and fragrance of the orchard in bloom. Her son would stroll through the orchard with Silanti, the uncommunicative peasant caretaker, and try to prod information from him about the details of his work. Silanti loved every tree in the orchard; he had brought them up from saplings, tending them like children.

But this spring the master and mistress fail to arrive. Instead the Revolution has come bringing with it a Soviet schoolteacher and a crowd of noisy children who occupy the manor house. A vague foreboding creeps into the uncomprehending mind of Silanti. The children swarm through the orchard, breaking the branches of an apple tree, and Silanti wrathfully drives them out only to be rebuked by the teacher. When the whole colony of children go to town for a day, Silanti sets the house on fire. Sitting on the ground near by, embracing his knees with his veiny arms, he stolidly gazes into the consuming flames.

Silanti is a casualty of the Revolution, of the struggle between the old and the new. This peaceful house and orchard were his whole existence and when he believed them lost, like Akaki Akakievich in Gogol's tale "The Overcoat," whose precious coat was lost, life had no further meaning for him. There is a psychological difference, of course, in Silanti's motive in destroying what he loved rather than have others irreverently use it, whereas Gogol's hero had lost what he loved through no fault of his own. In the eyes of Soviet critics that difference placed Silanti among the "enemies of the people," made him a "potential kulak," and placed his creator among the petty-bourgeois writers.

Not much of Fedin's personal philosophy or the future development of his artistic concentration can be discerned in this first published collection of stories. He obviously sympathizes with the lonely, off-center people he portrays, with Anna, Savel, and Silanti; his is a compassion born of their sufferings and failures in life. But style and method rather than content seem to be the main concern of the author. Here the influence of the Serapion Brothers, with their notion—borrowed from the Formalist critics—that a literary work is merely the sum of its stylistic devices, is everywhere apparent. Except for the pruned, austere language of the earlier "The Orchard," the other stories in *The Wasteland* reveal varied patterns of conscious experimentation in language

—rhythmic sentences, inversions, extreme figures of speech, and poetic devices. At times, as in "Anna Timofevna" and at the end of "A Tale of One Morning," the language reaches a point of emotional lyricism not far removed from the special quality of verse.

The Wasteland did not attract much favorable attention to Fedin at the outset of his career. Communist Party-minded critics expressed amazement that a writer, in a period of great historic upheaval, should isolate himself from the main stream of contemporary social activity and dwell upon the individualistic experiences of men and women of the past who seemed outside of history. But this appears to have been a conscious choice on Fedin's part at a time when it was possible in the Soviet Union for writers to make such choices. Instead of utilizing the class struggle and social existence of the moment he fell back on what he knew best—the inspiration and themes of the great prerevolutionary writers. What is new in these first efforts is experimentation in form and language. To be sure, he might have been indicating an artistic preference as well as a revulsion to his own initial revolutionary experiences and the strident demands of Soviet critics for fiction that would reflect the Party version of the reality of the present. And throughout the remainder of Fedin's career one can detect elements of this nostalgia for the past however much he has submitted to the categorical imperatives of the Party. Thus, years later, as though he felt it necessary to explain this "deviation" of his youth, Fedin wrote to a correspondent: "The thematic substance of *The Wasteland* ought not to surprise you. The little man, the hero of *The Wasteland,* was the subject of my predilections over a long series of years. . . . This was the fruit of my life in the old literature, of my tight, hermetically sealed school, of my secret dreams. I had to be *reborn* or else the fruit of death in me would have poisoned me. *Cities and Years* is a direct answer to your perplexity. . . . But before that time, I was freed from the past with the appearance of *The Wasteland*." *

THE TRAGEDY OF INDIVIDUALISM. *Cities and Years* is Fedin's first major effort in fiction. In it he partly escapes from the wasteland of the past and grapples with the reality of the Russian revolutionary present. Its appearance in 1924 was a significant event, for it heralded the beginning of the first school of Soviet realistic fiction which produced some interesting novels before the controls of the Communist Party stifled what creative freedom its authors possessed. As his first published novel *Cities and Years* is a very ambitious attempt and stands as a striking contrast to the limited circumference which Fedin had revealed in his writing up to this point. Though the main theme is the tragedy of individualism in an epoch of revolution, it is projected against an enveloping background of "cities and years," of time and space, of war and social revolt. The whole is penetrated by the author's personal philosophy born of the anguish of disillusioned hopes in a world of violence.

In fact, the principal failing of the novel—though a few critics consider it a virtue—is the subordination of characters and plot to this extensive background of social, political, and cultural material. Fedin develops an elaborate symphonic structure of war and revolution in Germany and Russia between 1914 and 1922. The main theme, the life of the hero, is muted again and again for the sake of subsidiary but connected motifs of "cities and years," genre pictures during specific years of crisis in Petrograd, Moscow, and Semidol in Russia, and in Nuremberg, Erlangen, and Bischofsberg in Germany. The pattern is mixed chronologically, apparently for heightened dramatic effect, and the scene shifts back and

* Quoted from a manuscript letter in B. Brainina, *Konstantin Fedin,* pp. 47–48.

forth from Russia to Germany. Thus the novel opens in 1922 in Petrograd with the death of the hero, moves back to 1919 in the next chapter, to 1914 in Germany in the third chapter, and then moves forward year by year until it reaches 1922 again in the last chapter.

What Fedin is obviously trying to do here is to show, within a limited time sequence, the contrasting impacts of war and revolution on the national characteristics of Germans and Russians. Drawing upon his own experiences in Germany from 1914 to 1918, he describes the external appearances of these small German cities and how they harmonize with the psychology of the people. The prewar temper is one of complacency. The people are in love with trifles because the trifles are theirs. The smooth machinery of dull burgher life is lubricated by the oil of patriotism which is plentifully supplied, Fedin suggests, by the ruling class. One may justly quarrel with this picture of provincial bourgeois Philistinism, banality, and narrow-mindedness as representative of prewar Germany. The satirical and didactic intent of the picture is as patent as its half-truths, but the picture is nevertheless brilliantly drawn.

By contrast the effects of the war on this German population are depicted with still greater power and convincingness. The horrors of war are brought out in a series of telling incidents, such as the hiding of cripples from their relatives, the treatment of conscientious objectors, and the hospital scene of the mutilated veteran, sightless and deaf, pleading repeatedly for his wife who stood over him but whom he could neither see nor hear. Inspired by such incidents, Fedin generalizes quite subjectively on the theme of war. In passages that are sometimes lyrical or ironic or witheringly satiric, he attacks the insanity of war, the hypocrisy of those who glorify it, its purposelessness and its suppression of the human personality; or with romantic pathos he expresses his compassion for the heroic victims of war who had been sacrificed for its deceitful ideals. In such passages he grasps the tragedy of a whole epoch in a style that is often beautifully expressive in a rhetorical sense.

The images of these German cities, where war and hatred for the enemy are taught as ends in themselves, are many-faceted. Fedin brings out the opposition of certain elements of the Social Democrats to the war and in scenes of thrilling action he describes how this opposition finally erupts in the organization of a Soviet of Workers' and Soldiers' Deputies in provincial Bischofsberg. The German cities are shown in their variation and alteration from one year to another under the impact of changing political and social experiences. Such antagonisms are hardly reflected in the Russian cities which Fedin describes. To be sure, the war was over by the time the Russian cities began to play a part in the novel, and Fedin leads us to suppose that the Revolution had already enveloped the entire city life. However, political and social opposition in the Soviet Union in 1919 and 1920 was rife, and Fedin's failure to reflect it in his images of the Russian cities is an obvious evasion and a realistic and aesthetic fault in the neatly balanced structure of his novel.

In an article for a 1952 edition of *Cities and Years* Fedin admitted that he might wish to alter certain aspects of the characters if he were to rewrite the novel. But he insisted that his characterizations of the German cities and people would remain the same, especially after his experiences with the Nazi invasion of Russia during the Second World War. Indeed there is a temptation to regard these treatments of the German cities, which form so large a part of the novel, as separate psychological studies in themselves. This would be a mistake, however, for these studies and the main characters of the novel are closely connected. The events influencing the cities and the general psychology of the populace provide a key to an understanding of the actions and individual psychology of the characters. This is especially true of Andrei Startsov, the hero of *Cities and Years,* whose stay in Germany helped to form his ideas and to define the mission of his life.

Andrei Startsov is a young Russian who comes to Germany to study just before the outbreak of the First World War. He is a sensitive intellectual, gentle, idealistic, a hater of violence, and an "internationalist" in the sense that he passionately believes that above all nations is humanity. A deep admiration for Western European art and culture is the bond that first unites him with the young German artist Kurt Wahn. Andrei's devotion and deference to Kurt are difficult to understand because their friendship is one asserted by the author rather than one that develops through progressive intercourse.

Vulgar chauvinistic demonstrations in Erlangen at the beginning of the war and later manifestations of war hysteria, which are described in a mingled comic and serious vein by Fedin, reveal to Andrei characteristic traits of the Germans which he had not suspected previously. And the moral shuffling of Social Democrat friends in the face of the patriotic German upsurge grates on his cosmopolitan sensibilities. He begins to doubt the efficacy of the European culture he revered and he falls back on his friend Kurt for a solution of his perplexity. But now Kurt, either because of fear at being seen any longer with an "enemy" or because of his own patriotic feelings, crassly rejects and avoids Andrei, who is finally interned in Bischofsberg as a civilian prisoner of war.

Watched by the police and daily exposed to sentiments of hatred and violence engendered by the war among the populace of this provincial German town, Andrei is increasingly disillusioned with European humanism and his inner craving for the solution of peace forces him more and more to contemplate the desirability of political rebellion against the architects of war. But in the last analysis he shrinks from the path of blood. In his loneliness he falls in love with Mari Urbach, or perhaps it might be more correct to say that she falls in love with him, since the essence of Andrei's nature is passivity. Mari, the impetuous, restless daughter of the esteemed family of Urbachs, had recently been the fiancée of the leading citizen of Bischofsberg, Markgraf von Schönau, a fact which she conceals from Andrei. She turns to this strange Russian because he responds to a dim groping in her own mind for a focus of thought that would condemn the meaninglessness of the war. Andrei, happy at last with having found a convert, overwhelms her with conversation about his doctrines of compassion, of nonviolence, of peace.

With Mari's help and urging Andrei tries to escape across the Czech border but he is arrested and sent back. This attempt brings him in contact with Von Schönau, an officer in the German army, who already has his orders to go to the Eastern front. Von Schönau is an aristocrat of the Prussian junker type and a collector of paintings. He had bought up all of Kurt Wahn's canvases because of a conviction of Kurt's future promise; this talented young man had been reduced virtually to the position of a "kept" artist by his imperious patron who would not permit him to sell to anyone else. The apprehended Andrei, now in danger of prison or something worse, is aided by Von Schönau because Andrei recognizes a picture of Kurt on his wall and tells of his friendship with the artist.

At the end of the war Andrei returns to Russia, again at the urging of Mari, who hopes to join him there. But when the main action of the novel shifts to Russia, Fedin is forced into a schematic plot arrangement that tries the patience of coincidence. Both Kurt Wahn and Von Schönau turn up there as prisoners of war, and rather improbably all three principals are thrown together again. Ultimately Mari Urbach also makes her way to Russia, and now the influence of the cities and years of the Bolshevik Revolution completes the ideological development of these main characters and resolves their individual fates.

Andrei and Kurt renew their friendship in Moscow. The meeting brings out the sharp differences in their natures as

well as Andrei's painful striving to identify himself with the
new revolutionary outlook of Kurt. For this former German
patriot and dreamer-artist has become an enthusiastic and
active Communist in the course of his experiences in revolutionary Russia. In the long conversation at their reunion Kurt
blames himself for not having understood the import of
Andrei's love of humanity and peace for all, as he now connects these "internationalist" views with the catchwords of
early Bolshevik propaganda. The gentle Andrei, however, shyly
remarks: "Now you think otherwise. But neither then nor now
does war frighten you. Has anything really changed in you? I
remain as formerly: war is literally repulsive to me."

Kurt stoutly counters this with the typical Communist argument: there are different kinds of wars, those waged to oppress
mankind and those designed to free mankind forever. If war
is necessary to end war, there is no other path. "Blood, blood,"
he declares, "is what terrifies you. And this eternal fear that
evil begets evil. . . . How am I to achieve good if evil is all
around? Show me that it is impossible to attain good by evil
means."

Weakly Andrei replies: "I cannot prove this." Everything in
his nature cries out against the Communist doctrine that moral
ends justify unmoral means. Like many intellectuals in the
early years of the Revolution, he wanted to embrace the
utopian ideals of the movement but rejected the bloody struggle that was carried on in their name.

Pleased with Andrei's apparent submission, Kurt persuades
him to accompany him to Semidol, a remote town in eastern
Russia, to help arrange for the evacuation of prisoners of war.
During the remainder of the evening Andrei pours out all that
happened to him in Bischofsberg. At one point the memory
of Mari forces from him the wish that he would like to be back
in Germany again, and in eager, nostalgic words he tells Kurt
of his love for Mari. The puzzled Kurt drily asks: "This means
that the greatest thing in your life over these years was love."

And when Andrei agrees, his friend coolly comments: "Well, in mine it was hate."

Hatred was the reality of bitter revolutionary strife, love the idealistic emotion of misguided bourgeois intellectuals out of the past. "It is you Startsovs," declares Golosov, the cocky young head of the Semidol Party Executive Committee, "who constantly whirl about in the confusion of principles. You always want to reconcile the ideal with the real. We know that it is impossible to reconcile them. . . ." Despite Golosov's reprimand, one of Andrei's first actions in Semidol was to drift into love with a stray girl, Rita, whose image reminded him of Mari and whose caress he accepted as a kind of proxy of his distant sweetheart.

With Kurt's prompting and help, however, Andrei enters into the stream of Bolshevik activities at Semidol. He wants to be accepted by these men of action, for he feels a desperate need to be a man of the present, to still the endless debate between good and evil that goes on in his mind. Von Schönau appears as the leader of an anti-Bolshevik revolt among the Mordvinians of this region, and Andrei participates in the punitive expedition sent out to quell them. In the violent action of battle a revolutionary ardor seizes him, and after the engagement he happily confesses to Kurt that for the first time he has understood his own measure of guilt for the horrors of contemporary life: "It was a false notion that I did not bear any responsibility for the horrors which occur in the world. . . . I realize that I must take upon myself the full burden of these horrors and not avoid them by regarding the world as being guilty of them and not I. . . . I cannot live now as I have previously."

There is something almost Dostoevskian here in Andrei's desire to share the guilt of others for the crimes they have visited upon humanity. But the position of the conscience-stricken intellectual in the cause of the Revolution was essentially foreign to Andrei's emotional nature; he soon betrays that cause, as well as his friend, by stealing papers from Kurt's desk that will enable Von Schönau to escape certain death at the hands of the Bolsheviks and to make his way back to Germany. The motives for the betrayal are intensely human: Andrei is moved both by Von Schönau's plea for his life in return for the good service he had rendered Andrei out of his friendship for Kurt in Bischofsberg and by his willingness to deliver a letter to Mari back in Germany. Then, shocked by his action and longing to recapture his lost revolutionary ardor, Andrei requests to be sent to the front at the time of the Yudenich offensive on Petrograd. Instead he is given an office job at army headquarters in the city.

Various adverse circumstances now begin to impose a tragic conclusion to Andrei's life. The privations, suspicions, and inhumanity of a Petrograd in the throes of civil war undermine his will to go on living. The pregnant Rita seeks him out in the city and his compassion for her plight is only deepened by his incapacity and his poignant memories of Mari. Then one day Mari stands at the door of his room (Von Schönau had delivered Andrei's letter and she had made her way to Russia with great difficulty to rejoin her lover). The sight of the pregnant Rita and the look on her face tell Mari everything; she flees down the stairs, heedless of his despairing cries.

More than anything else, however, it is Andrei's sense of futility, his feeling that he is unwanted in this bright new world of revolutionary action, that preys on his mind. In a last despairing letter to Mari, he writes: "I remember one winter evening I came across a little dog that was scratching a closed door with its front paws. Its master was either asleep or perhaps did not want to open the door; there was a snowstorm outside. I went up to the door and saw red tracks on the trodden snow from the dog's paws. The little dog had bloodied its paws scratching the door. It could not understand that it was not wanted on this earth. But I understand this. That is, about myself. . . . All my life I tried to be in the center of things, so everything would revolve about me. But I was always washed away, thrust aside. . . . In short, I stopped scratching."

Andrei's story ends with his mad wanderings about Petrograd, tormented by the failure of his life and haunted by his lost love and the betrayal of his friend. Kurt, the relentless Bolshevik and man of hate, discovers the theft of the papers from his desk and suspects Andrei. He tracks him down and under the pretense of renewing the confidences of their old friendship he wheedles a confession from the distracted Andrei. The subsequent conclusion is to be found in Kurt's stark report to an investigating committee of the Party: "I knew that all this was the result of unfortunate circumstances in his personal life. Therefore I approached his confession with great caution. However, I had trained myself to think objectively and to act according to reasonable conclusions. . . . No doubt remained: for personal motives he saved the life of our enemy and he betrayed the cause which we all serve. As a man he had become hateful to me, as a friend—and I was his friend—he had become loathsome. I killed him."

As in the case of many of the characters in Fedin's early short stories, the influence of nineteenth-century Russian fiction is apparent in the characterization of Andrei Startsov. In his high idealism and reforming instinct accompanied by an incapacity for action, he falls into the celebrated category of the "superfluous heroes" of Turgenev and of other novelists of the Russian past. His hatred of violence, his pacifism, and his conviction of the evil-begetting power of evil echo well-known ideas of Leo Tolstoy. And Andrei's moral ambivalence, which in the end leads him into a chaos of tormenting doubts and self-condemnations, recalls the behavior of some of Dostoevsky's heroes.

However, these possible literary influences do not detract from the validity of Andrei Startsov as a rather convincing representative of those members of the intelligentsia who were the victims of the struggle between old and new in the early years of the Revolution. In one form or another it was to become a favorite theme of Fedin, as well as of Leonov and other Soviet writers. Like many of the old intelligentsia, Andrei had a deep sense of social responsibility which he translated into a humanitarian philosophy of love and service to mankind. But it is a personal and essentially a passive philosophy entirely unequal to coping with the harsh realities of the Bolshevik Revolution. Psychologically alienated from the Bolsheviks, he naively tried to adjust himself to their world in a spirit of class harmony rather than of class conflict. As an individualist, however, he could not place the collective above the free human personality any more than he could realize that for the Communists there was no longer any question of acceptance or nonacceptance of the Revolution. The debate had ended. And those who failed to understand this were not wanted. Like the little dog in his letter, Andrei must either seek a new home or die—the tragic dilemma of all those members of the intelligentsia who failed to conform. The characterization of Andrei Startsov served as a model for many similar ones to follow in Soviet literature. Unfortunately Fedin too often sacrificed this central figure to the other varied motifs of his novel, for when Andrei is off the stage interest in the story element diminishes.

Basically *Cities and Years* is not a novel of characters; the men and women in it seem rather like illustrations of varying points of view in a deliberately wrought pattern of ideological struggle. The hero achieves some measure of reality perhaps because he is obviously derived from the substance of the author himself. The secondary characters, however effectively they may serve as mouthpieces of points of view, do not gain our sympathy as living human beings. Though the Kurt Wahn of 1914, the apolitical artist who loves nature and European culture and is a devoted friend, is initially interesting, the transformation of this chauvinistic German five years later in

Russia into a hard, cold, hating Bolshevik, eager to murder his closest friend for the good of the cause, is unbelievable.

Similarly Mari Urbach has the making of a vivid personality as Fedin portrays her lively childhood and adolescence, but from the time she falls in love with the indecisive Andrei the characterization becomes schematic and psychologically unmotivated. Given her particular upper-middle-class German background, and even making allowances for Andrei's emancipating influence on her—an influence more conjectured than demonstrated—the reader is left entirely puzzled as to why this rather carefree girl should suddenly change into a young lady of extraordinary decision. Where does she get the capacity to organize a Soviet of Soldiers' Deputies in Bischofsberg? And why does she nearly become a Bolshevik and then accept the chilly refuge of a worker in a children's home in Petrograd after her love for Andrei is shattered? The reader must accept all this on faith, and the result is that after the first part of the novel Mari becomes a lifeless symbol of something that the reader has long since forgotten.

Von Schönau is likewise only a symbol, but he is more consistently drawn and more interesting than the other secondary characters. Fedin all too plainly reveals his scorn for Von Schönau as an aristocratic and often supercilious representative of German militarism in the days of the Kaiser. Von Schönau's destruction of all Kurt Wahn's paintings, which he had so assiduously collected, as a gesture of contempt for a compatriot who had turned Bolshevik, and his mean insistence upon informing Andrei, after the latter had saved his life, that he had enjoyed an aristocrat's right of the "first night," so to speak, with Mari—these actions are entirely of a piece with his character.

Various minor characters in *Cities and Years* make their swift entrances and exits as contrived representatives of classes, such as the peasant Lependin who is hanged by Von Schönau's men, and the proletarian Communist Golosov. Others are exponents of ideas or are illustrative figures in the social background, such as the German Social Democrats Meyer and Hennig, and the colorful Professor Sergei Shchepov in Petrograd. If, in general, too many of the characters in *Cities and Years* seem to live in a kind of author's laboratory where they undergo artificial growth, this is perhaps because the whole center of gravity of the novel is in the numerous descriptive, dramatic, and anecdotal digressions calculated to reveal the social tragedy of cities and of years. This approach lends innovation and originality. Though in this scheme of things the basic plot and even the characters are often lost sight of, there are compensations in these powerfully written digressions, such as the descriptions of the festive day at Erlangen, a sunny morning in Bischofsberg, the digging of the trenches in Petrograd, all of which contribute to the total effect that Fedin is aiming at.

The reaction of Soviet critics to *Cities and Years* was mixed. Nearly all praised the power, emotional intensity, and originality of the work, but they differed on the relative success of the realization of various characters and particularly on how faithfully these characters represented the ideological complexities that emerged from the events of these troubled years. Most of the critics perceived the autobiographical content of the novel and even the close resemblance of Fedin's psychological condition and world view at this time to those of the hero, Andrei Startsov. Both men were products of the prerevolutionary intelligentsia and culture which, in turn, created in both similar ideological responses to the demands of the Bolshevik Revolution. In a number of the digressions Fedin exposes his own views on war and pacifism, on art and culture, on the government and politics of Western Europe, and on the class struggle and iron discipline of Communism; and in many respects they are like the views of Andrei Startsov.

On the other hand, though Fedin reveals a sympathetic understanding of his hero's human weaknesses and political uncertainties he also wishes to make it clear that he condemns Andrei's passive failure in life at a time of exacting revolutionary demands. Speaking in the novel of Kurt's "execution" of Andrei, Fedin writes: "Kurt did for Andrei everything that a comrade, a friend, and an artist ought to have done." And again expressing his own opinion of Andrei at the end of the work, Fedin declares: "Oh, if only he had allowed himself just one blemish or had even trampled one flower! Perhaps then our pity for him would have grown to love and we would not have consigned him so painfully and so insignificantly to destruction. But up to the last moment he never completed a single action and only waited for the wind that would take him to the shore which he wanted to reach."

It is as though Fedin, in killing Andrei Startsov, were announcing the death of some outmoded aspect of his own personality. He realized that the "superfluous man" could never find a place in the Russia of Communism. However, Fedin probably appreciated the truth of a pointed observation made by one Marxist critic in analyzing the characterization of Andrei Startsov: "To diagnose your own sickness does not mean that you have been cured of it." * And Fedin's future creative path bears witness to the correctness of this observation.

THE STRUGGLE BETWEEN THE OLD AND THE NEW. The heroic and sympathetically drawn Lependin in *Cities and Years* is only a transient peasant type. Fedin now turned his attention in a serious way to the treatment of the peasant and peasant life in fiction. He drew upon his experiences in the villages of the Smolensk area, where he lived between 1923 and 1926, for a series of three tales which appeared in book form in 1927 under the title *Transvaal.* All three stories deal with peasant life, but the longest, the title story "Transvaal" (the other two are

---

* Yu. Dobranov, "Tvorcheskii put K. Fedina," *Russkii yazyk v sovetskoi shkole,* No. 5 (1930), p. 190.

"The Muzhiks" and "Morning in Viazhnoe"), is easily the best and perhaps his most successful artistic achievement in this genre.

"Transvaal" is an absorbing and psychologically profound character study of Svaaker, a Boer by origin who had been driven from Estonia by the war and takes up living in a Russian village in the Smolensk district. (The portrait of Svaaker was based on a real person whom Fedin met during his stay in this region of Russia.) Ugly in appearance, with a glass eye and false teeth, speaking a broken Russian, this foreigner is regarded as a mysterious, almost supernatural, being by the simple peasants. He has a contempt for these Russians and has the strong will and energy to exploit them. When the Revolution enters the village he is cunning enough to exploit is also, using its power to serve his own ends. Svaaker masks his ambitions and greed by an outward appearance of kindness and humility. He is ever ready to shed crocodile tears over the very injustices he contemplates or has already committed, or to assuage his victims by quotations from the Bible. Step by step he uses his superior intelligence to bring the whole economy of the village under his control and even drives out the local landowner, a remnant of the old regime, and marries his cultured daughter whose spirit he then remorsely crushes by his mingled unctuous and authoritarian behavior. The story ends on a note of triumph for Svaaker as he dreams aloud of extending his little village empire over the whole district while his broken wife listlessly agrees that he can do anything.

"Transvaal" provoked a furor among Soviet critics, many of whom saw in it an apology for the kulak in that Svaaker is portrayed as successfully improving the economy of the village by exploiting the peasants and is left unpunished at the end. A few critics, however, praised the story as a condemnation of the kulak type in the sense that Svaaker is presented as a thoroughly repulsive and morally reprehensible character. Both views seem a bit pointless, for there is no evidence that Fedin was attempting to convey an ideological position about the kulak in describing the career of a foreigner in a Russian village in the early days of the Revolution. If any social implications are to be drawn from "Transvaal," they derive from the thoroughly realistic picture of the stagnant, shiftless, and ignorant existence of the peasantry in a typical Russian village. Here Fedin is again working in the best tradition of the great nineteenth-century novelists. It is not a social but a biological emphasis that predominates in the brilliant characterization of Svaaker, and the poetic quality of the style in this story, as in the other two tales in the collection, marks an advance over the style of any of Fedin's works up to this point.

While he was working on his second novel, *The Brothers,* published in 1928, Fedin wrote to Gorky: "In a word I have become reconciled, to the end of my days, to love only the wretched and the unwanted." With some vexation Gorky stigmatized this as a failing in Fedin, an unhealthy inheritance from the past: "Nowhere," he replied, "do people suffer with such satisfaction as in Holy Rus." An element of literary legacy (particularly the influence of Dostoevsky) was indeed present, but what Gorky failed to realize was that Fedin's refined, sensitive nature was peculiarly attuned to the suffering without end which he found in his native land. And Nikita Karev, the hero of *The Brothers,* is a figure out of the past whose artistic nature is almost crushed in his efforts to adjust himself to the revolutionary present.

Once again Fedin draws upon his own biography: his childhood memories, his love of music (he studied the violin), and to some extent his German experiences. Nikita, as a child, is compelled to take violin lessons by his well-to-do and domineering Cossack father. His youthful experiences of country life in a large family, his experiences in the city of Uralsk where he studied with a Jewish violin teacher and was witness to a pogrom and the suppression of a revolutionary up-

rising in 1905, parallel to some extent the youthful experiences
of Fedin in Saratov. On the other hand, Nikita's early memories were dear to him—his loving mother, his older and
younger brothers Matvei and Rostislav, the peasant servant
Evgraf who taught him to manage horses, and the strange and
beautiful young girl Varvara, the daughter of the Sherstobitovs,
a merchant family. Later in life he often returned to these
memories in moments of emotional stress.

Music took a firm hold on the talented Nikita; as a young
man he went up to Moscow to study piano in the conservatory
and eventually turned to composing. Shortly before the outbreak of the First World War he went on to Dresden to continue his musical studies. Life in Germany brings out the
psychological complexities of Nikita's nature. In his loneliness
and struggle to express himself creatively, it soon becomes
clear that he lacks faith in his artistic destiny. He falls into
a neurotic state in which the image of death obsesses his
thought. At this critical juncture chance brings him into contact with Anna, a charming German girl whose love and in-
tuitive understanding of his artistic needs act as a catalyst on
his creative powers. Their life together is an idyl of emotional
harmony and artistic fulfillment for Nikita. After the successful
performance of his first extensive organ composition, their
mutual unspoken rapture over the miracle of art, as they stroll
hand in hand outside the church, is sensitively analyzed by
Fedin.

The fulcrum of Nikita's precariously balanced artistic nature
is removed by Anna's death, a very important event in the life
of his hero which Fedin unfortunately simply announces rather
than describes. Apparently it had taken place toward the end
of the war, for it is not until the Bolshevik Revolution has
turned into civil war that Nikita makes his way back to Russia.
On his way home to Uralsk he meets his younger brother
Rostislav who is in command of a Red detachment bent on

winning over the region to the side of the Revolution. Rostislav
at once confronts his brother with the harsh ideological problem of political allegiance. The pull of the past, its traditions,
and all his training predispose Nikita, as in the case of Andrei
Startsov in *Cities and Years*, to reject the new in favor of the
old. An individualist and an artist, he has no interest in politics,
loathes violence, and tends to retreat into his own little world,
even into his childhood memories, rather than face the realities
of the present.

In Uralsk, Nikita recaptures something of his lost musical
inspiration by escaping from the ominous life of the present
into a private world of memories, and for a time his work on
a projected symphony progresses. One of these childhood
memories is the merchant's daughter Varvara, who has now
blossomed into captivating womanhood. On one of Nikita's
trips home from Dresden she had revealed her love for him,
but the face of Anna stood between them. Now Varvara appears again, determined to remain in Uralsk because Nikita is
there, although all her family has left upon receipt of the
news that the Reds are approaching the town.

The characterization of Varvara is plainly inspired by the
"infernal women" of Dostoevsky, such as Nastasia Filippovna
in *The Idiot*. Varvara's haunting, exotic beauty masks a cruel,
perverse nature which compulsively seeks expression in wild,
dramatic scenes of personal self-abasement alternating with
willful assertions of her dominance over men. She has reduced
the Smerdiakov-like Vitka, a family servitor, to a submissive
slave to her every whim while tantalizing him with the forbidden fruit after which he vainly languishes. On the other
hand, she bows down before Nikita in the unassailable conviction that her destiny must be joined with his. The evil in
Dostoevsky's infernal women is somehow sublimated by a
spiritual striving, however misdirected or unrealized, for truth,
goodness, or moral betterment, and it is this that makes them

believable as human beings. But the evil in Varvara is unrelieved by any attribute of goodness and hence she never seems quite real.

The dreamworld of Nikita is finally disrupted by the Red attack on Uralsk and despite his assumed disinterest in the struggle and declared intention of remaining under any circumstances, he flees with his family and the rest of the Whites. Harsh privations on the road in winter as a refugee, the callous treatment accorded him by the Whites, and news of the death of Rostislav in combat, all contrive at last to thrust upon his consciousness a realization of the immanent nature of the class struggle. Here, he is the lonely, wretched, unwanted individualist whose little world of his own making has dissolved in the chaos of contending forces of which he is not even a part. It is significant that in the end he turns back to Uralsk, now held by the Reds, in a symbolic gesture of acquiescence to, if not genuine acceptance of, this side in the struggle.

Nikita's adjustment to the new revolutionary order was difficult. This order was antipathetic to the culture of the past which he represented, and he doubted its interest in the kind of music he wished to compose. After two lonely and discouraging years of working on his symphony in Petrograd, during which time he slipped back into his own little world, he attends a concert, a very rare event for him. Fedin uses this important and effective scene to mark a turning point in the ideological and artistic orientation of his hero. The concert had been arranged on behalf of the trade unions and large numbers of workers were present. Before the start of the performance he thinks the workers noisy and vulgar and incongruous in these surroundings, but once the music begins he observes with surprise their rapt attention and is astounded at their enthusiastic appreciation of often difficult pieces.

On the way out from the concert, Nikita meets his niece Irina, the pretty, vivacious seventeen-year-old daughter of his older brother Matvei, now a distinguished physician and pro-

fessor of medicine. He cheerfully tells her that he has just discovered that music is needed not only for musicians. They sit
and chat and Irina scolds him for being such a hermit, for not
visiting her family, and for failing to proceed with his symphony. He replies by describing the reactions he has just had
to the workers at the concert, and he adds: "Then I thought
that I must definitely compose, end the piece soon, and let
them hear it; that I do not have the right to be silent if, as it is
said, I am obligated to all these people to give everything I
have." As they talk Irina's fresh, sensitive responses, her enthusiasm for his work, and her expression of faith in him
resurrect the image of the dead Anna and she and Irina unconsciously merge in his mind. He cannot resist the urge to
tell her of a "dear friend" in the past who had inspired his
work, and the clever Irina guesses that the "dear friend" was a
lover. "I am sorry for you," Irina declares, "in that you . . .
feel compelled to pity yourself . . . when you ought to be
strong, strong, strong." The identification of the two women
seems complete. Already half in love with Irina, Nikita returns
home in a state of exaltation which he has not experienced
since his Dresden days. His ideological awakening had been
combined with what was essential to his creative nature—the
love, inspiration, and faith in his destiny which an Anna, now
transmuted into Irina, could provide.

Nikita's symphony is a great success. In a formal printed
review of it, which Fedin states is written by a distinguished
composer, the influence of Western music on Nikita's style is
stressed as much as is its Russian lyrical content. Only in one
place does the reviewer mention that the symphony contains
"that greatness which has brought us to the Revolution." Indeed, it becomes increasingly clear that it is not so much his
newly found revolutionary idealism, but the face of Irina that
has inspired his symphony. But as this face fades, for he finally
realizes the hopelessness of his love for his seventeen-year-old
niece, the will to follow up the success of his symphony dwin-

dles. He understands now that he has identified Irina with Anna in a search for his original inspiration. Yet he confesses to himself that "it was necessary for him to find one face on which he would like to rest his glance for the remainder of his life." And in his visions the beautiful face of Varvara at last begins to mingle with those of Anna and Irina.

In fact, Varvara, who had married the Communist Rodion Chorbov, an uncouth peasant river pilot, has come up to Petrograd to continue her pursuit of Nikita. She stalks him as a hunter stalks his prey. Fedin verges on the ridiculous in these unnatural scenes, in which Varvara manifests her passion, her jealousy of Irina, and her determination to have a child by Nikita. There is a compelling psychological logic in this situation, however, for Fedin from the outset has carefully stressed Varvara's developing monomaniacal nature in the circumstances of a repeatedly frustrated passion for Nikita. The pursuit comes to an end in a moment of lost hope when Nikita paradoxically bargains away his devotion to music, which Varvara hates, for "a face on which he would like to rest his glance for the remainder of his life."

In *Cities and Years* Andrei Startsov, a product of the old culture, was mercilessly destroyed by the Revolution because he could not subordinate his individuality to it. In *The Brothers* Fedin seems determined to assimilate the old and the new in the person of his artist-hero. But throughout the novel the integrity of the literary artist prevented Fedin from surrendering his own individuality to a Soviet pattern of life with which he obviously did not wholly sympathize and which perhaps he did not as yet wholly comprehend. The depiction of the new Soviet people in the book is minimal, and they are completely overshadowed by figures from the past. The most brilliant pictures are those of the early, prerevolutionary life of the Karev family, of the merchant family of Sherstobitovs, and of Nikita's prewar existence in Dresden. Even the best postrevolutionary scenes, such as the nameday party at Dr. Matvei

Karev's and the performance of Nikita's symphony, have the characteristic quality and aura of nineteenth-century Russian realistic fiction. The most effective characterizations are of people from the past: the wonderful old Cossack father Karev, who might almost have stepped out of the pages of Leo Tolstoy; the dedicated violin teacher Yakov Goldman and his proud father; the humorous peasant Evgraf whose habit of devotion to the Karev family undermines his naive questing after revolutionary glory; the distinguished but weary and society-surfeited older brother, Dr. Matvei Karev, who adores his pretty daughter, ignores his vain wife, and runs his household like a character out of one of Chekhov's stories; and the inimitable old Professor Bakh with the perfect profile and courtly graces who lives among his dusty tomes and faded glories of the past.

In contrast, what could be described as characteristically Soviet is meager and often only tangential to the narrative core of the novel. There are three Communists. The youngest Karev brother Rostislav flashes across the pages in one brief bright scene where his youthful political convictions are no doubt intended to contrast with the weak, apolitical nature of his artist-brother Nikita, but the next we hear of him is Evgraf's description of his meaningless death, and that a street in Uralsk has been named by the Reds in his honor. Not much more space is devoted to the old Bolshevik Shering. He is an important Party member, the commander of an armed Volga flotilla, but he is more hallowed in the author's reminiscences about him than by any heroic action in which he participates in the novel. We next see him on his deathbed where his son, in what appears to be deliberate satire on Fedin's part, accuses this old Bolshevik of a degree of infantile leftism, in short, of being a Communist deviator.

Shering is the revolutionary hero of Rodion Chorbov, the one fully drawn Communist whose life of action is interwoven with the fates of the principal characters in *The Brothers*.

Soviet critics regard him as an early exemplar of the positive hero type, a man dedicated to changing the world according to the doctrine of Marx. A peasant playmate of Nikita on the Karev family estate, Rodion became a sailor on the Volga boats, joined the revolutionary movement at an early age, and was imprisoned by the tsar's police. He grows up to be an irascible, fiery Communist whose overwhelming zeal for the cause is matched only by his peasant naïveté in comprehending its dialectical niceties. He is captivated by the beauty of Varvara, whom he meets as Shering's secretary, a position she has taken to save her own skin from the Reds. And though he appears to consider marriage as some outmoded bourgeois survival, he succumbs to her, apparently unaware that she has taken this way out to save the life of her devoted slave Vitka, whom Rodion had caught in an infraction of Red military discipline.

The birth of a daughter preserves this unequal marriage for several years, while Varvara constantly chafes at Rodion's parroting of Party dogma. In an amusing scene, filled with satiric jibes at his political faith, Rodion objects to her reading fairy tales to their daughter. Varvara mildly queries why he is so worried since he was brought up on fairy tales and yet had become a good Communist. "How bored I am with you," she frankly tells him. "You carry on like a chicken laying an egg. And you cluck together with the rest of them: children must be brought up according to the working-class formulae—fairy tales are survivals of superstition, religion is opium for the people. . . . Lord, what boredom, but mainly it doesn't suit you and is terribly difficult for you. Indeed, you are just a healthy muzhik!" And when he furiously accuses her of still loving Nikita, she boldly admits it and leaves him.

It is difficult to find anything sympathetic in the characterization of Rodion, and it is unlikely that Fedin did, yet the author allows him to stand as a symbol of the triumph of the new over the old, for in the end he marries Irina. Perhaps it might be better to say that in this union of a Communist peasant striving to enter the ranks of the new Soviet intelligentsia with a daughter of a member of the old intelligentsia, Fedin saw a possible solution to the struggle between the old and the new.

Fedin's deep sympathy for Nikita, however, this artist-product of an older culture, is everywhere apparent in the novel, although he often scolds him for his ideological ambivalence and weakness of will. At the conclusion of the novel Varvara, after they have lived together only a few months, tells Nikita that she has realized all the time that she came to him just when Irina had rejected him and that she received him as a gift from Irina. "I begin to fulfill for you only a role of service," she asserts, for she understands now that he will remain forever dedicated to his music. Then this "infernal woman" brutally informs him that she too had her purpose in winning him—to have a child by him. She is now pregnant, she says, and no longer cares whether she lives with him. Her renunciation seems almost like an act of vengeance in return for the long painful years she had waited for him.

In despair Nikita rushes from the room. He returned to Uralsk, Fedin writes, "in order to continue the life from which he fled." And the author concludes the novel with the cryptic comment: "The world rejected Nikita Karev in order to receive him." The suggestion is that out of the fullness of his experiences and unhappiness in the old world that had rejected him, he could create still greater music in the new world that had received him.

There was not a great deal which the Party-minded critics in 1929 could find to praise in *The Brothers*. A few defenders saw in it a powerful and proper resolution of a controversy that was then going on in artistic theory—the development of a new Soviet national art as opposed to a regurgitation of the Russian art of the past or of an art oriented to Western Europe. The artist cannot isolate himself from life or even be contented with merely observing life, declared the critics, he must be an active participant in the process of changing life. Such critics regarded Nikita's struggle to express himself in music as a triumph and affirmation of the unity of nationalism and the Revolution in art. They pointed out that Nikita had to learn the spiritual powerlessness of art which tears itself away from the national soil, rejects the revolutionary movement of the masses, and creates in a language alien to the people. It is true that Fedin theorizes much on this score in the novel and appears to take the Soviet point of view, yet it is strange that Nikita's successful symphony is in no sense described as a reflection of Soviet demands in art. As a matter of fact, that "new Soviet man," Rodion, in a passage studiously overlooked by all the critics, condemns the symphony as a "damnable concert. . . . It is not our music. It is bad music. Bad music."

What the Party literary critics especially singled out for favorable mention was the fact that Nikita Karev, unlike Andrei Startsov, eventually comes to an acceptance of the Soviet way of life. This was hailed as an indication that Fedin had at last resolved his own ideological dualism in the struggle between the old and the new. And such a resolution may have been deliberately suggested in the epigraph to *The Brothers*, Byron's lines:

> Fare thee well! and if for ever,
> Still for ever, fare *thee well*.

Such a forthright conclusion, however, is not fully supported by the evidence of the novel. Perhaps the critics, like Fedin in his own efforts to adjust to the new, were indulging in wishful thinking. Nikita's struggle with his past and with the artistic problems of expression in music is a profoundly individualistic one, very little influenced by the clamor of the Soviet marketplace. He had to live in this Soviet world, but his return to his childhood home at the end of the novel, "in order to continue the life from which he fled," could also be regarded as symbolizing a rejection of the new Soviet world.

Nor does Fedin himself advance in the novel a wholehearted rejection of the past. In a remarkable scene in which he describes a debate on this vital question between the Communist Rodion and old Professor Bakh, the passionate pleading of the professor no doubt represented Fedin's own conviction at this time: "We do not know the beauty which you create. We do not know how you will experience your new beauty. But you will never repeat our feelings because you will never repeat the man of our epoch. Yet we were able to feel, Rodion, we were able to create the beautiful and to be enriched by it! And I am sorry, Rodion, that the new man mercilessly discards us from life. . . . We bear in ourselves those feelings which you regard as hostile not because they are harmful, but because you do not possess them, do not wish to see their significance. . . . Oh, for us time does not exist for we, in truth, are immortal!"

If you are immortal, quips Rodion, "Then why do you complain that the new people discard you?"

One gathers from this discussion that the struggle between the old and new had by no means resolved itself in either the political ideology or artistic consciousness of Fedin.

WINDOW ON EUROPE. After finishing *The Brothers*, Fedin spent the larger part of the next seven years (1928–34) in extensive traveling throughout much of Western Europe. If we include the four years that he lived in Germany during the First World War, then no prominent Soviet author can claim as wide and varied an experience with the people and nations of the West as Fedin. And the impact of this experience on the development of his creative art, as well as on his hesitant political and social views, is clearly apparent in his fiction. An authority and a Western "flavor" in the handling of scenes laid in Germany in his first two novels often contrast with an unsureness of grasp in his treatment of Soviet life in these works. With perhaps the exception of Ilya Ehrenburg, Fedin is easily the most Western of all Soviet novelists. Indeed, up to this point in his career, he seems more "at home," as it were, in describing life in the West than that in the Soviet Union. This effect is very striking in his next novel, *The Rape of Europe,* the first volume of which came out in 1934, the second in 1935.

Fedin's travels through Western European countries in the depression years after 1929 provided the inspiration and material for his new work. The basic plan was a simple one—to contrast and compare the deteriorating social and economic existence of the West under the influence of the depression with the full employment and the tremendous economic upsurge that resulted from the first two Five-Year Plans in the Soviet Union. Neither picture is objective, but curiously enough that of the West is more convincing in its verisimilitude and far more interesting in its artistic grasp of character and action.

Fedin was too much an artist, however, to allow the hobbyhorse of politics to gallop off with the narrative interest of the story which is centered in the Dutch family of Van Rossums, importers of lumber and operators of ocean transportation. For fifty years the firm had controlled a timber concession in Russia, and it had grown rich on this business as well as on its shipping activities. Fedin describes the family during the period when its fortunes are beginning to decline because of the depression. Franz Van Rossum, nephew and agent in Russia of the two brothers Lodewick and Philip who run the firm, writes that the Soviet government is interfering with the concession and that production has been cut by striking workers. Transportation assignments are also dwindling. Under these stresses and strains the firm stoops to shady dealings such as buying up and heavily insuring old cargo-carrying ships in the expectation that they will sink.

The Van Rossums and their associates symbolize for Fedin the capitalistic West and the mounting demoralization of its way of life in a world riven by new social and economic forces. In effective realistic vignettes he contrasts the life of the rich and the poor: beggars on the streets of Rotterdam, the slum section and a strike of workers in Amsterdam, the layoff because of a lack of orders in a Silesian manufacturing town, and the pathetic story of the stoker Rudolph Kvast, a suicide because of unemployment; then the mad, financial scramble of speculators in the Rotterdam stock exchange, and the luxurious life of the Dutch oil king Eldering Heuser, whose huge, custom-built Rolls Royce attracted as much attention outside the concert hall at Bayreuth as the music of Wagner inside. There is the plush dinner party of the German son-in-law of Philip Van Rossum, Kaspar Krieg, and the clever satire on the after-dinner conversation of the well-fed male guests bewailing the bad state of business, in contrast with the chatter of their wives on such then socially correct topics as pan-idealism, nudism, and the need for a great leader in these troubled times—a sinister forewarning of the rise of Hitler.

Though the deliberate Soviet emphasis of Fedin is apparent in these contrasting scenes and characters drawn from the life of the rich and the poor, the total effect is not one of hopelessly biased propaganda. Socially minded European literary critics in the early 1930s might have quarreled with the tone but hardly with the realism of these pictures. Portrayals of the wealthy bear no resemblance to the bloated caricatures of capitalism so common in Soviet fiction. Philip Van Rossum, for example, the central figure in *The Rape of Europe,* is sensitively and convincingly delineated. At sixty he is a logical human product of all those forces and factors of the successful business world and of the high society in which he has lived. He is a lover of art, a student of international affairs and foreign languages, cultured, and discriminating in his tastes. He enjoys the perquisites of wealth but does not flaunt them. With his nephew's wife he philanders with a certain delicacy, not forgetting the affection he owes his mistress. Though the ruthless competition of high finance has dulled his feelings, he can still throw a bone of comfort to a begging unemployed

worker or express genuine sorrow over the tragic death of his
beloved daughter Elena. Making money, however, is the driving force in Philip Van Rossum's life and his devotion to this
purpose has left him spiritually atrophied. When Lodewick is
dying, Philip's first concern is the terms of his brother's will;
his worry over the death of his nephew Franz is limited largely
to the thought that he will not be able to replace him easily as
the firm's agent in Russia.

In fact, Philip Van Rossum's conviction that he can carry
on gainful business with the Soviet Union is almost the only
reason that he opposes the hostility of his colleagues to that
country. The "Russian question" occupies a prominent place
in the novel as it did in reality in the minds of many thinking
people in the West and America in the early 1930s. One may
well imagine that Fedin heard it endlessly discussed in his
wanderings through the countries of Western Europe, and
in the debates among his characters on this question he faithfully reflects the sharp differences of opinion that were voiced
everywhere in the West at that time. In the face of the depression businessmen were eager to trade with the Soviet
Union but at the same time feared future competition for
world markets. Others, like the oil king Eldering Heuser, try
to persuade Western capitalists to boycott the Soviet Union,
for they see no point in supporting a communist system dedicated to the destruction of capitalism. On the other hand, the
timber king Philip Van Rossum, already deep in business dealings with the Soviet Union, justifies his position by the familiar
hope of those days that Communism would ultimately fail
whereas the capitalist economy of the West would go on as
always. Yet a Swiss engineer, Kaspi, just returned from a visit
to the Soviet Union, tells the doubting guests at the Krieg
dinner party of the tremendous outpouring of energy inspired
by the five-year plans and states that in his opinion the
Soviets will succeed in their huge industrialization program
and may eventually surpass the West in this respect.

In a number of conversations of this sort Fedin's intention is to emphasize that the primary interest of the Western business world in the Soviet Union is self-interest which crassly subordinates the human and social problems involved in this vast socialistic experiment to "business as usual." And consistent with his concern for the "little people" in his previous fiction, he now points out that it is the unemployed workers in the West, the impoverished victims of the depression, who understand in a dim, fumbling way the human hope" that the Soviet Union holds out for the needy proletariat. Clearly Fedin was moving closer to the traditional Party line, but it is interesting that he does so under the influence of observed economic conditions in the depression of the West which also turned the thoughts of many Western European intellectuals and workers in the same direction.

Love had played a more or less significant role in the two preceding novels of Fedin, and it is not denied an appropriate place in *The Rape of Europe*. In fact, the love story threatens to swallow up the political message of the book even though it is designed to illustrate it, for it is intensely realized and its various human involvements are always interesting. The love affair between Ivan Rogov and Klavdia, the beautiful Russian wife of Franz Van Rossum, is not exactly a study in depth of "the science of the tender passion," as Pushkin described the emotion, but it is the kind of sophisticated, sentient handling of the theme which is extremely rare among Soviet novelists. Rogov is hardly a Russian Romeo. Nondescript in appearance, painfully lamed by a bullet in the civil war, always quick to resent the slightest criticism of his country, he cuts a rather sorry figure in the company of these Western capitalists. In Ivan Rogov, however, there is more than a trace of the intellectual questing of Andrei Startsov. Fighting in the civil war had partly satisfied a youthful desire to live actively and heroically, but the heroic is curiously mingled with fantasy in Rogov. He roams over Europe, a

Soviet journalist without any apparent assignment, and finally comes to rest in Holland at the feet of Klavdia Van Rossum, whose husband he had known in Leningrad. He begins to wonder if Klavdia is not the object of his quest, the answer to his loneliness.

Their affinity for each other transcends the fact that they are both Russians in an alien land. There is also the intellectual attraction of opposite political convictions which arouses the proselytizing zeal of each. When she tells him of her escape from the Soviet Union as a girl, and he blames her for not being sterner with herself, she frankly answers: "I'm not a heroine. I am one of the ordinary persons who make up the world. Perhaps I behaved unfaithfully, but why should I condemn myself for this? I ran away from boredom, from misery. I was unable to find a place for myself. I yearned for ease, jollity, variety. But our life there . . . We were not even able to relax. In those days I always had the feeling that I was chained to a wheelbarrow."

Rogov angrily accuses her of being a foreigner and not a Russian, and he unwillingly perceives that she is a sensuous creature who prefers her life of luxury as the wife of a rich man to the harsh existence which his socialist idealism justifies. But his idealism and reforming zeal melt under the spell of a bewitching Amsterdam night when she seeks him out in his loneliness and pain. It is a charming scene of mingled poetry and pathos, humor and wise humanity.

In the second volume of *The Rape of Europe,* the scene of action shifts to the Soviet Union where Philip Van Rossum had come to join his nephew Franz in an effort to save the firm's timber concession. The second volume contains the answer of Soviet socialism to the economic defeatism of Western capitalism revealed in the first volume. The answer is rather crude and unconvincing both as a rationale and as an artistically embodied contrast of ways of life. Perhaps Fedin's long absence from the Soviet Union had something to do with the failure, but his own objectivity and critical reaction to some of the absurdities of five-year planning also contributed to it.

When Philip Van Rossum arrives at the village of Sorok in Northern Russia, he is overwhelmed by the comic opera, carnival spirit of the workers who greet him and his sailors at the dock with an orchestra, speeches, and general jubilation. Sergeich, boss of the local sawmill and leading Communist of Sorok, begins his intolerably long speech of welcome: "Dear comrades, foreign mariners. You have just set foot on a land whose masters are the workers and peasants. All these people here are sawmill workers. A sixth of the earth's surface belongs to them, the first workers' government in the world, the beloved country of all the toilers." It all sounds like a parody of Lenin in 1918.

The Dutch capitalist finds these Soviet toilers a humorless lot. Indeed, they are less believable in their heroic feats of labor than are Fedin's portrayals of resentful Western workers caught up in the poverty of the depression. The workers' brigade leader Volodia Glushkov and the eager-beaver Komsomol member Senia Ershov are nothing more than enthusiastic manikins of mass production. When the pretty, idealizing Komsomolets, Shura, is introduced to Klavdia, her "heart beats faster," for she immediately concludes that Klavdia is a White Guard, "a real one in the living flesh." Shura is more a subject of gentle satire than of realistic delineation. And Sergeich, obviously the intended hero of the second volume and the Communist ideological foil of Philip Van Rossum, dwindles to a mere mouthpiece of Soviet dogmas.

The picture that Fedin was trying to convey of a huge release of national energy during the early five-year plans and of widespread labor enthusiasm was real enough. But somehow he failed to grasp it with imaginative power and artistic authenticity, as though he himself were not entirely convinced of either its aims or its necessity. Nor was Philip

Van Rossum convinced. He is amazed at the fervor for work which he sees on every hand, and he listens incredulously to Shura's simple reasoning about why she participates in the unpaid collective laboring on Saturdays. Yet he observes the low standards of existence of the workers and comments to Sergeich: "You really ought not to base an industrial plan for the country on the hunger of the population." Sergeich calmly agrees but insists that it will be worth it in the end and that in any event the people will not starve to death. The pointed contrast which Fedin persistently draws is the idealism behind this huge, self-sacrificing effort in the Soviet Union and the cynical self-interest of Western capitalism. He generalizes on those, like the Van Rossums, who come to do business with the Soviet Union: "For businessmen socialism was not a curiosity like sunrise over the Kremlin. As in the case of any client, socialism could be interesting or not interesting. It was interesting if it bought goods and paid for them. And it simply did not exist if it did not want to go shopping."

The Van Rossums, however, soon discover that the Soviet government can trade as sharply as any cynical capitalist. When the uncle and nephew appear at the ministry to deliver their charges of interference and government regulation of prices, which is contrary to the agreement in the old concession, they are coolly told by the official in charge: "This, however, is our internal affair; in a planned economy, regulation of prices is entirely natural. . . . Surely we could not permit the concession to regulate the price; only the government can do that." Further, the Soviet official countercharges the Van Rossums with violation of the terms of the concession by their wasteful cutting of timber and by their unlawful treatment of the workers. Despite Philip Van Rossum's pleas he is told that the concession is canceled, with the alternative of negotiating a new agreement with the Soviet government.

As in the first volume, the solid narrative interest here is to be found in the continued love story of Klavdia Van Rossum

and Ivan Rogov, both of whom now turn up in the Soviet
Union. Rogov's love for his mistress has grown deeper as their
ideological differences have sharpened. He wanted possession
of both body and mind and cannot seem to understand that
she regards their relations as an inevitably passing affair
which must under no circumstances be allowed to ruin the
security of her life with her husband, whom she professes still
to love.

Fedin details a conversation of the lovers as they stroll about
the streets of Leningrad. It is a frank, sophisticated, and effective piece of dialogue, perhaps unique in such a situation
in any Soviet novel written at this time. The focus is always
love but the ambit is their ever-widening political estrangement
which Rogov cannot resist fingering. At one point he asks
Klavdia her reaction to his latest newspaper article and she replies:

"In everything that now takes place, and especially in everything that is written, there is one simply impossible feature. This
is arrogance. And Rogov does not avoid it. So much the worse for
Rogov."

"Let it be the worse for Rogov! But why do you take it into your
head to read a moral? Why suddenly is arrogance bad?"

"Because there is no adequate reason for it."

"Even if there isn't any adequate reason for it, who can properly
reproach us for the sin of arrogance? Was it not the humble West
that for centuries repeated again and again that we as a country
were the most impoverished, the most ignorant, the most pitiful?
Always the chimneyless hovel! And now when we prove that we
are not behind but ahead of others, that we . . ."

"But it is not proved, only asserted!"

"We stand at the very beginning of our revolution, and the
affirmation here is the will to action, to achievement . . ."

"But please! What are you getting so burned up over? I positively have nothing against such pride, and I'm very happy that at
last we are becoming like other people! But I'm saying—how is all
this manifested? Sometimes in very childish forms. For example—
the insanity of great numbers. You have grown a Japanese radish
somewhere of eighteen pounds, and you rejoice. But why? What

are you going to do with it, with your radish? Just listen, and you hear: the greatest, the longest . . ."

"The most powerful," prompted Rogov.

"A passion for everything great—this is a disease. It is the quite well-known disease of Americanism. What it has led the Americans to, you already know. They have reduced the whole meaning of life to figures. They reckon and reckon to the very day of their death—complex percentages in the brain, pen and checkbook in their hand. Why do you think that this reverence for 'the greatest' will bring you where you wish to go and not to that same checkbook?"

"I rejoice to hear you defend life against the checkbook. Touching! The checkbook is a naughty child. Is it true? The checkbook, let us say, of Philip Van Rossum. Phui! Is that it?"

Rogov's thrust struck home, but on this occasion, as on other similar ones, they composed their differences in an embrace of love in a hideout that Klavdia had thoughtfully provided. One may suspect, however, that her criticism of Soviet arrogance and greatest-in-the-world boastfulness reflected also Fedin's views, for these exaggerations were offensive by-products of the propaganda drive that accompanied the first Five-Year Plan. Likewise the undiscriminating Soviet reverence for the more material achievements of American industry, a commonplace then, warranted a satiric jibe, however misplaced it may be in this passage.

Rogov is not a Communist nor is he a very perceptive lover. Klavdia takes fright at his persistent demand that she desert her husband and live with him, and when he deliberately reveals his passion to Franz she abruptly terminates the whole affair. Klavdia perhaps minded less the beatings from her outraged husband than the thought of what the loss of his love might mean to her material security. And she rather expectedly takes the easy way out of becoming the mistress of Franz's rich uncle, Philip Van Rossum, who had long had an eye on her. A suspicion of this fact contributes to Franz's accidental death, and shortly thereafter Klavdia and Philip leave the country, he consoling himself over the loss of his concession

in the Soviet Union with the possession of a beautiful mistress, she mourning her dead husband and yet curiously con-
juring up through the mist of her tears an image of Rogov
waving her a farewell from the shore.

From the point of view of what Fedin set out to do in
this novel, *The Rape of Europe* may be regarded as something
of a failure. However, absorbing scenes and situations of
European life on several economic levels during the depression years abound in the first volume. Fedin's satire and irony
were never more effective, especially in his portrayal of Philip
Van Rossum and Klavdia, yet these bourgeois types are easily
the best character creations in the novel. Ivan Rogov, on the
other hand, is hardly a captivating image of the new Soviet
intellectual, a man of inner richness and complexity, as Fedin
obviously intended him to be. Beneath the varnish of Soviet
idealism one plainly discerns the grain of the old Russian
intellectual of nineteenth-century fiction. He is lame, frequently ill, and surprisingly self-centered in his "bourgeois"
passion for Klavdia. In fact, he remains human and interesting
simply because he fails as a representative of the new Soviet
intellectual. In the end Fedin tries to dignify his Sovietism by
making him—most improbably—play the part of a patriotic
sleuth tracking down a hostile financial conspiracy of Philip
Van Rossum, and by placing in his mouth the moral of the
novel, pronounced in a speech at a meeting of Komsomol
youth at Sorok: "The country of the Soviets is a country of
peace. We are for agreements, but only on the basis of equal
rights. . . . Either equal rights or nothing—these are the conditions on which we are ready to trade honorably with the
West."

Fedin, no doubt, conceived Sergeich as the fountain of
pure Party wisdom. He is that and nothing more. Unconvincing
as they are, there is at least a suggestion of reality in Fedin's
previous portrayals of Communists, Kurt Wahn (*Cities and
Years*), Rostislav and Rodion (*The Brothers*), but Sergeich

seems to exist solely as an abstract Party virtue in a Soviet
morality play.

Fedin regarded *The Rape of Europe* as a political novel, as
an effort on his part, after much uncertainty, to identify himself with the socialist hopes and aspirations of the Soviet
regime. The new doctrine of work and the achievements of
the first Five-Year Plan which contrasted so vividly with the
defeatism of the depressed capitalist West undoubtedly contributed to his growing convictions in this respect, as they did
in the case of a number of other fellow-traveling Soviet writers
at this time. The novel itself, however, bears testimony to his
hesitation in accepting unthinkingly all that he saw around
him in the Soviet Union. Perhaps this fact, more than anything
else, accounts for his inability to argue persuasively and to
embody with artistic success the central theme of *The Rape
of Europe*. Shortly after the completion of the novel he
candidly tried to explain some of the reasons for his failure:

I had long thought that the complex, ossifying character of capitalist Europe had been resisting the great historical and majestic
process of the *dawning* of a new character among us in the Soviet
Union. I thought that in the West the form, which had long since
ended, had already disintegrated and had begun to reek; in the
Soviet Union there is the intensive education of the new man, the
gathering together of his future features into a unity which we
merely know in our dreams. Therefore I opposed to the finished
character of the principal hero of my novel—the capitalist Philip
Van Rossum—a whole gamut of the separate features and characteristics of Soviet persons. But I at once realized that in this case
Western Europe would be concretized in an artistic image which
would be more powerful than the Soviet world opposed to it. I
understood that it would be absolutely necessary to provide con-
crete Soviet images. But I could not find the real circumstances of
"business" existence in which the capitalist would conflict with
equivalent forms from the Soviet world. Nevertheless the novel
is based on the materials of so-called "business" developments.
Roughly speaking, I ought to have analyzed the "Soviet counterbalance" in Rogov, a quite refined person, and in the Communist
Sergeich, a person of expansive and transparent moral qualities.

But what happened? Europe emerges in the novel through the language largely of one hero, the Soviet Union through the speech of two. I had hoped that the thousands of circumstances in our country working against Philip would supplant the hero. Now I see that this is a mistake in construction arising out of the over-all design. But I speak frankly: for my novel I have not yet discovered the "counterbalance" of Philip, though I confess that the creation of a Soviet hero, bearing, so to speak, an "individual" impress, the impress of his Western European antipode, is still the problem of our literature.[*]

A SOVIET MAGIC MOUNTAIN. Nor did Fedin succeed in solving the problem in his next work, the short novel *Arctur Sanatorium*, which appeared in 1940. Western European experiences continued to dominate his creative impulses. A severe tuberculosis condition was one of the reasons he went abroad. Gorky, himself afflicted with the disease, encouraged Fedin to seek a permanent cure and aided him to enter a sanatorium in the Swiss mountain valley of Davos. Thus Fedin's short novel has an autobiographical basis, but the storyteller's art has transformed a lengthy and uneventful personal experience into a psychological study of illness, a study of some power and of mingled pathos and humor.

The central figure is Dr. Klebe, an Austrian physician who owns and runs Arctur Sanatorium, which Fedin placed in the picturesque Swiss valley of Davos. He is one of Fedin's "blameless drudges" of the early stories, a Chaplinesque creation whose natural goodness is tragically distorted by a losing struggle against creditors and disease in a futile effort to maintain his beloved sanatorium. As the unpaid bills mount panic seizes him. The physician's normal desire to cure his patients conflicts with the secret hope that their illness will be prolonged. A single empty room becomes a catastrophe. In these circumstances the distracted Dr. Klebe drifts into unethical practices—misinforming a patient of the state of his health and falsifying the negative laboratory report of another.

[*] *Literaturnyi Leningrad*, No. 17 (1936), p. 162.

The situation is further complicated by the suspicion, which at first he is afraid to test, that he himself has tuberculosis. Growing fear and self-pity undermine the effectiveness with which he carries on his daily duties in the sanatorium. All think about themselves, he complains, and no one about him. He tries to escape into the unreal world of Edgar Wallace's detective stories, the only books that he will read, and he imagines himself as the strong-jawed, dynamic hero. Or he daydreams, when listening to music, of becoming a celebrated conductor, or of becoming a great athlete as he watches a skiing competition. Meanwhile his small staff and even some of the patients, whom he approaches always with unfailing kindness, perceive the tragicomic aspects of his rapid disintegration. "Our good Klebe," remarks one of the patients, "desires many years for all his sick ones. But only many years in Arctur Sanatorium."

Fedin subtly connects the fate of Dr. Klebe with the resolution of the central situation of the novel, a love triangle involving two women—the pretty young patient, Inga Krechmar, and the attractive Dr. Hoffman, a staff assistant—and the young Soviet engineer Levshin, who has almost recovered his health in the sanatorium. The psychology of the sick is brilliantly grasped and reflected by Fedin in his portrayal of Inga, the best characterization after Dr. Klebe. Alternate hope and fear obsess Inga in her fight against the ravages of tuberculosis. The able Dr. Shtum, half in love with her himself, tries to instill in Inga a sense of spiritual triumph over her condition. Despite her efforts, however, the will to get better succumbs to both the realities and the symbols of despair. "I don't want eternally to share my life with: *it is possible, it may*," she declares. In her sick imagination, inflamed by the reading of exotic novels, she sails in strange ships to unknown lands, "dooming herself to destruction," writes Fedin, "to a passionless, shameless love." Love, indeed, the need for which was intensified by the disease itself, might have provided Inga with that increment of will which she so lacked in her struggle to go on living. She sought it in Levshin who responded, but more out of a sense of pity than from sincere love. And when he leaves the sanatorium for a brief period, submitting to a design of the frantic Klebe who thought he could retain the more profitable long-paying patient Levshin if he could get rid of Inga who was annoying him by her attentions, she too prepares to go. Her decision becomes final when her rival Dr. Hoffman, who has returned from a rendezvous with Levshin in his mountain refuge, confronts Inga with her passion and peevishly tells her that it would be better for all if she left the sanatorium.

The last thread joining Inga to the desire to live has been snapped. When the deeply sympathetic Dr. Shtum tries once again to impress her with the absolute necessity of obeying her doctor, she quietly replies: "I think I could have obeyed one man. . . . But he has gone." The scene in which Fedin describes Inga's departure from the sanatorium is admirably executed. Though aware of the desperate condition of her health, she imagines herself as one of the cured, going away from this place out to a new and fresh life. And she makes a point, with what little remaining strength she can summon up, of going to the patients and bidding each of them an elaborate farewell, as though sorry that they must remain in the sanatorium. She is returned by the authorities from the next railroad station and dies the following day, but not before she has called for Levshin, who takes a pathetic farewell of her.

Levshin constitutes the only Soviet element in this most European of all Fedin's novels, and the portrayal has confused and annoyed Soviet critics, as in fact has the whole novel. In contrast to either Dr. Klebe, Inga, or Major Pashich—another patient—Levshin does represent the triumph of the spirit over disease, of the will to live. And Fedin leaves no doubt in his reader's mind that the source of this conviction is precisely the fact that Levshin is a product of Soviet society. He dreams of the great engineering tasks back home and regrets that he is not participating in them. "And again with renewed strength," writes Fedin, "the resolve seized him: to get well, to get well, to get well and to return home to the meaning and purpose of the whole future!"

But as in *The Rape of Europe*, Fedin's art seems to desert him when he is faced with the task of creating a convincing Soviet hero. Levshin is the least interesting character in the book. He has nothing of the psychological depth and humanity of Klebe or Inga, or even of the lesser figures Dr. Hoffman and Dr. Shtum. He never seems to be a part of the society of living people around him. And the minor humorous characters —the odd Major Pashich, the jack-of-all-trades Karl, the cleaning woman Lizl, the rich patient Mme. Rivash, the amusing English pastor and his wife—all have dimensions of human interest not accorded Levshin. Further, he is a bit of a cad in his love-making. Though he has given Inga some encouragement he lies to her about his going away, because "her suffering oppressed him and he did not want to be a nurse in her illness." And while thinking rather ashamedly of Inga pining for him in the sanatorium, he makes love to Dr. Hoffman in his mountain hideout. Yet after Inga's death and his own decision to return to the Soviet Union, he easily dismisses both her and Dr. Hoffman from his thoughts as though they had never existed.

The only other concession Fedin makes to the ideological sensibilities of Party-minded Soviet critics occurs at the end of *Arctur Sanatorium*. Dr. Klebe, overwhelmed with debts, the loss of patients, and the now certain knowledge that he has tuberculosis, loses touch with reality, and in a powerful, mad scene in which he tramples under foot his copies of Edgar Wallace's novels, listens to the music of Grieg, and indulges in fantastic thoughts about the horrible irrevocableness of his past and his present insignificance, he finally commits suicide. He leaves behind him a letter in which he says: "At times I dreamed about a miracle which would save me. But the miracle never took place. And this is understandable: the miracle is money, and there is no money. They say that there is a country in the world where miracles happen to people who have no money. If I were healthy, I would go there in order to convince myself that this is a fairy tale. But I need money to go there."

This transparent reference to the Soviet Union puzzles Dr. Shtum and he asks Levshin about it. The latter informs him that there is such a country but that it was no place for Klebe. On the other hand, remarks Levshin, the successful, able, well-adjusted Dr. Shtum should visit there. The latter, however, declines for he believes that his services are necessary to his patients in Davos.

Beside the excellent characterizations and realistic scenes of life in the sanatorium, there are beautiful descriptions of Alpine scenery in this short novel and not a few well-turned, thoughtful passages on the burden of disease and on the frailty and courage of the human spirit in the face of death. Some Soviet critics regard *Arctur Sanatorium* as a polemical answer to Thomas Mann's *Magic Mountain* with its emphasis on the tragic helplessness of man before the cruel and blind laws of biology. It is very likely that *The Magic Mountain* contributed to the conception of Fedin's novel. The settings of both are the same, and both reveal the life of the sick in a sanatorium. *The Magic Mountain* is one book which Dr. Klebe will not permit in Arctur Sanatorium. It is a "sea of pessimism," he declares. And one may see an indirect criticism of Mann's work in the comment of Klebe: "Too often in life we allow ourselves to become the spectators of a debauched, amoral psyche in order, as it were, to study the ugliness of a soul as is done in a novel."

Soviet critics continue the comparison by professing to see a sweeping condemnation of the moral degeneration of the bourgeois intelligentsia in Fedin's work, as well as an affirmation of life in Levshin instead of what is imagined to be man's submission to his fate among the sick in *The Magic Mountain.* The two works, however, do not bear comparison: *The Magic Mountain* is a major artistic effort and *Arctur Sanatorium* is a minor and not altogether successful short novel. Nor does Fedin seem bent on condemning Dr. Klebe or Inga; in fact, he seems to have infinite pity for these two victims of life. Then, too, Dr. Shtum, a member of the bourgeois intelligentsia, is sympathetically portrayed by Fedin as a successful and estimable physician. And the ideological message of Levshin, so stressed by the Soviet critics as a direct refutation of Mann's emphasis in his novel, is, on the contrary, quite similar to the final position of Hans Castorp in *The Magic Mountain:* "For the sake of goodness and love, man shall let death have no sovereignty over his thoughts." The difference, of course, lies in Levshin's motivation: for the sake of the "meaning and purpose of the whole future." The reason for this important difference—the socialist future—was beginning to loom larger and larger in Fedin's political and artistic speculations.

THE SEARCH FOR A COMMUNIST HERO. The year after *Arctur Sanatorium* was published the Nazi armies invaded the Soviet Union. The next eight years (1941–48) were Fedin's busiest and most productive, a period in which he achieved full maturity as a writer and at the same time resolved certain artistic and ideological problems which had been troubling him from the beginning of his career. The first of a projected three-volume work, Fedin's tribute to a great author who had influenced him in important ways, *Gorky Amongst Us,* appeared in 1943 and was widely praised. The Presidium of the Union of Soviet Writers publicly acclaimed Fedin as possessing that "eternal restlessness which is the quality of great artists and men of action," and described the book as one of the best that had been written about Gorky. The second volume

of *Gorky Amongst Us* (1944), however, was widely condemned, culminating in an official reprimand in *Pravda* (July
28, 1944). The final volume was never written and the first
two have been excluded from subsequent editions of Fedin's
writings.

Gorky Amongst Us was designed as a series of literary
memoirs growing out of the extensive correspondence of Fedin
and Gorky and covering the years from 1919 to 1936 (the
second volume ends with 1928). Though Fedin's unbiased
appreciation of certain literary figures out of sympathy with
the Soviet regime provoked most of the denunciations of the
second volume, another reason for the attacks was the revelation of his own social and artistic views which had little in
common with the Party line in these matters. The very charges
leveled against him present a true image of the man and his
outlook. He was accused of being objective and skeptical, of
defending the contemplative artist and apolitical art, of preaching toleration and a dispassionate relation to the reactionary
ideas of the past, and of being willing to sacrifice socialist individuality in an effort to restore individualism in general.
True enough, Fedin had attempted to remain objective in de-
picting life, even Soviet life, in his books. Not the clamorous
social demands of the Party but only the emotions can direct
the creative process, he clearly implies in *Gorky Amongst Us*.
Art may be tendentious, he says in the same work, but the
artist himself is not tendentious; he creates unconsciously, as
it were.

A harsh but rather pointless accusation was that in *Gorky
Amongst Us* Fedin had remained outside of politics at a time
when his country was fighting for its life. As a matter of fact
the war exercised a powerful influence on him, as it did on
a number of distinguished Soviet authors. He spent much time
at the front as a reporter and witnessed the frightful destruction of villages and whole cities and the terrible depredation
and loss of life visited upon the Russians by the enemy. A

deep feeling of patriotism and new convictions about the purpose and ultimate destiny of the Soviet regime grew out of these experiences and were quickly reflected in a war play, *A Test of Feelings* (1943), and in two volumes of sketches and tales.

These new experiences no doubt also played their part in the creation of Fedin's masterpiece, a work that won him a First Stalin Prize. In an autobiographical account in the 1952 edition of his writings, he tells us of the inception and purpose of the work:

During the war years I began to work on a trilogy long since contemplated, and in the course of 1943–48 I completed two parts of it, *Early Joys* and *No Ordinary Summer*. My turning to pure Russian material—for all my previous novels had been more or less linked with the theme of the West—was not only dictated by a powerful desire, but it was also an expression of my search for a great contemporary hero. In those years, when the fate of our country was being decided in the Great Fatherland War, the conviction had grown much more strong than formerly that the future of Russian life was inseparably joined with the Soviet regime, and that a truly great hero of contemporary times must and should be a Communist whose active will was synonymous with Victory. I have attempted to make the principal character of these two novels such a hero, showing his development in prerevolutionary Russia and during the civil war.

This Communist hero is Kirill Izvekov, and it is perhaps significant that Fedin, like Leonov and Sholokhov, once again seeks to identify his chief protagonist with the historical past. An escape into the past may betray a negative judgment on the present as a creator of the heroic, or a sense of inadequacy or even fear of portraying the contemporary type of hero which the official Soviet critics were incessantly demanding. Certainly Fedin seemed incapable of imagining a real Communist hero whose formative roots were not in the past, a period when revolutionary idealism was ennobled by the simple virtues of sincerity and integrity.

But in another sense the past was essential to the larger scheme of Fedin's trilogy. An awareness of the historical continuity between the past and present, in his opinion, was a vital concomitant of existing society. In fact, the image of historical time dominates the trilogy which is planned as three separate novels linked by leading characters and an inner unity of theme. The action is concentrated in three separate years within a period of some thirty years. If time changes people, the heroic actions of people also accelerate historical time in a vast canvas filled with movement, numerous characters, and various circles of society in which the realistic pictures of daily life blend with history and the romance of heroism.

Early Joys, the initial volume of a trilogy began to appear serially in *New World* in 1945. It took the war-weary Soviet readers back to the peaceful year of 1910 and to Saratov, Fedin's birthplace, a provincial town "of gingham, retired generals, and flour kings." The delightfully described love between the youthful Kirill Izvekov and Lisa Meshkova is suddenly shattered by Kirill's arrest. He is a strong, manly, idealistic youth of eighteen, the idol of his widowed mother, and a bright student at the technical school. Lisa, the pretty daughter of a grubby merchant—a rigidly righteous, religious fanatic of a man—is a charming composite of gentleness and ardor, of dutiful submissiveness to the wishes of her stern father and flights of rebellion against his oppressive demands. Nowhere in Soviet fiction has young love been treated with such charm and psychological insight—the secret walks on warm spring evenings, the glorious arguments on the eternal verities, the mysterious chemistry of accidental physical contact, and the wonderfully chaste castle-building in the future when at last they "would be together."

The only secret Kirill kept from Lisa and from everybody else was his revolutionary activity. He had come under the influence of the worker Pyotr Ragozin, who for a short time had been exiled for participating in the 1905 Revolution. By 1910 governmental reaction had intensified and the opposition of the underground workers' movement grew apace. The hut of the zealous Ragozin and his devoted wife Xenia became the center for the illegal printing of revolutionary manifestoes in Saratov. Fedin had thus selected 1910 as the historic year at which to begin the revolutionary education of a future Bolshevik leader—Kirill Izvekov.

The visionary expectations of young Kirill, which the older and experienced Ragozin kindly but firmly debunks, are quickly transformed into practical revolutionary tasks. It is hardest of all for Kirill to keep his secret from Lisa who herself is for him a mystery arisen out of a dream. Both mysteries strangely fuse in his mind and he confidently imagines that the time will come when Lisa will see the political shape of the future as he does. Then the sudden descent of the police on Ragozin's hut and the discovery of the printing press end all these hopes.

The love of Kirill and Lisa, caught up in the web of underground political conspiracy, is the novel's central action which touches, directly or indirectly, the lives of nearly all the other characters. These characters in turn have been deliberately selected by Fedin as a representative cross section of the social stratification of Saratov. The intellectual and artistic stratum is represented by the actor and town dramatic idol Tsvetukhin, and by the young playwright Pastukhov, who has enjoyed a small success in Moscow and has returned to his native town upon the death of his father. Tsvetukhin, warmhearted, generous, ebullient, irresponsible, and vain, is the uninhibited artist incarnate, the inseparable friend and intellectual foil of Pastukhov, and the flirtatious admirer of Lisa, in whom he correctly divines and encourages an ambition to be an actress.

Pastukhov, on the other hand, is a man of pure intellect, devoid of social conscience, or perhaps it would be more correct to say that he lacks the courage to oppose social evil when such opposition might deprive him of the comfortable way of life which he values above all things. He is cool, calculating, and wounding in his wit; his flabby face habitually takes on a plaster smile in polite conversation; but his "eyes had the inquisitiveness of a pike—greedy, cold, fishy eyes." Pastukhov is an outstanding characterization in a gallery of excellent ones in *Early Joys*.

In the vigorous discussions on art between the two friends, Tsvetukhin and Pastukhov, Fedin returns to a theme which long concerned him in his fiction, especially in *Cities and Years* and in *The Brothers*. Pastukhov condemns Tsvetukhin's conviction that art is simply an imitation of life and he does not discern any man-made rule or political necessity as a guiding principle. His authorities are Balzac and Tolstoy who believed that the creative instinct manifests itself independently of the artist's will. "The life of the imagination," declares Pastukhov, "this is the essence of the artist or of the outstanding mind. . . . Hail the artist! and down with the copyist! Hail Tolstoy! and down with Zola! Hail the lord of Art—imagination!"

Later in the novel a new element is thrust into Pastukhov's consideration of art. After a performance of Gorky's *The Lower Depths*, Kirill, much to Lisa's mortification, accuses Tsvetukhin of having overplayed and sentimentalized the part of the Baron. Tsvetukhin is amazed. "An actor must stir the public," he answers, and did not the audience acclaim his performance? Lisa supports him by remarking that his conception of the part has been a revelation. "It's the author who made the revelation by looking beneath the surface of life," insists Kirill. And he goes on: "Not every dramatist sees what's hidden beneath the surface. . . . It's not enough to be even a poet; for that you have to be a revolutionary!"

Kirill's observation sets Pastukhov to wondering whether so arbitrary a thing as imagination is enough, whether its brother—foresight, divination, the power to prophesy—is not a higher manifestation of the artistic mind. And in the end he begins to doubt whether art is guided by any laws. "They [the laws] did not exist," he tells himself, "they were embodied in action. If art was effective, then it was legitimate. If it was dead to perception, then what law could animate it?" In all this Fedin may well be expressing his own criticism of the Party's determination to propound Soviet "laws" on the creation of art. However, in the light of the endless Soviet controversy on this subject, Fedin may have preferred Pastukhov's less reverent position. On parting, at the conclusion of the novel, Tsvetukhin exclaims: "We didn't even drink to art," and Pastukhov replies: "Art, art! You can never settle everything in art, just as you can never say everything in love. Art without misunderstanding is like a banquet where nobody gets tipsy."

In the quest for "material from life" on which to model his portrayal of the Baron, Tsvetukhin and Pastukhov visit a flophouse, which enables Fedin to introduce representatives of the "lower depths," specifically the Parabukin family which must surely have been suggested by the Marmeladovs in *Crime and Punishment*. The father, an unemployed stevedore and chronic drunkard, a handsome hairy giant of a man, combines the dignity and even poetry of the poor with the clownish behavior of an incurable sot. And his work-worn wife Olga with her compulsive chatter, alternately scolding and protecting her baby Pavlik and nine-year-old Annochka, seeks proud comfort for her poverty in memories of better days. Annochka, who plays an important part in the novel, is one of those "thinking children" of Dostoevsky, both spritely and grave, yet wise with the wisdom that comes from adversity. She understands the misery of grownups for she has known only misery herself, and she comforts the distraught mother of Kirill after his arrest by that unspoken childlike concern which finds its only expression in an effort to be helpful. The theater, to which Tsvetukhin introduces Annochka, fascinates her, and that remarkable scene in which she steals into the dark empty playhouse to watch a rehearsal symbolizes not only a desire to escape from her own world of drab reality, but also a vague yearning to identify herself with the make-believe world of the theater.

Fedin also introduces the tsarist officialdom of Saratov, especially the town prosecutor Polotensev, who is the examining officer of the secret police, and his minion Oznobishin, a timid but ambitious officer of the law. The play of irony and humor with which their activities are described only serves to emphasize the cruelty and relentlessness of the police pursuit of those under suspicion. Ragozin escapes, but his pregnant wife Xenia is jailed and brutally treated because of her refusal to inform against her husband. The extreme of human callousness is manifested when Polotensev temporarily interrupts his departure for a ball one evening and hurries to the prison at the news that Xenia is near death after bearing a child, for he hopes to extract a morsel of confession from the dying woman. All who were even remotely and innocently acquainted with Ragozin and Kirill, including Parabukin, Meshkov, Tsvetukhin, and Pastukhov, are swept into the police net and grilled. Fedin imparts an intense detective story element to this section of the novel, but at the same time he aims to reveal realistically an aspect of tsarist life which unwittingly contributed to cementing the brotherhood of political revolutionists in those days.

The collision of revolutionary idealism and harsh reality in the prison questioning and treatment of Kirill matures without embittering him. Though he worships Ragozin and is influenced by him, his political quest is anchored in an emergent independent philosophy which compels him to probe his relation to society in terms of the progressive movement of his day. Even his love for Lisa grows stronger and more manly under the trials of his bitter experience. He manages to get a letter to her from his place of exile in the north, to which he has been sentenced for three years. She must feel free to give her affections to another, he writes. "I won't take offense. Your freedom and independence are dearer to me than all else." Then he jealously asks if she's attracted to Tsvetukhin. He cannot have anything against it, he adds, but if it is not so he will be happier than before and perhaps some day they will be together.

The charming, eighteen-year-old Lisa, however, is not made of such stern stuff. After vainly trying to help Kirill in his plight, she is worn down by the dogged insistence of her father and marries Shubnikov, the spoiled, foppish, unstable nephew of a rich woman merchant. Lisa cannot overcome the sense of duty to her parents inculcated in her from childhood though she fully realizes that she has a still more important duty to herself. Her sensitive nature is crushed by this loveless marriage and she understands too late that she has transgressed against love, for the image of Kirill remains as strong as ever in her heart.

Soviet readers as old as Fedin must have marveled at the recreation in *Early Joys* of a Russian past never to return. For the author recalls with loving realism the Saratov scenes of his childhood—the gay colorful carnival, drama at the provincial theater, picnics in the fields outside the town, boating on the Volga, and the hauling and singing of the picturesque stevedores at the docks. The novel is full of the sights and sounds of the streets, of the movement of people and nature, all of which suggests impending social change accompanying a sense of political change. Vividly constructed genre pictures, such as the scenes in the flophouse, the drunken scenes at Mefody's and Tsvetukhin's, the raid at Ragozin's house, the prison scenes, and the brilliantly described society charity ball, serve both to advance the action and illuminate the manners and customs of the town's social strata.

A sense of history, however, influences these characters.

Fedin had purposely singled out 1910 as the year of action of his novel. The vast shadow of the great Tolstoy hung over Russia in this year of his death and darkened the lives of people who seemed to feel that with his passing would vanish also the conscience of the nation. Fedin vividly recaptured the universal concern reflected in the citizens of Saratov as they stood about the newspaper offices anxiously waiting for the next bulletin from the tiny railroad siding of Astapovo where the dying sage lingered on. The final message of death signalized the end of cherished hopes and the beginning of an era of change which would renounce the master's doctrine of nonviolence. In the novel Tolstoy is clearly regarded as a symbol of the inevitability of much-needed change, a "mirror of the Russian Revolution," as Lenin described him. But there is an unwarranted distortion in the implication that Tolstoy's call for a moral change in the hearts of men was the inspiration for the revolutionary changes brought about by the bloody events of 1917. In the connection of the two movements, however, a connection significantly reflected in Kirill Izvekov's declaration that Tolstoy "is among my great men," Fedin may have been trying to suggest the measure of idealism which influenced the thinking of the early revolutionists.

Indeed, it is only the truth of Tolstoy that seems capable of arousing momentarily the dormant social conscience of the intellectual Pastukhov. Tolstoy had been his literary hero, but now the great man's death awakens him to the larger purpose of Tolstoy's life and thought, and he weeps bitter tears as over a personal loss. "I'm not a prophet," he tells Tsvetukhin, "I don't want to foretell the future. I shall say only one thing. He [Tolstoy] has left us a rule as plain as a word. Here is the earth. Here is man on the earth. And here is a task: a life good for man must be built up on earth."

In short, Pastukhov glimpses a vision of the progressive heritage of Tolstoy: a new life for man on earth. Though Pastukhov's conscience has been stirred, it is Fedin's purpose to reveal the incapacity of such intellectuals—unlike Ragozin, Kirill, and their proletarian followers—to act positively upon their convictions. Pastukhov confesses to himself that in 1905 he wanted to take a place at the barricades, but he lacked the courage. When Kirill's mother pleads with him, as a prominent person, to help her imprisoned son, he coldly refuses. In a contemplative mood, at the end of the novel, when he is preparing to leave Saratov for Moscow, Pastukhov comments on their idle life to Tsvetukhin, and thinking of what the future may have in store for them, he remarks: "And somewhere, hard by, someone is forging our future for us, and, through the wild untrodden woods, torn and bleeding, pushes on towards the goal. . . . I mean some good-for-nothing boy."

This is a plain reference to the exiled Kirill Izvekov. The generous explosive Tsvetukhin catches the hint and conjectures that it would have been easier for them if they had been deservedly, instead of mistakenly, accused of being part of the Ragozin conspiracy. "The mistake was, perhaps, that we were not doing the things we were accused of."

But the cautious Pastukhov laughs off this challenge and sums it all up by an intellectual's typical observation: "We live too much in the mind, my friends. I want to drink to our participation in life, less in the mind and more in the body!"

THE COMMUNIST HERO REALIZED. The "good-for-nothing boy," Kirill Izvekov, turns up nine years later as the positive Bolshevik hero of *No Ordinary Summer* (1948), the second novel of the trilogy. After creating, with indifferent success, a series of Party figures in his early works Fedin now attempts to solve "the problem of our literature," which he had mentioned after the completion of *The Rape of Europe*: "the creation of a Soviet hero" who would compare favorably with the best heroic characterizations of Western European literature.

Once again the action centers largely in Saratov at a time

when—Fedin remarks toward the end of the novel—young Soviet Russia "had triumphantly scaled the peak of the civil war in the not ordinary year of 1919." In short, history, or more properly now, a Marxian view of history, continues to rule the action of the novel and in one way or another affects the lives of nearly all the participants. Most of the characters of *Early Joys* reappear but the canvas is much broader, the action more varied, and the historical circumstances entirely altered. These circumstances are memorably reflected in the opening scenes of *No Ordinary Summer* where Fedin vividly describes the effects of revolution and civil war on the countryside as seen by a new character, Dibich, a former tsarist officer, returning from German captivity to his home in the center of European Russia.

Tsarist Saratov of *Early Joys* is now under Soviet rule. In the bitter struggle between the old and the new, accentuated by the civil war which has overtaken the town and its inhabitants, Fedin is keenly aware of the pathos of the individual tragedies involved, although he appears to accept them as the inevitable consequences of the operation of history's laws. It seems almost that he willingly takes refuge in historical determinism as the only "logical" explanation which his sensitive nature can tolerate of the vast human misery brought about by violent revolution.

For Kirill Izvekov, historical determinism explains everything. "Our aims," he declares, "serve the historical interests of Russia, and in decisive moments in the life of the people our aims and their interests become one." After his release from exile he had served the Party under an assumed name as a propaganda agent first among workers and then as a soldier in the First World War. In 1919 he returns to Saratov, as secretary of the town Soviet, a stocky, broad-shouldered, square-jawed, clear-eyed, indomitable fighter in the cause of the Revolution. What saves him from the fate of taking his place among the endless dull, gray stream of similar Bolshevik heroes in Soviet literature is his creator's capacity to humanize him.

Though there is an element of the eternal boy scout in Kirill, there are also spiritual and emotional depths in his nature as well as moments of profound doubt as to the rightness of his behavior if not of the cause he serves. In most respects the youthful, idealistic, lovesick fellow of *Early Joys* has not changed; he has only developed. We observe Kirill now in manifold activities in the town Soviet and at Party meetings, in making recruitment speeches and in mobilizing and leading a punitive expedition against counterrevolutionaries. We see him also in relaxation, going to the theater, visiting museums, collecting books for his library, and even fishing on the Volga. But unlike the hero stereotypes of so much Soviet fiction, Kirill's personal life is not entirely sacrificed to his Party duties, though his dedication to them creates the major conflicts of his harassed existence.

On the punitive expedition Kirill is one of a military tribunal that sits in judgment over Lisa's husband Shubnikov, who has committed a serious act of sabotage. He votes for execution but he will not sign the death warrant, because Shubnikov accuses him of a personal grudge. Alone with his tormented thoughts, he wonders what his mother and others would think of his condemning the father of Lisa's son. Would they think he did it because he hated this man with a hate that was purely personal? It is a rather dubious ethical point, yet Fedin feels it necessary to defend this personal and quite un-Communist decision: "By refusing to sign the sentence Kirill exposed the calumny that Shubnikov had been victimized by Izvekov." However, as though to convince the Party judges that he is not opposed to the death penalty, Kirill almost eagerly signs the execution warrant of Zubinsky, a fellow conspirator of Shubnikov.

On this same expedition Lisa's father Meshkov is apprehended with illegally concealed gold on his person while he is in the company of the disguised Polotensev, the examining police officer of *Early Joys*. Here again the Bolshevik Kirill's moral scruples and personal feelings are sorely tried. He sends Meshkov to prison, but when the unhappy Lisa learns of her father's plight she finds the courage to appeal to her former lover. It is an intensely moving scene compounded of the memories of a once tender love now forsworn and the blind, cruel tragedies of revolution. Kirill stands on the letter of the law and has the unkindness to remind Lisa of the part her father has played in determining her fate. He is her father, she protests, and she would defend him even as she would defend her hated husband as the father of her child. "Why such blindness?" asks the Bolshevik Kirill. "Don't you hear the witchcraft of those words—husband, father? Behind the words stand people, and behind the people—their deeds. Cain also bore the name of brother." And she indignantly demands: "What are you accusing me of? Of the fact that my relatives are my relatives? That they are near and dear to me?"

In the end the Communist gives way to the human sympathy which Party discipline never quite subdues in Kirill. He promises to help and actually does use his influence to bring about the release of Lisa's father.

Fedin is obviously concerned with the ideological purity of his hero, who makes nice distinctions between the calculated good that one does in the interests of the masses and well-intentioned actions prompted by egotistical and personal motives. Certainly Kirill's stern demands on himself, his moral strength, and clarity of vision differentiate him sharply from the ambivalent heroes of much nineteenth-century Russian literature and even from the heroes of Fedin's earlier novels *Cities and Years* and *The Brothers*. But his love of life and his sense of humor for its oddities neutralize the doctrinaire in him. For example, he is the first of Fedin's heroes who is altogether happy in love, a state of bliss achieved only after the sad experience of his affair with Lisa.

Lisa had left a deep and painful scar on Kirill, which nine years of absence from Saratov had not effaced. Upon his return, helpless before the unexpectedness of his fits of memory, he questions his mother closely about her. Lisa had written him only once, and that about her marriage, asking him not to blame her in his heart. The further story of Lisa's fate in this second novel of the trilogy is told with deep sympathy and psychological understanding. When Shubnikov's mad antics had threatened the well-being of her son, Lisa left her husband for good. She began to discover her own will only after losing Kirill, for one does not mature until one has experienced grief. Saddened by the death of her mother and impoverished by the Revolution, Lisa lives with her little son and her old Soviet-hating father whom she pities but no longer respects. Lonely and ill she drifts into a second marriage with the equally lonely and miserable Oznobishin, former tsarist law official.

The charming vision of the eighteen-year-old Lisa he had once loved Kirill now discovers in Annochka Parabukina, the clever child of *Early Joys,* who has grown into a lovely young lady of spirit, humor, and intelligence, at turns delightfully naive and strangely mature about the profession of acting to which she is dedicated. The most memorable scenes of *No Ordinary Summer* are devoted to the story of their love—from the emotional alchemy of their first meeting, the storms and stresses of little jealousies, the difficulty posed by devotion to duty, to that ecstatic evening of consummation in her room before his departure for the front, when he finds the courage, on a hint from her, to blow out the light. Here the Bolshevik hero is sublimated in the ordinary but eternally interesting theme of a man in love. And it is at this level of life with its mysteries and values that Fedin is quite supreme among Soviet novelists in his delicacy, understanding, and psychological grasp. He succeeds where Leonov so often fails and where Sholokhov also triumphs but on a less sophisticated level.

In the work of the Party, Kirill shares the spotlight with the old Bolshevik Ragozin, who also returns to Saratov after the Revolution. Fedin deftly contrasts the Communist master and his disciple. Ragozin by derivation is a worker, and in his speech, behavior, and reactions to given situations he always remains a worker, though one molded by Party precepts. When the task of managing the town's finances is thrust upon him by the Party, he joyfully escapes to the docks for a few hours a day to pound away at iron mountings for river gunboats. His pleas for a life of real action away from deskwork are finally heeded when he is made commissar of a Volga flotilla, confident that his Communist faith will somehow compensate for his ignorance of this kind of activity. The image of Ragozin, however, is not devoid of emotional depth and spiritual dignity. His fatherly affection for Kirill, with its curious reticence, is warm and inspiring, and his patient search for the lost son born to his beloved Xenia in prison reveals an appealingly tender and attractive dimension of his otherwise stern Bolshevik nature. And when he finally discovers Ivan, there is something both movingly pathetic and ennobling in his fumbling efforts to bridge the gap of nine years between this half-wild waif and an unknown father. It is Ragozin who reminds Kirill of the danger of becoming estranged from people in striving to achieve a Communist society, and of failing to see "just a bit of the future in the people of today."

One is struck by the sharp contrast of Saratov in 1910 in *Early Joys* and Saratov in 1919 in *No Ordinary Summer*. With stark realism Fedin brings out the gray existence of the citizens, the privations they undergo, and the prevalence of fear among them as well as of enthusiasm for the Soviets among adherents of the new order. The large element of improvisation in the rule of the new masters has its laughable as well as its grim sides. While obviously sympathizing with the stubborn idealism and self-sacrifice of the leaders, Fedin ridicules the early Communist faddism of some of the intellectuals, such as the schoolteachers who declare: "With our children, 'home' is a conception that will eventually die out," or "Homework is an old-fashioned teaching method," or "We are trying to destroy the sense of private property in children."

No mercy is shown to the former "privileged" people of the tsarist regime. One form of persecution has been exchanged for another, only now it is more precisely a class persecution. Old merchant Meshkov is dispossessed of his business and all the wealth he has patiently accumulated over the years, save for the few gold coins that he illegally conceals. The same fate befalls the inherited business and wealth of the playboy Shubnikov. Oznobishin's legal career and social status are submerged in the menial job of notary clerk. The rancor of these and other dispossessed in the novel is intensified by their bewilderment over a fate which they feel they have done nothing to deserve. As Oznobishin phrases it: "As though I intentionally got born and grew up under the tsarist regime."

The adjustment to the Soviet scheme of things by those two remarkable friends of *Early Joys*—Tsvetukhin the actor and Pastukhov the playwright—inspires a number of the most absorbing chapters of the second novel of the trilogy. The formerly ebullient Tsvetukhin, now older and much cowed by the return of his virago of a wife, is suddenly aroused to new visions of art by the appeal of a group of young people, led by Annochka Parabukina, to help them in their theatrical activities. By a kind of self-hypnotization, he swallows in one gulp (though he also has a roving eye for the pretty Annochka) the new revolutionary fervor for an art that will carry the theater to the people, that will identify drama with life. With boundless enthusiasm, using his eager young Soviet-minded pupils as bait, this provincial matinee idol appeals vigorously to Kirill and Ragozin, and to anyone who will listen, for financial support for a traveling theatrical troupe. Fedin uses the occasion to indulge in delicious satire on the extreme theatrical experimentation of the early revolutionary years.

At the same time Fedin employs this situation to continue the debate on art which occupied so prominent a place in *Early Joys*. The Revolution, however, has brought about a shift in the emphasis of the discussion, to the collective, mass responsibility of art as opposed to the individualism of art. Tsvetukhin, Kirill, and Annochka support the new revolutionary position from varying points of view. In his enthusiasm for the people, Tsvetukhin demands an art that will penetrate the lives of the spectators who will then merge with art and by becoming a part of it will help to create art. The youthful Annochka is naturally more modest in her views. She disclaims any knowledge of what art will be in the future, but at present, she declares, it is part of life. As a devoted pupil of Tsvetukhin she shares his ardor for art for the masses and under his direction achieves popular success in a leading role. But Tsvetukhin's ideas on art for the masses are not unmixed with designs on the purity of the pretty young actress. This she eventually discovers, to her chagrin.

Kirill represents the Party position on art but in the rather attenuated form in which it existed in the early days of Bolshevism. He is deeply interested in art as a means of influencing people and significantly identifies this objective with his own "art" of influencing people politically. "An artist," he asserts, "should express all people through himself, and express them as they actually are. Otherwise he will not be understood." Though he distrusts Tsvetukhin and understands that he is sponsoring not revolutionary art but the romance of an actor already well on in years, Kirill feels that he must put personal considerations aside and support the endeavor of a man who believes that art should be allied with revolution.

Pastukhov, now a successful and well-known playwright, offers the only pointed opposition in the novel to these views on art. Over the years he has moved away from the Tolstoyan position he took on art in *Early Joys*. In fact, he has grown weary of discussions on art, although he feels that he knows more about the subject than most of the people who argue with him. Actually he has a contempt for schools and tendencies in art and is convinced that everything of artistic value has been created in spite of them. Besides this, he has come to the conclusion that postrevolutionary times are irrational and that reason is being applied to things which, like the dance, defy reason. In all this Fedin is no doubt offering a criticism of the numerous and contentious schools and theories of art which sprang up in the early years of the Revolution and vied with each other for popular support.

On the other hand, Fedin implies that Pastukhov's dissent grows out of his inability to adjust his dramatic muse to the needs of the Revolution. Pastukhov is irritated by Tsvetukhin's naive faith in the originality of his dream of a mobile theater and rejects his request that he write a revolutionary play for it by scornfully quoting Lomonosov's reply to his patron: "The muses are not wenches to be had for the asking!" He cynically reminds Annochka of the debt she is incurring to Tsvetukhin: "I know stage producers only too well. Come to your senses, my dear girl. They may promise you fame, but they demand a very high price for it!"

The real essence of Pastukhov's distrust of the new regime's intentions in art is revealed most clearly in his argument with Kirill in the stirring scene where Tsvetukhin and Annochka appeal to the local Soviet authorities for financial aid for their new theater. What if we suggest a theme, Kirill counters to Pastukhov's insistence that the Revolution has so far not inspired him with the subject of a play.

"Probably not suggest, but—order?" Pastukhov deliberately queries.

"If you wish to put it that way."

"But an author's freedom lies in his choice of subject," Pastukhov asserts.

Kirill then tries to rationalize this deprivation of the writer's freedom by explaining the Marxian doctrine that freedom is necessity. The Communists, he declares to Pastukhov, have freed him from dependence for his success on a particular layer of society. Now his art depends on the masses for its success.

"By transferring this freedom to yourselves," answers Pastukhov, "and making me dependent on it, you deprive me of my freedom."

"It belongs to us," insists Kirill. "This freedom is represented by our taste."

To illustrate his objection Pastukhov quotes the comment of Ryabushinsky, the tsarist millionaire patron of authors: "I am convinced that there is little difference between a writer and a prostitute. A writer is just as willing to sell himself to anybody who comes along, and will allow the highest bidder to do whatever he wants with him."

Apparently not perceiving the point that for Pastukhov there is no difference between the artistic success which depends on the favor of a millionaire patron and that which depends upon pleasing the Communist Party, Kirill eagerly asserts: "We have emancipated you from the Ryabushinskys."

"Thank you," Pastukhov drily retorts. "Then please allow me to enjoy my emancipation."

Pastukhov learns, however, that there is no emancipation and no real freedom of choice under the new regime. In fact, there is not even the freedom not to choose, which troubled him most of all. In 1919 history compelled allegiance for or against the Bolsheviks, and one's personal well-being, even one's life, depended on this enforced choice. In these terms the characterization of the intellectual and writer Pastukhov is a superior achievement of *No Ordinary Summer,* and Fedin's own troubled ideological adjustment to the Soviet regime over the years must have contributed greatly to the convincingness of the portrait.

Hunger had driven Pastukhov out of Petrograd, along with his beautiful wife Asya and his young son Alyosha. This well-dressed, cultured family, accompanied by a nursemaid, seems like an anachronism in provincial Saratov, impoverished by the Revolution and civil war and torn by divided loyalties. With his sharp intelligence Pastukhov understands what has happened in the Russian world, but he cannot reconcile himself to it intellectually or emotionally. He realizes that now not merely dissenters or Tolstoys but an entire people has risen up, yet whether it is for a new way of life or for a myth he cannot be sure. His very plays are already out of date, but artistically he is unable to grasp the present epoch and its search for the new which implies repudiation of the old. As he walks about the town impeccably clothed and inquiring with his courtly grace where Tsvetukhin lives, he begins sadly to wonder: "Was not he himself a part of the last century? A broken bit of the cornice of some shattered edifice?"

At heart Pastukhov is a traditionalist accustomed to resisting every new idea, yet he now plunges into reading Russian history in an effort to discover some sense of continuity between the past that he knew and the present that baffles him. The only continuity he finds is the fact of rebellion, in which the masses in the violence of their vengeance deepen the roots of the past they are trying to uproot. Then he begins to wonder if it is not history that is slowly but surely crushing him, and in a brilliantly written chapter Fedin presents Pastukhov's momentary defiance of the "history, the times, the calendar, the hands of the clock" which have sentenced him. He is guilty of nothing, his death has not the slightest meaning to anyone, so why should he be sacrificed? He is neither a Red nor a White, so why should he be forced to join either side? "A choice, a choice, that was what Pastukhov had to make! The meaning of his whole life, its very essence, boiled down to one thing—a choice." Yet he will not make a choice.

Threatened with being put out on the street with his family because the military has requisitioned his two rooms, Pastukhov appeals to Kirill Izvekov for aid. It was the most difficult thing for this proud man to do, and yet, at the outset of the conversation, provoked by this young Bolshevik's praise of the Soviets, Pastukhov rejoins: "So far as I can see, human misery all comes from these teachings about leveling down. You can't create a form of life which is uniform and common to all, any more than you can create a form of happiness which is uniform and common to all." In the discussion that follows Kirill presents all the stock arguments of the Communist Party in defense of the Revolution, the civil war, and the dispossession of the middle class. Pastukhov's effective rebuttal is as much a tribute to Fedin's artistic insistence upon this character's intellectual superiority over Kirill as it is to his own objectivity. For example, when Kirill repeats the Leninist principle that the war the Reds fight is a just one because it is for a noble purpose, Pastukhov quietly replies: "I am not so naive, or, in the last analysis, so despicable, as to fear a fight which has some meaning. But I must confess that I am horrified to see how much evil man commits in the name of good." In the end, however, Kirill demands that Pastukhov make his choice of the side of the Reds or be considered a deserter. Instead, Pastukhov decides to flee Saratov.

Fedin, however, leads Pastukhov through a series of harsh experiences which eventually convince him of history's right to exact a choice as the price of human happiness or even survival. He is thrown into a stinking prison by the Whites in the town of Kozlov, and there, in the face of possible death, he undergoes a prolonged self-examination of his life. He sees now that he is subject to nature's laws, the biological law that makes him want to live, and the social-historical law that compels him to live within society. He seeks justice for himself because life has become hard for him, but he had not sought it for others when life had been easy for him. Always he had wanted to receive without giving, and only now does he begin to perceive that if man could build life unerringly, like nature, then we could have a happy society.

When the Reds retake the town Pastukhov is released and, dazed and scarcely believing that he is alive, he rejoins his family. Still under the spell of his terrifying prison experience, he continues his searching self-examination, now aided by the questioning of his adoring wife who has made herself over in his image and has no thoughts but his. She had been reading Tolstoy's *War and Peace* and had found its philosophy of history puzzling and even false. Contrary to Tolstoy, says Asya, history directs man's course like an instrument.

Pastukhov replies that he does not wish to analyze which interpretation of history is false, but he has at last learned that "it is necessary to identify yourself with whatever is propelling history forward." However, if he must submit to the course of events regardless of circumstances, "at least it is within my power to choose which of the various forces influencing this course I shall submit to." And now, he tells Asya firmly, he has no intention of floundering among the wreckage, of perishing because of some fool misunderstanding. His choice, he declares, is the side of the Reds.

However, it is the logic of events rather than the labor of the intellect that brings about Pastukhov's conversion. He had promised himself that if he ever got out of the local branch of Dante's Inferno alive, he would write to Kirill Izvekov to confess what an ass he had been. And like the hero of Stendhal's novel, whose misery made his soul accessible to art, Pastukhov now enthusiastically promises the delighted director of the Kozlov theater that he will write an apotheosis for him and that its title will be "Liberation." Pastukhov could be sincerely happy in his conversion, for unlike Tolstoy's passive victims of history he was not merely submitting to circumstances. Rather by his own free will he would contribute to the development of circumstances. Pastukhov had finally come to believe that the sum of such free choices was one of the forces determining history. "In other words," he asserts, in Marxian terms, "to a certain degree history is created by the free will of man. By *my* free will." This is a conviction, it appears, that Fedin had also reached by the time he wrote *No Ordinary Summer.*

With the continuation of characters from *Early Joys* and the introduction of new ones the plot complications increase, but Fedin handles them now with the skill of a mature novelist. The Parabukins, older and a little better off economically under the Revolution, continue to be related to the main action and to provide the same tragicomic element of the earlier novel. Old Parabukin and the ex-actor Mefody have become boon drinking companions. Under the spell of vodka and influenced by their curious job of tearing up confiscated books to make wrapping paper, they philosophize lugubriously about the sin of drunkenness, the blessings of religion, and the future of Russia. The death of the old mother of this family, worn out by toil, is beautifully narrated with sentiment that never verges on sentimentality. Pavlik Parabukin, a baby in *Early Joys*, is now a boy of ten deftly schooled in all the ways of exploiting the Revolution. He, Lisa's son, the entrepreneur Vitya, and Alyosha, the shy, grave son of Pastukhov, form a trio of active, explosive youngsters who claim many of Fedin's best narrative pages as well as some of his most acute psychological insights into human nature. The life of the boys is centered in old "shaggy-locks" Dorogomilov, a new character in the trilogy and one of the most fascinating. Tragedy in his early life had slightly warped his mind and turned him into an odd, lonely figure who sought a kind of compensation by becoming the gentle leader and preceptor of all the boys in the neighborhood. He won their fervent devotion by teaching them the lore and adventure of childhood in hiking, fishing, and in the captivating stories they found in his well-stocked library. But there was another side of Dorogomilov, an idealistic radicalism which had early drawn him into the revolutionary movement. It was he, we learn, who had concealed Ragozin in *Early Joys* when the tsarist police were seeking him. Though Dorogomilov dies in *No Ordinary Summer*, his devoted young friends Pavlik, Vitya, and Alyosha, are no doubt intended by Fedin to be among the leading characters of the third volume of the trilogy, the action of which will take place some twenty years later.

Through many of the pages of *No Ordinary Summer* runs the theme of the civil war in southern Russia in 1919. In his previous fiction, much of it concentrated on the years of Revolution and civil war, Fedin patently avoided whenever possible the violence of combat. Temperamentally he seemed to have a distaste for a subject that became a commonplace in early Soviet fiction. *No Ordinary Summer*, however, requires extensive treatment of war and it is the least satisfactory part of the novel. Unlike Sholokhov, Fedin has little interest in the excitement of violence, in the thrill of a cavalry charge, or in the stirring spectacle of clashing armies. His artistic range does not include the mass movements of men. Like that other artist Pastukhov, he perceives the world through an isolated being. It is not human suffering as an abstract concept that he sees, but the living individual who is suffering.

Consequently, Fedin's descriptions of war in *No Ordinary Summer* are only adequate. Such is the punitive expedition led by Kirill, in which Dibich, the ex-tsarist officer turned Red, loses his life, or the expedition of the gunboat flotilla under Ragozin. For the most part Fedin limits himself to a dry "historical" account of the civil war in the south, interpolating dull quotations from official documents and statements of

Lenin and Stalin. Indeed, the whole account is arrant propaganda, for Fedin insinuates that the "treachery" of the commander-in-chief of the Red Armies, Trotsky, whose forbidden name he never mentions, was responsible for the failure of the initial campaign in the south, and that victory was achieved only after Stalin took over at Tsaritsyn. This, of course, is the official Soviet version of the campaign; a further excuse is that the account was written in the postwar period when the national propagandized acclaim of Stalin as the "great military genius" was at its height. Since his death this particular aspect of his fame has been officially debunked, a belated correction that simply compounds Fedin's error.

The conclusion of *No Ordinary Summer* symbolically foretells the future of Kirill Izvekov. Shortly before he leaves for the front he realistically analyzes his character, his hopes and dreams for Annochka, as though gently warning her that her love must be great enough to stand the test of living with a man who is compelled by his nature to serve a still higher love. I cannot change, he says. "I shall pound the earth until it is hard enough for me to ascend. So that later we can climb to heights undreamed of. The vision of those heights is with me always—do you believe me?" This motif is carried on when he arrives at the front, sees an inspiring review of Budyonny's cavalry, and meets and talks with Voroshilov and Stalin. To the enraptured Kirill it seems that he is actually glimpsing the onward march of history. "And his present elation," concludes Fedin, "was due to the fact that he, Kirill Izvekov, had added his small but loyal step to this thundrous stride."

BUILDING COMMUNISM. To date (1957) only one chapter of the last novel of the trilogy has appeared in print.* From Fedin's note on it, one gathers that the action will cover the second half of 1941, will center in Moscow, Tula, and the surrounding

---

* "V Yasnoi Poliane," (At Yasnaya Polyana), in *Literaturnaia Moskva* (Literary Moscow), (Moscow, 1956), pp. 7–38.

area, and will concern, apart from several new figures, the further development of characters in the first two novels, especially the children who have now grown up.

The chapter takes up the story with the beginning of the wanderings of Pastukhov, now in his sixties, who has been evacuated from besieged Leningrad. He has been a successful playwright under the Soviets, but apparently neither in his personal life—he has quarreled with his son Alyosha, who is in the Red Army—nor in his spiritual and ideological life has he achieved the happiness he seeks. Memories of his past fill him with a sense of guilt which is intensified by the German invasion of his country. It is perhaps significant that he makes Yasnaya Polyana, the former estate of his literary hero Leo Tolstoy, the first stop in his wanderings. And he vividly recalls how in his youth, as related in *Early Joys,* he had wept over the news of Tolstoy's death, and, thinking of *War and Peace,* he wonders how the great author, if he were alive, would write about this second invasion of his native land. The chapter ends with Pastukhov setting off to visit Tolstoy's grave at Yasnaya Polyana. "I will go to ask forgiveness," he declares, "that I am not the man I want to be." Even on the basis of this slight evidence it is safe to conclude that Fedin will make use of the final development of Pastukhov's characterization to represent the last act of his own spiritual and ideological reconciliation with the Soviets. Yet it is perhaps symbolic of the ultimate resolution of Pastukhov's long moral struggle that he asks forgiveness for what he considers the central failure of his life from one of the great dead of Russia's past, its foremost apostle of nonviolence.

Whatever contribution the last novel, when completed, may make to the total artistic achievement of the trilogy, *Early Joys* and *No Ordinary Summer* emphatically confirm Fedin's position among the three or four best novelists of Soviet literature. Further, these two connected novels are easily the most impressive fiction that has appeared in the Soviet Union since the war. These works mark the artistic fulfillment of a fine talent that has developed slowly but surely in a creative career of some thirty years. The novels are leisurely paced and rich in dramatic situations that are organically joined in a plot structure of considerable complexity which rarely depends upon coincidence, miracle, or mystery for its effects. The symbolic content is always functional in that it contributes to an understanding of the over-all design of the work. A wealth of descriptive detail, especially of landscape, testifies to Fedin's consummate control of the surface features of fiction. Though the major characterizations are still unfinished, Fedin has never done better in the novelist's fine art of creating living human beings. Kirill Izvekov may well turn out to be one of the very few artistically acceptable portraits of a positive Soviet hero simply because Fedin has been unwilling to eliminate or subordinate immemorial human qualities and failings for the sake of achieving a two-dimensional replica of Party perfection. Even in his unfinished state, Pastukhov is well on the way to becoming one of the great characterizations of Soviet fiction, the morally and emotionally tormented intellectual of the past who must adjust himself, in order to live at all, to the exacting and often cruel demands of a new way of life. As for the many secondary and minor characters, especially the women, these are nearly always treated with psychological authority and abundant human warmth and sympathy. The content of the novels is enriched by many philosophical discussions of art, history, and morality to which Fedin brings learning, wisdom, and a degree of detachment rarely found in Soviet fiction. And the ornamental prose of Fedin's early writing is replaced, in *Early Joys* and *No Ordinary Summer,* by a style which is poetic in texture but remarkable for its simplicity, clarity, and precision. Throughout these two volumes there is an intensification of a quality which Fedin had exhibited in his earlier works, a quality of feeling, a profound emotional involvement in the individual tragedy of man living in a world where tragic suffering has become a commonplace of daily existence. This is a quality inimical to the official optimism of Soviet literary canons which exclude "the wretched and unwanted," the beings whom Fedin loves above all.

The extent to which Fedin's art is a continuation of the great Russian realistic tradition of the nineteenth century has been indicated, and the direct influence of some of its authors on him, especially Dostoevsky, has been pointed out. It is perhaps of consequence that in *Early Joys* and *No Ordinary Summer* he moves away from Dostoevsky, whom the Soviets have always disliked ideologically, and seeks inspiration from Leo Tolstoy, a more favored author of the past. In fact, in an unpublished note Fedin writes: "After the twenties Dostoevsky began to yield to Leo Tolstoy in my efforts to make another beginning. However, none of this was direct influence, but only a passionate stimulation to work and to search for my own form of expression." * In Fedin's trilogy Tolstoy, as we have seen, plays the part of an active symbol of the past, but more importantly *War and Peace* is the obvious inspiration behind the trilogy which in a real sense is a Soviet "War and Peace." There, however, apart from certain artistic details and matters of construction, the comparison should end, although Fedin must be credited with a good deal of innovating skill for the manner in which he has reworked the classical heritage of Russian fiction into a new synthesis and adapted it so successfully to the Soviet scene. Thus, for example, Tolstoy's philosophy of history in *War and Peace,* which amounts to man's helpless surrender to the arbitrariness of historical action, becomes in Fedin's trilogy a philosophy of the ordered laws of history which man can help to direct and fulfill by intelligently participating in events.

As a creative artist in the Soviet Union, Fedin could hardly be accused of believing that a writer's talent is inversely proportional to his political activity and to his understanding of

* Quoted by B. Brainina, *Konstantin Fedin*, p. 273.

politics. Yet for most of his artistic life he has attempted to avoid entanglements in Party or literary politics while living under a regime that has aggressively identified politics with literature. The emotions, he believes, and not a rationale of life should direct the artist. His objectivity and intense concern for the inner moral problems of his characters seem to be attributes of this aloofness. So too, perhaps, is the atmosphere of keenly observed life which recalls that of the best nineteenth-century Russian fiction, and yet is so unlike the turgid atmosphere of contrived struggle and dubious class contradictions in most Soviet novels.

Fedin's prolonged ideological uncertainties, reflected in most of his fiction, were finally resolved by the time he began his trilogy. The forces and circumstances that influenced his decision can only be guessed at, but as already suggested the horrors of the Nazi invasion and the united efforts of Party, government, and people in defense of the country undoubtedly had much to do with the positive convictions he formed. In his speech at the Second All-Union Congress of Soviet Writers (December 26, 1954), a few of his statements invoke the unspoken reasons which quelled his last doubts and led him to identify his ideology with that of the Party. Speaking of the relation between Soviet literature and the development of its new hero type, and perhaps thinking of himself and his creation of Kirill Izvekov, he declares: "The writer educates this new man in himself, becomes the new man and introduces new features into his art." Then, overcoming all doubt, he boldly asserts: "The Soviet artist has become an artist of socialist realism because he has belonged and now belongs to a people who are building Communism."

Leonid Maximovich Leonov, 1899-

Leonid Leonov

"The purpose of poetry is poetry," Pushkin testily replied to a friend who demanded to know the purpose of one of his poems. Art as a value in itself, however, has rarely been regarded by native critics as the ethos of Russian literature. From Belinsky's view in the first half of the nineteenth century that literature is the conscience of the nation, to the Soviet dictum today that it must reflect the spirit of the Communist Party, critics have sought to identify the universal elements of Russian verse and prose with temporal causes. They have not willingly understood that the artist is confronted with questions which transcend those of his own age, that the insights which art affords into the meaning of existence are not necessarily relevant to the social or ideological preoccupations of the present. In the Soviet Union in particular, literature must serve the optimistic socialist present in terms of a utopian Communist future. Leonid Leonov, like Fedin, is one of the few Soviet novelists whose image of the present reflects the past and whose concern with life often represents a search beyond time and space for the universal determinants of human behavior.

If the young generation of Soviet writers since World War II are often the historians of the present, it is an official, embellished present they report, divorced from tragedy and steeped in the Party theology of socialist perfectibility. Life is

good and happy and its only evils are trifling "bourgeois survivals" which the positive hero easily vanquishes. Neither youth
nor Party regimentation account entirely for the low gray
level of artistic achievement of these younger writers. They
have no roots in the past and their vision of the future is pre-
ordained. Their works—if not their personal existence—are
officially denied the tragic experience of life out of which
great art often emerges. Perhaps the older generation of Soviet
writers succeeded so well because they had roots in the past
and because they themselves lived through the tragic struggle
between the old and the new which inspired much of their
best writing. Leonov belonged to the older generation, and no
Soviet writer felt more deeply this prevailing tragedy of the
Revolution.

ARTISTIC APPRENTICESHIP. Though Leonov was only eighteen
when revolution broke out in 1917, he had already read widely
in the works of the great masters of Russian fiction of the
nineteenth century and had found his cultural moorings in the
old intelligentsia to which his father, a radical journalist and
self-taught poet, aspired to belong. Life in the Moscow suburb
where he was born, then in the city itself, and finally in distant
Archangel, to which his father had been exiled in 1910, provided the young Leonov with a rich store of experience which
he was to draw upon later in his writings. And his knowledge
of the city and the provincial intelligentsia was supplemented
by his contacts with the countryside and peasantry in his work
on a Red Army newspaper during the civil war in the Crimea.

At the age of fifteen Leonov had begun to publish verse in
his father's Archangel newspaper, and a strong lyric sense
suffuses the form and language of his earliest short stories, as
do symbolic devices which were undoubtedly influenced by
the Symbolists Andrei Bely and Aleksei Remizov. But equally
prominent in these tales is a realistic content often psychologically interpreted in terms of a nonrational or mystical atti-

tude toward life, which reveals the powerful influence of Dostoevsky. This influence was certainly the dominant factor in the development of Leonov's creative art.

The early intellectual and emotional gropings born of the fierce destructiveness and human wastage of the Revolution find poignant expression in *The End of a Petty Man* (1924), a *novella* which is properly regarded as the artistic culmination of Leonov's period of apprenticeship. In the macabre, death-lurking atmosphere of freezing, starving, morally depraved Petrograd of 1919, the old and renowned Professor Likharev struggles to complete his definitive study of Mesozoic fossils. The end of the old clashes fatally with the new just being born. Confronted with the dissolution of their world, various representatives of the old intelligentsia who might have aided the professor in his efforts reveal the manners, pettiness, and bankruptcy of their lives. Not they but a black-market specu-lator, Isaak Mukholovich, who seeks to ennoble his meaning-less life with a vision of cultural achievement, encourages Likharev's work. The professor condemns the Bolsheviks for their violence and crime, but out of hunger he himself commits a crime—he steals a decaying horse's head. And during a heart attack he undergoes an experience similar to that of Ivan Kara-mazov—his double appears and accuses him of being no better than the Bolsheviks and urges him to burn his manuscript. In the end Likharev comes to believe that his own class has no more interest in culture than the Bolsheviks and he burns the manuscript in a final gesture of despair. The only one to regret the act is the black-market speculator.

Leonov, like Professor Likharev, saw much to condemn in those survivors of the old who revealed the emptiness of their lives when faced with the terrible challenge to all that they had believed in. Many of the young intellectuals who had some of their roots in the past welcomed the Revolution. They hoped that it would destroy the ugliness of the old regime but would spare all that was fine and beautiful. The young intellectuals were not opposed to the new but they grew disillusioned—again like Likharev—when the flames of revolt consumed, along with the dross, all that they admired in the culture of the past. In short, Leonov had cast his lot with those early Soviet writers who were known as "fellow travelers." Leon Trotsky, in his book *Literature and Revolution,* rather perceptively but a little unfairly described them as men "who fail to grasp the Revolution in its entirety, its final Communist aim being alien to them. . . . They are not the artists of the proletarian revolution, but only its artistic fellow travelers." And it was as an "artistic fellow traveler" that Leonov wrote his first full-length novel, *The Badgers* (1925).

With few exceptions the Party critics praised *The Badgers* as a marked advance over his mystical and symbolic early tales with their mannered prose, and Leonov was hailed as an important new force in the young Soviet literature. The novel's artistic worth alone could hardly have evoked such uniform praise if at the same time there had been any serious question of its ideological acceptability. The central theme—the struggle between the peasant village and the proletarianized city— was regarded by the critics as having been resolved in favor of the workers. Or rather the peasants in the novel had been compelled by force to recognize the interdependence of village and city under the leadership of the Communist Party. It was the age-old Russian peasant question inherited from the past but acquiring a Soviet twist in the early 1920s—the period of strife treated in the novel—when the government requisitioned food from recalcitrant peasants to aid the starving cities.

A careful reading of *The Badgers,* however, suggests that Leonov, while not assuming an overt ideological position in the novel, leaves the profound contradictions between city and village essentially unresolved. Rather, he appears to be attempting to use the power of art to break through the surface limitation of class strife and Party dictation in order to pose a broader solution of these contradictions. Before the

Revolution two brothers, Semyon and Pavel, like so many peasants then, are forced by poverty to desert their village and come to the city to seek their fortune. In this brilliant first part of the novel Leonov describes the corrupting influence of the city on peasant workers. The strong are transformed into money-grubbing hucksters, the weak are irretrievably crushed, and the positive spiritual qualities which both groups had absorbed from their contacts with the soil and with nature are destroyed by the city. Leonov seems to identify himself with the human spirit of the peasants and with nature rather than with the city and the proletariat. Semyon, who returns to the village after the Revolution and leads the bloody opposition of the "Badgers" (for the most part deserters from the Red Army) on behalf of the peasants in their struggle against the food-requisitioning city Communists, is the real hero and the most sympathetically portrayed and realized character. On the other hand, his brother Pavel, who becomes first a factory worker and then a Bolshevik commissar, has his orders to quell the peasant revolt and disperse the Badgers. He is a hard-bitten, shadowy character, appearing rarely, and is unsympathetically portrayed by his creator. Yet critics professed to see in Pavel an early prototype of the purposeful, leather-jacketed, positive hero, the Soviet Communist "new man," a type that Leonov was to become increasingly interested in as his own ideology shifted and his creative powers deepened.

On this slight foundation of plot Leonov erected a substantial edifice of story curiously overlaid with baroque ornamentation in incident and situation: the absurd and ancient dispute of two villages over the ownership of a meadow; the tactless efforts of Communist officials to requisition food; the massacre of Soviet sympathizers by the peasants and the drunken orgy that follows; the full-scale revolt of the villagers as fear-ridden peasants join the Badgers in the woods; and finally the hopeless plight of the peasants, their submission, and the crushing of the Badgers. Interwoven with this activity is the love tri-

angle of Semyon, the bandit Zhibanda, and the Communist-
hating bourgeois Nastya. But it is a pale, unconvincing affair
bedeviled by mixed motivation—the female in love is an
artistic weakness in Leonov's fiction which he rarely overcomes to the satisfaction of his readers.

The concentration of the novel, however, is on the peasantry,
on their present misery and their uncertain future. Like Leo
Tolstoy, Leonov understands the Russian peasant, but he is
unable to translate that understanding into the creation of living human beings with the artistry of Tolstoy, although Semyon,
at least, is given a characterization that is substantial. Another
peasant character, Chmeliev, represents a kind of symbolic
bridge between the city and the village. Encouraged by an
agronomist, he had tried to educate himself and had become
a Communist. Chmeliev preaches the economic and cultural
value of the city to the peasants, but he believes that nothing
will ever come of this unless the city is able to understand
and appreciate the peasant's psychology and cultural needs.
It is perhaps significant that this peasant Bolshevik is killed in
the revolt.

At the end of the novel Leonov does not allow us to listen
in on the conversation in which Pavel is supposed to have
convinced his brother to give up the fight and accept the
authority of the Party. At best, Semyon seems only half convinced and we are led to believe that the peasant hostility
to the Bolsheviks and to the city which the Bolsheviks sym-
bolized must go on. By his art Leonov dramatized this ancient
problem which had assumed an acute form under the Soviets,
and at the same time he revealed the tragic irreconcilability
of the opposing forces, the futility of a rational Communist
approach to an almost primitive peasantry whose irrational
instincts and superstitions, as well as their spirituality, were
formed by the forces of nature that controlled their lives. Indeed, this important struggle between the rational man and

the man of nature was to echo again in Leonov's second novel, *The Thief* (1927).

A SOVIET RASKOLNIKOV. Up to this point fellow traveler Leonov had a vision of art singularly unsuited to the demands of a ruling Party that had already become aroused to the possibilities of art as a medium for forming and controlling the minds of men. It was a vision inspired by the great Russian classics of the past, in which man the individual with his transient joys and sorrows, successes and failures, had been transmuted by art into an image of universal man. In a society in a state of revolutionary flux Leonov wished to discover more permanent values, to create enduring human embodiments of the struggle between good and evil. Perhaps it was quite natural that the young author should have taken as his model the extraordinary art of Dostoevsky with its compassion for the insulted and injured, its spiritual intensity, its doctrine of salvation by suffering, and its view of the Russian man as the messianic microcosm of the great future world destiny of the Russian nation. Dostoevsky's contempt for rational socialism as a panacea for the ills of society and his profound but peculiarly individualistic religious faith were not shared by Leonov. But Dostoevsky's belief that the Russian man and the nation as a whole would achieve personal and national salvation only through sin and suffering and thus would earn the right to guide the destinies of the rest of the world attracted the young Leonov. For him Golgotha followed the 1917 Revolution, when the terrible sufferings of the Russian people would entitle them to the salvation of Communism which for Leonov had now become invested with a kind of mystical halo.

More than once Leonov has paid tribute to Dostoevsky in print and in public speeches even though this great author has never found favor among the leaders of the Communist

Party. Dostoevsky's influence on Leonov is not limited to the larger doctrinal issues mentioned above; it may also be observed in various details of plot, characterization, scene, situation, and dramatic device. However, Leonov is not a slavish imitator of Dostoevsky; he has completely assimilated this influence in writing fiction that is highly original and very much his own.

If Dostoevsky had lived in the Soviet Union at the time of the New Economic Policy (NEP), one imagines that he would have sought its artistic epicenter where Leonov placed it in *The Thief*—in the Moscow underworld whose ambivalent heroes and heroines of crime reflect the pathos of degeneration in a society that had lost its political and social idealism. For Lenin's "planned retreat" to petty-bourgeois capitalism had resulted in an orgy of greedy speculation, get-rich-quick schemes, thievery, and a deep sense of disillusionment among those who had fought for the Revolution and for its promise to eliminate the bourgeoisie as a class. The only "heroes" now spawned by the Revolution (the period of action covered by the novel is 1924–25) are heroes of crime. This cynical barb of satire by Leonov seems to be aimed against those who believed that Communism represented a rational approach to life.

It is just such a "hero" that Firssov, the uncouth, bespectacled author of the novel within *The Thief*, who is endlessly sniffing around with notebook in hand, discovers in Dmitri (Mitka) Vekshin, former commissar in the Red Army, "daredevil boy, darling of the regiment," now king of the thieves in Moscow's underworld. He had come from the village, worked with proletarians, joined the Party, and fought against the Whites with conspicuous bravery. But Mitka's glorious career in the army is ended by a searing traumatic experience—he murders in cold blood a captive White officer who had killed Mitka's beloved horse. Obsessed by a feeling of guilt and disillusioned in his political convictions, he comes up to Moscow only to discover that revolutionary heroes have no place of honor among the money-mad Nepmen of the capital, and he turns thief to revenge himself on this society and on everything he had held dear.

Mitka is a Raskolnikov-like character with more than a touch of Dmitri Karamazov's passionate sense of honor. And Leonov's psychological analysis of his tormenting dualism reveals the method of Dostoevsky if not his profound penetration and convincingness. The trouble is that Leonov has blurred the image by clothing Mitka in some of the extraordinary trappings of Stavrogin, that titanic self-willed character of *The Possessed*. In this guise he looks a bit ridiculous—the strong, silent, guilt-ridden type, with the clear gaze and the mark of Cain on his brow, but whose soul, as the philosophical pot-mender Puchov puts it, is as "tender as a girl's, and sick from always searching and never finding another like itself."

Such a kindred soul was the beautiful Masha Dolomanova, but fate and Leonov keep her and Mitka apart. Like Varvara in Fedin's *The Brothers*, she is one of those "infernal women" of Dostoevsky's novels. Masha, like Nastasia in *The Idiot*, whose whole life was tainted by the moral hurt she suffered as a girl, can never forgive Mitka for refusing her offer to run away with him when, as a youth, he was threatened with arrest and had to flee. She had then been raped by that fearsome bandit and incredible stage prop Agey and has elected to live with him out of a desire for self-violation and in a spirit of revenge on Mitka. Eventually, it appears, she betrays Agey to the police and he is killed in a raid, which then leaves the field open again for Mitka. However, she must first break his pride, the initial cause of their estrangement. Pride, indeed, is at the center of this intense love duel between two well-matched antagonists. "Yes, he's hard as steel!" Masha tells her rival, the plump and simple Zinka, whose anguished love for Mitka is unreturned, "but you've got to meet pride with pride." Zinka acutely observes that Masha's heart is too near her head, yet Masha tells Curly Donka, the poetic thief to whom she has submitted to spite Mitka: "Do you know the richest treasure that a woman can possess? A man like Mitka."

If in this second novel Leonov falters before achieving full and effective realization of the psychologically complex na-tures of his chief protagonists, he succeeds admirably with some of his secondary characters. Nikolka Zavarikin, the cunning peasant who comes up from the village to Moscow to exploit the Revolution, delighted Soviet critics as a perfect personification of the Nepman. Huge, strong, and ruthless, de-void of conscience, and scorning friendship, he had come into the world with his fists clenched, as he says, and is determined to be top dog. He despises weak people because to pity them would detract from his own strength. When he woos Tanya, the gentle, charming sister of Mitka and a famous circus star, who seeks comfort for her loneliness and weakness in Zavari-kin's force and assertiveness, he assails her like a country bumpkin bargaining at a fair. And when she surprises him by a visit to his tiny room, where he sits alone eating boiled eels and spitting the bones into a jampot, he is so embarrassed that he rushes around the room with the eel's head in his hand and regales her with a story of how the village shepherdess tried to seduce him in the bathhouse. "There she stood, bare as my fist, in front of me," he related.

"And what did you do?" Tanya bent her head.

"I? . . . I let her have a whack on her bare belly with my stick and took to my heels."

This pushy peasant, rapidly on the way to achieving a bourgeois status through shady speculations, stands in striking contrast to Manyukin, "the last of the Russian noblemen," a victim of the Revolution who now survives by playing the buffoon and telling fantastic stories in barrooms to tipsy clerks who embezzle the government's money. He is a wonder-ful, drunken, Marmeladov-like character, the central attraction in powerful Dostoevskian scenes of human degradation. Beneath the unintentional pomposity, genteel manners, and culture of Manyukin, there is revealed a suffering soul fallen to the social bottom of ignominy and wretchedness. Throughout the novel runs a baffling thread of narrative which connects Mitka with Manyukin as his illegitimate son. It is hard to discover the purpose behind this motiveless mystification, for nothing much is made of it in the plot, though Leonov may be attempting to suggest that the incongruously fine bearing, appearance, and feelings of Mitka the thief are somehow to be explained by his "noble" birth.

Chikelyov, the disagreeable roommate of Manyukin, is perhaps the most original and brilliantly portrayed character in *The Thief*. Firssov loathes Chikelyov as "a degenerate epigone with a wound instead of a face," but he is much more complex and perhaps deserving of more sympathy and understanding than Firssov will allow. For Chikelyov is the product of all the vileness of his unhappy childhood. In order to exist and then to succeed, both in the time of the tsars and under the Soviets, he has turned himself into a variation of Uriah Heep, humble to his superiors and a tyrant to everyone else. This repulsive, bandy-legged scarecrow of a little man is a Philistine incarnate, petty and mean in human relations and ready to sacrifice all moral values in order to advantage himself. So thoroughly has he adapted himself to his own conception of the new order that he has projected it into the future, when everyone will be kept under observation and won't be allowed to run around without control. "Thought," he declares, "that is the cause of suffering. The man who can eradicate thought will be held in everlasting remembrance by a grateful mankind." (In this Orwellian bit Leonov may be satirizing the future Communist state and its rationalism.) Yet Chikelyov yearns to be like other people; he wants to marry and have a child, though he translates even this ambition in terms of doing his duty to the Soviet state. And his pathetic attempt

to woo the suspicious Zinka by displaying endless care and
tenderness for her little daughter reveals an element of genuine
humanity in this wretched, love-starved creature.

The burden of Communist ideology is a very light one—
almost heretically so in a Soviet novel, even in this early NEP
period. Perhaps Leonov anticipated this accusation in the
work itself in a rebuttal to the critics' charge of the "political
unsoundness" of Firssov's novel on the subject of *The Thief*:
"[They] did not realize that an artistically honest work can
scarcely ever be ideologically false." The only two functioning
Communists among the many characters—Atashez, former
comrade-in-arms of Mitka, and Zinka's brother Matvey—are
shadowy figures with very minor parts. Certainly one of the
unlabored themes of the novel is to reveal the degrading aspects of the "retreat to capitalism" and the moral hurt Mitka's
revolutionary idealism suffered because of it. But this was an
anti-Party manifestation at that time, as Atashez tries to explain to Mitka. Leonov makes it plain, however, that Mitka
retains more than a modicum of faith in the new order. And
there is at least one suggestion in the novel that he owes something of his incredible and repeated successes as a thief to the
"protection" of the Party, which was cognizant of his past
services and convinced of his future rehabilitation. For despite
his political disillusion, Mitka will not permit anybody to run
down the Revolution in his presence. Like Commissar Pavel in
The Badgers, he recognizes that the peasants must be led by
the Party. When the homely philosopher Puchov narrates a
little fable of how the devil is leading the blind masses in a
futile pursuit of progress, Mitka passionately exclaims: "And
good too! But when we get there, we'll become the masters
ourselves. You're on the wrong track, Puchov. Men must go on
advancing further and further."

The main theme of *The Thief*, however, has very little connection with political ideology; it is the personal tragedy of
Mitka the lonely individualist who has suffered a psychic

wound and rebels against a society in which he can no longer find happiness. He is a romantic rebel nostalgically yearning to recapture the mysterious, innocent glow of childhood love for Masha and the revolutionary enthusiasm of warm comradeship which he had experienced in the Red Army. Yet he deliberately sacrifices the two links with his idyllic past which might have brought comfort to his anguished spirit. His cynical and ungenerous behavior toward Sanka, his endlessly devoted comrade in battle and now in thievery, turns Sanka into an informer. After Agey's death Mitka might have found solace in the arms of Masha, who still passionately adored him. But pride and the emptiness in his soul forbade it. "He, Mitka, as Masha's husband! . . . It would have ruined him in a year," he scornfully imagines.

"Is it wrong to kill a man . . . an unarmed man?" Mitka demands of the psychiatrist to whom he has gone for help. His conscience, tormented by his murder of the defenseless White officer, gives him no rest. Like Raskolnikov, he must expiate this crime and his many thefts by suffering. "You must suffer, Mitka," Puchov tells him, "till the fire of your soul burns you clean." He seeks solace by returning to nature and the village scenes of his childhood but the furies continue to pursue him and he plunges once again into a life of crime. Finally, physically and morally ill over the thought of his lost honor, he flees the city in a train for the east. How he regains his good name through exhausting toil as a lumberman, work in a factory, and by study is another story, Leonov tells us at the end.

Party critics deplored this novel and regarded it as marking a sharp decline after *The Badgers*. The Moscow underworld as a setting and a Communist turned thief for a hero were features for which they understandably had no sympathy; *The Thief* is conspicuously absent from the latest Soviet edition of Leonov's collected works. Yet in certain respects it is his most artistic novel and rarely surpassed in power by the others to come, and it certainly represents a considerable advance over *The Badgers.*

In form this second novel reveals Leonov in an experimental mood. The form is intensely dramatic, an approach no doubt again suggested by his study of Dostoevsky. Leonov has no mercy on his readers, for he willingly sacrifices sequential narrative in order to achieve striking dramatic effects. The device of the novel within a novel, though not original in itself, results in a dialectical presentation of characters that is often highly original. Time and space coalesce in bewildering patterns of structural ambiguity in plot. Normal chronology is abandoned, much is said about characters before they are actually introduced, and the order of events is sometimes reversed. Such devices contribute to the element of mystery, a legitimate artistic concern of the writer of fiction, but when they create confusion, as occasionally happens in *The Thief,* they defeat the artist's purpose. In the mystification, the indiscriminate piling up of verbiage, and the violation of the reader's right to understand the mixed motivation of thought and action of these complex characters, the total effect is rather Faulknerian. Tanya, Mitka's sister, remarks to a foreigner: "But you'll never understand how we Russians live through every tiny detail of our trouble." However, it is the novelist's business to enable the reader, even the foreign reader, to understand this, which is one of the artistic achievements of Dostoevsky, the master of Leonov.

Despite its faults, however, *The Thief* is absorbing reading. Leonov was never again to exercise so completely the free spirit of creative independence which artistically dignifies this novel. For in his next effort, the fellow traveler heeded the "social command" for fiction that would further the purpose of the Communist Party.

A FIVE-YEAR-PLAN NOVEL. The First Five-Year Plan (1928–32), which succeeded the period of the NEP, engulfed the Soviet

Union in a second revolution, this time a revolution from above. Perhaps even more so than the October Revolution, this dynamic national program of industrialization and agricultural collectivization at an incredibly swift tempo affected the personal lives of masses of the people. National habits of shiftlessness and passivity were altered by a nationwide campaign of ruthless action which, in the case of agricultural collectivization, often descended into shocking brutality. Never before in history had the doctrine of work so seized the imagination and compelled the attention of a whole nation. Propaganda slogans on the virtues of worker shock brigades, labor fronts, and socialist competition were daily drummed into the consciousness of people who in turn performed prodigies of human labor. The Communists, disillusioned with the "return to normalcy" of the NEP, now came into their own as the enthusiastic leaders of this first tremendous push in the direction of socialism. Hard and fast lines were drawn by them. Being for or against the Plan was a primary test of loyalty, and those who failed to support it were branded as enemies of the regime.

Literature was also mobilized to support the Five-Year Plan. The Party instructed government publishing firms to suggest to authors themes which would glorify achievements of industrial construction and agricultural collectivization, and the Russian Association of Proletarian Writers (RAPP), which dominated the literary scene at the time and was favored by the Party, used its authority to coerce writers into following the Five-Year Plan "line." The fellow travelers in particular objected to this literature of social command, and most of it that appeared dropped stillborn from the presses. Boring sameness of theme, plot, and characters, and artificiality of motivation stamped these works for what they were—overt propaganda masquerading as belles-lettres.

Many writers, however, and Leonov among them, no doubt sincerely responded to this tremendous, elemental, driving energy which was transforming the whole face of the country with a variety of massive constructions. Gone was the old, fatal inertia. This was a new and different Russia struggling to banish the age-old backwardness and to take her place among the leading nations of the world. If this was what socialism meant, then they were for it. Hitherto the Revolution had in part signified for Leonov the indiscriminate destruction of both good and bad cultural values of the past in the name of a rational solution of society which had resulted in all the human misery and waste of the civil war and the loosened moral fabric and sniggering indecency of the NEP. The achievements of the Five-Year Plan clearly caught his imagination and opened up for him a whole new field of artistic creation. Here was a revolution that justified the sacrifices made in its name, the "advancing further and further" which Mitka Vekshin had enthusiastically foretold to Puchov. But Leonov insisted on telling this story in his own way. However unwittingly he may have been submitting to the propaganda climate of the moment, he publicly rebuked those who espoused a literature of social command. As a result he wrote two Five-Year Plan novels which are among the best of the very few good ones dealing with this theme.

Though Leonov was only thirty-one when *Sot* (1930) was published, the great Gorky paid him a handsome compliment by writing an introduction to it in which he described the young author as a prominent continuer of the best traditions of Russian classic literature, and he compared favorably certain of his effects in the novel, in style, description, and characterization, with those of Tolstoy and Lermontov. "Quite consciously do I measure Leonov by so high a standard," he wrote, "quite consciously place him in one rank with the greatest figures of our old literature—Leonid Leonov himself forces one to approach him thus with the highest claims."

Gorky asserts that *Sot* represents a substantial artistic advance over *The Badgers* and *The Thief*. However, *Sot* is. not easily comparable to these earlier works, for it is cast on a different thematic level which in turn requires a different focus of verbal and structural devices as well as a shifting of ideological focus from the two previous novels. The theme is one of construction, the building of a paper mill on the River Sot in an almost primitive district of Northern Russia. But the tiresome stereotypes of feverish activity, intense work competitions, and challenging shock brigades of so much Five-Year-Plan fiction are overshadowed in *Sot* by Leonov's favorite artistic preoccupation—the struggle between the old and the new. Only the struggle now is not primarily between individuals, but rather between the old Russian way of life and the new socialist way of the First Five-Year Plan. And the people involved are subordinated to the almost mystical intensity of the strife, which perhaps accounts for the limited use of that penetrating psychological analysis of character which had been so striking a feature of Leonov's artistic development in *The Thief*.

The novel opens with a lyric description of the beauties of nature on the banks of the Sot. On one side of the turbulent river is the little village of Makarikha slumbering comfortably in accumulated dirt and squalor, its peasant inhabitants submerged in the superstitions and ignorance of the Russian ages. On the other side is an ancient monastery whose filthy, ragged monks are hardly less ignorant and superstitious than the peasants. Oblomovism—a do-nothing attitude—like a smog hangs over this region in which the slow habits of the old empire still reign. Then one day, at the beginning of the Five-Year Plan, the Communist Uvadiev arrives in this primitive stagnating backwater, shouting to his lagging aides: "Hurry, hurry, comrades, you are building socialism!"

Soon a paper factory begins to rise on the bank of the Sot; preparations are made to harness the river for water power, to strip the forests for pulp; and the sleepy village, in the way of the factory site, is torn up by the roots, moved a distance off, refurbished, proletarianized and Sovietized complete with a workers' club and Party cell meetings. And the ancient monastery, like some huge rotting old oak in the forest, a dispensable relic of the past, is also marked for destruction.

Who are the invaders of this sylvan paradise bent on exploiting the forces of nature for the glory of socialism and the Five-Year Plan? The romantic Potemkin has dreamt this idea (Bolsheviks must be able to dream, said Lenin), and by sheer will power and the aid of Jeglov and Uvadiev, he finally crams it through the Soviet circumlocution office. For his efforts Potemkin is made head of the project and months later, exhausted from overwork and unattended illness, he is invalided off to the Caucasus to die, one of the endless sacrifices of the Five-Year Plan. But in this novel he is never more than an idea, a symbol of the heroic expendables of socialism.

Uvadiev, the Party organizer of the project and the central figure of the novel, is made of sterner stuff. He is a version of that wraith, Commissar Pavel of *The Badgers,* but now terrifying because he is almost real. The Dostoevskian element of rebellion against life, which had characterized the last two heroes of Leonov, is replaced by an affirmation of life, but it is an affirmation of the life of the socialist future. Here is the new Soviet man who crucifies today in the conviction of its resurrection as a beautiful tomorrow.

Of proper proletarian origin, Uvadiev had suffered arrest for political conspiracy in the old regime, had served as a Bolshevik soldier-agent during the war, and after 1917 had become "a dray horse of the Revolution" while slowly climbing the Communist ladder of success. In turning him into a fanatical, dedicated priest of the dictatorship of the proletariat, the Revolution had sucked him dry of the sweeter juices of life. "He fled tenderness," remarks Leonov. Smoking and vodka, both of which he liked, are banished, because he considers such indulgences "against regulations." Love turns into a necessary evil annoyingly interfering with the exacting demands of his work; "It was merely a fuel to treble his strength on the next day's path." He callously casts off his faithful wife Natalia "who for nine years had mournfully stuck by him, like a traveling inkpot," for the pretty young worker Suzanne who soon drops him for the more human affections of the engineer Favorov. In his loneliness he strokes the fluffy curls of his typist Zoe and invites her to his quarters to partake of some dates, a rare delicacy then. When she arrives, however, Uvadiev "realized one thing," remarks the novelist; "This was the enemy." Apparently to calm his aching desires Uvadiev excuses himself to put through a purely business telephone call but when he returns to the room he finds the overeager Zoe, who had understandably regarded her boss's invitation to his apartment as something other than a summons to eat sticky dates, sitting stark naked before him with a timid smile on her lips, murmuring: "I got a surprise for you." But the stern-visaged, hard-working Bolshevik at once recovers his moral scruples: "Get out . . . you vermin, get out!" he shouts.

With discernment Potemkin describes Uvadiev: "He's not made of flesh and blood, but some kind of metal, red pig iron." The representative of the new Soviet man has been drained of spirituality. Nature for him is just a wanton female that causes the Sot to overflow its banks, messes up the roads in the spring and thus interferes with the swift tempo of work on the paper mill. The soul he dismisses with a shrug: "What is it made of?" he asks. "Where is it for sale?" All obstacles in the path of the success of his Five-Year-Plan project must be ruthlessly swept away. He has no sympathy to waste on the suicide of Suzanne's father Renne, the old timber expert unjustly persecuted as a saboteur. He arrogantly tells Potemkin, who tries to explain to him that Renne has his own way of managing things, his own ideas about what is right: "What's right is what I happen at any moment to think is right!" And when his friend and superior Jeglov tries to reveal Uvadiev's shortcomings to him by telling him: "You're a machine . . . a machine adapted to independent existence. You reckon your own nature unchangeable . . . you're not alive, only performing functions," he contemptuously answers: "I don't fear the judgment of those on account of whom I made myself so."

Uvadiev, however, and the other characters absorbed in this frenzied effort of construction are essentially impersonal symbols representing the new forces of Five-Year-Plan socialism struggling with the opposing forces of old Russia which in turn are represented by a group of characters equally impersonal. Leonov, to be sure, is able to make some of these characters of both types interesting as personalities, but their life of thought and action is demonstratively concentrated on one or the other aspects of the struggle between the old and the new. Even the forces of nature, which the Bolsheviks are trying to tame for their own uses, appear to take sides. Good weather and the abundant timber in the neighborhood speed up the construction of the factory. Then the heavy rains mire the roads, slow down the building, and the overflowing Sot releases the accumulated logs in the river and threatens to undermine the foundations of the factory. But unlike many authors of standardized Five-Year-Plan novels, Leonov is unwilling to let the new go uncriticized. The botching of plans, endless red tape, shortages of material, and the confusion of Soviet authorities are all realistically revealed. And there is a gentle note of criticism of excessive tempo, for when Uvadiev accuses the able and loyal chief engineer, Burago, of trying to brake the swift pace of socialism, the latter sharply replies: "I build factories, Uvadiev . . . and it makes little difference to me what you feel you have to call it. I'm with you to the end, but don't ask of me more than I can do. Socialism . . . yes . . . I don't know. But everything is possible in this country, down to the resurrection of the dead!"

Leonov, however, is manifestly on the side of change. He clearly sympathizes with Uvadiev's retort to Burago's com-

plaint that the people are getting tired: "All our people usually enjoy whining for the past because they lack faith in the
future." These "people" in the novel are largely superstitious
peasants (who see in the lubricating pipes of a traction engine
the very thing for a home brew still), the "kulak" exploiters in
the village, and the monks. In fact, the mysterious monk Vissarion, an ex-White officer, is the ideological leader of the
neighborhood sabotage effort directed against Soviet construction and social thinking and planning. As a character Vissarion
is a lesser Shigalov, the furious theoretician of the mad revolutionary movement in Dostoevsky's *The Possessed.* Vissarion's
destructive fury, however, is aimed equally at capitalism and
socialism, for he believes that both are destroying the soul of
mankind and its quintessential culture based on religion by
their materialism, rationalism, and mechanization. The pristine,
primitive state of mankind can be recovered, declares Vissarion, only after some modern Attila has purged the present
world with fire and sword. Vissarion's intellectual brilliance is
more or less lost on his ignorant audience, and his practical
attempts at sabotage ultimately fail and encompass his own
destruction.

The natural enemy of the new, the peasantry, is not entirely
immune to the propaganda and demands of the Five-Year
Plan, especially while they provide work and good pay. Some
of the peasants combine with the local Komsomol to break
up the celebration of a religious feast by the village and the
monastery, and a number of peasants strive mightily with the
workers to protect the construction against the flooding Sot.
Yet this brooding sense of peasant hostility to the new Soviet
power hangs in the atmosphere. It rests on that same dichotomy of the spiritual and the material which the peasant
Semyon had expressed in *The Badgers,* and it is revealed once
again, as though Leonov were still troubled by this central
problem, by the quaint peasant carpenter, Fadei Akishin, in
Sot. The materialist Uvadiev had wanted to know what the

soul was made of and whether it could be sold. The peasant
Fadei, who delights in building privies in his spare time and
philosophically justifies the wooden variety over the stone ones
because "the soul cannot live in stone," explains to an uncomprehending foreign engineer: "And as I've grown to understand, my dear, the soul nowadays keeps going out of the
world, because reason is coming in its place. Sometimes it
can't find out how to escape, and so goes about all covered
with scratches, and that's why the new master—well, doesn't
fit in. But again, on the other hand, religion . . . smooths it
smarter than a plane; not souls, but rafters we begin to have."

However, it is the new that triumphs over the old in the
novel, the rational Uvadievs over the nonrational Akishins.
Yet it is a joyless kind of triumph. The driving, hard-bitten
Uvadiev is a lonely, almost tragic figure, as are virtually all
of Leonov's new Soviet men. Their triumphs are secured
through endless self-sacrifice in the present with the conviction
of some better tomorrow—a parable of the reality of Soviet
life. Uvadiev is intolerant of happiness and inhuman in his contempt for the pleasanter amenities of living, traits which
worried the Soviet critics who otherwise hailed *Sot* as an
enormous ideological improvement over *The Thief*. His treatment of Natalia and Suzanne, characterizations which again
underscore Leonov's strange incapacity for the effective portrayal of women, amounts to something of a record in the
fictional history of man's obtuseness to the most elementary
demand of the female for human understanding. A suggestion
of human warmth emerges only in Uvadiev's feeling for his
mother. Here Leonov succeeds admirably, perhaps because
Varvara is one of those off-center individuals, a human oddity,
the characterizations of which, whether male or female, are
among the novelist's finest portraits. Varvara is immense, both
physically and spiritually, a woman grown so accustomed to
want, Leonov tells us, that she is maddened by even the
tiniest property. Mother and son go their separate ways, but

their bristling independence reveals rather than conceals their real affection for each other.

Uvadiev's granite-like personality again weakens in his relations with the young novice Gelasi, the only inhabitant of the condemned monastery whom he thought worth saving. Though the effort is initially one of Communist proselytizing, there is no doubt that Uvadiev dimly begins to think of Gelasi as a son. He is childless, one of the failures of Natalia that he could not forgive. And he wanted a child, not so much for the conventional reasons, but as a kind of justification of the bitter self-sacrifices of his life; a child who would grow up to enjoy, or whose progeny would enjoy, the fruits of everything he had labored to accomplish. The novel ends with Uvadiev sitting on a bluff overlooking the river and the lights of the rising construction, dreaming of the young Katyas of the future whose schoolbooks will be printed on the paper from his factory. And this only makes it all the clearer to him "that the face of the Sot was changing; altering also were the men upon its banks."

This was the ideological mirage of Leonov's novel: the Five-Year Plan was changing the face of Russia and the people were changing with it. In the fierce struggle between the old and the new, the official critics now welcomed a fellow traveler who had at last become an ally.

A HERO FROM THE INTELLIGENTSIA MAKES HIS ADJUSTMENT. Leonov's next Five-Year Plan novel, *Skutarevsky* (1932), also involves the struggle between the old and the new, or more exactly, the old adjusting itself to and finally accepting the new. Only now the focus shifts back again from impersonal social forces to living individuals. As a result *Skutarevsky* is a thoroughly interesting novel, rich in the perplexities of a period of Soviet life in which Leonov once again attempts artistically to elevate typical situations and characters by seeking in them universal solvents of human behavior.

Events in the Soviet Union between 1928 and 1931 set the
stage and suggested the plot of this novel. During this period
the Party press violently attacked technical experts among
the non-Party intelligentsia for sabotaging the Five-Year Plan
and conspiring with foreign agents to overthrow the regime.
A series of public trials took place such as the Ramzin trial
in 1930, in which industrial experts trained under the old
regime were convicted of deliberate wrecking activities and
were severely punished. Widespread suspicion, denunciation,
and persecution were rife, and the demoralization of the
intelligentsia became so extensive that it seriously interfered
with the progress of the Plan, for at that time not many
technical experts of experience, trained under the Soviets, were
available.

It is difficult to ascertain how much truth there was in
such charges; these members of the old intelligentsia may
simply have been the scapegoats for official failures in the
operation of the Plan or the victims of internecine Party
strife. The latter assumption now seems more reasonable in
the light of the exposure of the so-called "doctors' plot" after
Stalin's death. It is also possible that the Party consciously
employed public prosecution of the few to frighten the many
anti-Bolsheviks and fellow travelers among the intelligentsia
into full acceptance of the Soviet regime. However, the situation had become so harmful by 1931 that Stalin, in a speech
in June of that year, pointedly instructed the Party and the
country to end their campaign against the technical experts
of the old school.

In spirit and in cultural orientation, if not exactly in age and
training, Leonov belonged to this class of persecuted intelligentsia; this, however, had not prevented him from joining
in one of the many public denunciations of the so-called sabo-
teurs. As an intellectual fellow traveler who had already
passed from a phase of doubt to one of cooperation with the
Soviet regime, Leonov had a sympathetic understanding of the

cruel problems that confronted the old intelligentsia. He realized that harsh circumstances of material existence had compelled most of them to collaborate with the new order while clinging to their old beliefs and traditions. But he also knew that this was not enough, for during this period of continued class struggle in the First Five-Year Plan, the Party insistently demanded that all should take a definite stand— for the Revolution or the counterrevolution. It demanded that collaborating members of the old intelligentsia take still another step—that they abandon their old traditions and beliefs and accept unconditionally Bolshevik ideology. It was precisely this phase of final adjustment that Leonov seized upon as the central problem for the hero of his novel who is portrayed against a background of the tension, sabotage, political conspiracy, and public trials of the First Five-Year Plan. No doubt Stalin's 1931 speech served to encourage Leonov to strike a blow on behalf of the persecuted old intelligentsia.

Professor Skutarevsky had swallowed life at a gulp but had never really digested it. The son of a poverty-stricken furrier in the days of the tsar, he had had to fight for his education. No task was too menial if it aided his search for knowledge, no reward too great to spurn if it deflected him from his consuming ambition to become a great scientist. Incessant work, talent, original thinking, and inventive genius finally won him national and then international fame. As a youth he had coquetted with a Marxist group, but when the Revolution came it meant for him mostly an opportunity to increase his scientific activities. For Lenin entrusted him with a leading position in the electrification of the country, and he was placed at the head of a large scientific institute with the resources of the state to aid his experiments. Tremendously vital, sure of his power, dominating and irascible, he tirelessly drove himself and all his assistants to greater efforts. At the beginning of the Five-Year Plan, when the novel opens, Skutarevsky is engaged on an epoch-making experiment intimately linked with speeding

the development of the country's industry—a practical solution of the dream of wireless transmission of energy. En-
croaching age worries him and he fears that death may over-
take him before he finishes his last major effort. But he won't
surrender to these gloomy thoughts. Quite characteristically,
he declares to one of his aides: "Damn it, man, real life consists in not even having time to die!"

Like many famous men completely absorbed in their work,
Skutarevsky has no private life. He had drifted into marriage
as a young man but as he and his wife approach old age they
have become almost strangers to each other. If she fears for
his safety as his engineering colleagues begin to be arrested
in the anti-intelligentsia campaign, it is from a sense of the
material loss such a catastrophe will mean to her. For she
drains his income in pursuing her sole passion—cluttering up
their large Moscow home with *objets d'art* and canvases of
the old masters which, in the end, turn out to be forgeries.
Their only son, Arseny, who is a scientist, has also become a
stranger to his father. Skutarevsky sticks to a single attic room
in the large house. He is devoted to music; he attends the
opera; and sometimes at night, when he is tired, he will drive
his car aimlessly around Moscow. But his favorite relaxation
is to play on his "growler," his bassoon, in his little room; or as
a special treat he plays duets with his old institute assistant,
Herodov, who performs on the French horn.

One evening, learning by chance that Arseny and his young
friends are having a party at the house, Skutarevsky decides
that he will drop in and make amends for long neglect of
his son. He imagines the party a student one such as he himself enjoyed as a youth. To his dismay he finds the smoke-filled
room occupied by rakish youths, sleazy wenches, and a poetic
ex-prince reciting anti-Soviet verses. In this decadent setting
father and son talk in a corner and they learn how formidable
is the barrier which life in the Soviet Union has erected between them. Skutarevsky criticizes his son for deficiencies in

a power plant which Arseny had helped to design. The gloomy son bitterly replies: "In this country whenever there's a bad accident they always look for 'guilty' people instead of asking *why* it happened." And he goes on to condemn the intolerable conditions under which technicians work: "And you call that planned economy? I call it *enthusiastic hysterics,* father." His anger mounting, Arseny informs his father of the arrest of another distinguished scientist, a friend of Skutarevsky, and then brutally says:

I'm not going to lie. I am going to speak out. You lost my respect when . . . they shot Ignaty Fiodorovich and you didn't say a word. Afraid, all right that's all understandable enough. . . . No, I know your views about the country having a right to dispose of what you might call its stock of human material. And if the experiment fails, of course wash out the retort and pour it all down the drain. Or break the whole damn thing. Don't forget your own words—it's no use whining over every single vanished species. . . . Now, you bulwark of Soviet authority, tell me, where is the man in the name of whom all this is done?

It is perhaps significant that Leonov has no answer to put in Skutarevsky's mouth to this and much more criticism of the regime by Arseny. Instead Skutarevsky tries to get him back to the subject of the power plant and demands to know why his son has not spoken out about the defects he admits to knowing. "Squeal?" Arseny shot at him. "You always taught me not to be a squealer."

This remarkable scene has been worth dwelling upon for it shows Leonov's courage in making out a rather persuasive case against certain of the abuses of the regime, perhaps on behalf of those members of the intelligentsia who felt compelled to rebel. To be sure, the critic is a weak character who has already drifted into a conspiracy because—the novelist lamely explains—of "his vague dissatisfaction with the Soviet social order." (There is nothing vague about the social conditions that Arseny condemns.) And the conspiracy is as unconvincing as the plot of a comic opera. The leader of the conspiracy is

Skutarevsky's brother-in-law Petrygin, a highly successful
entrepreneur in the engineering field who carries over from the
old regime a massive hatred of the Soviets. Beneath a hale and
hearty appearance set off by a jocose manner of speech, Petrygin is supposed to conceal a sly and sinister nature. We see the
plotters in only one meeting; Arseny and Herodov are there
with a few faceless individuals, and Petrygin hopes to blackmail Skutarevsky into participation. Hints are thrown out
concerning industrial sabotage, contacts with foreign powers,
and preposterous ambitions to overthrow the government. It
is a conspiracy more honored in allusions than in actions, in
expressions of vague intentions than in forthright declarations
of purpose. Perhaps Leonov imagined that this method of
mystification, as in the case of Mitka's career of crime in *The
Thief*, would intensify the dramatic appeal. It results rather in
making the conspiracy barely believable and in arousing a
suspicion among the readers as to whether Leonov himself
believed in it. But if one purpose of the novel was to demon-
strate that members of the old intelligentsia, like Skutarevsky,
wanted to be loyal to the Soviet regime, then perhaps it was
thought wise, in the temper of the times, to balance this fact
by showing that others, like Petrygin and his group, could be
disloyal.

Both life at that time and the dialectic of the novel required
a Communist guide to lead the fellow traveler Skutarevsky
through the various circles of his purgatory up into the light
of his final adjustment to the masses and the Party. We have
this guide in Cherimov, the young apprentice glass blower
who shared civil war experiences with Arseny, obtained a
scientific education, and was eventually appointed as the
Party's representative on the staff of the institute. Though he
is one of the "new Soviet men," he bears little resemblance
to Uvadiev except in ideology. The man he is guiding,
Skutarevsky, the famous, daring, wonderfully individual and
human scientist, dwarfs Cherimov into insignificance. It was

Leonov's misfortune that his principal Communist figure in the novel had to stand comparison with so attractive and vital a hero as Skutarevsky. In their charges the critics seized upon the point and scathingly dismissed Cherimov as a non-typical Bolshevik, boring and humorless, whose views on science and society were not those of the Party.

One may perceive a form of Communist snobbery in this position. It is true that Cherimov is not as appealing or as live a character as Skutarevsky, but he occupies a large and important place in the novel, and there is much reason to suppose that the portrayal is quite faithful to the type he is supposed to represent in the Soviet life of that time. Cherimov is the young Soviet-trained Party specialist of the period who was frequently associated with older or foreign experts on government projects. He was there to gain practical experience, to spy, to detect malfeasance or sabotage, and to promote the ideological line of the Party. Cherimov reveres Skutarevsky's scientific achievement, but as a good Communist he wishes to lead him to an acceptance of the Party scheme of things. Yet he hardly understands the psychological difficulties of a man who, while adjusting to a collective society, has his roots deep in the past, is a pronounced individualist, and profoundly feels the value of his own personality. When Cherimov asks him flatly why he does not join the Party, Skutarevsky answers: "Do remember that from the very beginning you have had no other path before you. For me all *this* is only the final stage of immense storms and changes and catastrophes . . . which, damn it all, may never have existed at all."

Cherimov is a bit more humanized than Uvadiev—spring does quicken his pulse, and though he "had never been able to spend more than a half an hour a month for love," before the end of the novel he cautiously condescends to an affair of the heart. Otherwise he is wholly dedicated to the Party and its work. Thus he follows the Party line in favoring practical science as opposed to theoretical science in the current controversy of the times, and collectivist experiments rather than individual ones; in both of these positions he challenges Skutarevsky. Though it was acceptable Bolshevik ideology, there is an element of irony in Leonov's remark on Cherimov: "It must be added that his approach to any truth was directly dependent on the echo it found in the opinion of the masses." It is an approach that Skutarevsky finds difficult to accept, and though he develops a certain regard for Cherimov, he deplores his confusing science and politics. "Science in his eyes is a Party duty," Skutarevsky comments on Cherimov to an important commissar. And when the latter smilingly asks if there is anything bad in that, Skutarevsky tartly replies: "It is not sufficient."

Yet it is Cherimov who reads a lesson in Communist morality to this tough, unsociable teacher of his. He had ferreted out the whole conspiracy which had come so dangerously close to including Skutarevsky in its toils, but the latter, though he suspects the affair, has failed to reveal it to the authorities. Like Lisa Meshkova, in a similar situation in Fedin's *No Ordinary Summer*, he responds to the higher moral claim of kinship. "My son is my son, and means even more to me than I to myself," is Skutarevsky's anguished thought. And Cherimov's reaction is strikingly like that of the Bolshevik Kirill Izvekov in Fedin's novel: "It was the old conception of morals, based on a slavish, dishonorable form of sympathy. It was the whole complex of antiquated and sham conceptions of loyalty, of blood ties and social relationships, that prevented Skutarevsky from following a straight line of his own in the affair."

Meanwhile a kind of irrational component enters the personal life of the lonely old Skutarevsky. He brings home one night a young member of the Komsomol, Gene, whom he has almost knocked down in one of his mad automobile drives. She has come to Moscow from an outlying district to seek work and education. The inhospitable behavior of his son and his wife toward Gene when she falls ill in the large house forces upon Skutarevsky a decision he has been contemplating for some time—to leave his home and family. He and Gene accept Cherimov's offer to share his small apartment and Gene becomes Skutarevsky's secretary.

Gene is an attractive, guileless, sensitive girl, but once again Leonov fails to realize the potentialities of a feminine character. One reason perhaps is that her position in the novel is only peripheral. Like Cherimov, but less actively so, she typifies the cautious sympathy of the young Soviet person for a member of the old intelligentsia whose mind and heart are not irrevocably closed to the message of the new. She is in awe of Skutarevsky and endlessly flattered that she can be of some small help to the great scientist. Though their relations begin on a purely platonic level, ugly gossip quickly spreads. Skutarevsky's wife, stupidly unaware of the part she has played in her own marital bankruptcy, is convinced that Gene has taken her place and is her husband's mistress. On the other hand, a silly Komsomol youth from Gene's home town offers her a conventional Party lesson on this kind of relationship, a position which Leonov is obviously satirizing: "Your duty must be to reeducate your old specialist—give him faith in his work and make it more intensive. We do not say anything in advance about the form of your relationship. . . . Remember, no children by him. During this transitional period, with the old intelligentsia as a whole. . . ."

Like Fedin, Leonov is deeply interested in the function of art in a socialist society. He had used the novelist Firssov in *The Thief* to criticize the Party attitude toward art, and with equal courage he now returns to this subject and treats it at greater length, employing as his instrument the character Fiodor, the artist brother of Skutarevsky. Fiodor, however, is a better developed and more interesting character than Firssov, and he plays an additional functional role in the novel, a role identified with its main theme—the process of the old intelligentsia adjusting itself to and accepting the new Soviet scheme of things. Before the Revolution the talented Fiodor had bartered his artistic integrity as a painter for conventional bourgeois success. Even then he sensed the balefulness of this degree of artistic self-violation and struggled against it. After 1917 Fiodor loses himself in the maze of conflicting ideologies; he falls into dissipation and extreme poverty, and for a time, under the evil influence of a former bourgeois connoisseur of art, Osip Struff, one of those human oddities that Leonov characterizes so brilliantly, he fakes old masterpieces, many of which are palmed off by Struff as originals on the gullible Mrs. Skutarevsky. But with the growth and success of socialist planning Fiodor discovers a fulcrum on which he can balance his conflicting views on art. He sees that capitalism is dead in Russia and that the artist must associate himself with the vast outpouring of energy brought about by socialism if he is to represent faithfully in art the new reality of life. But like Leonov, he insists upon the artist's independent right to filter these realities through his consciousness so that they assume artistic patterns dictated by his own individual creative spirit. Fiodor appeals to his brother and to Cherimov for aid in his artistic theorizing, but he finds that their views conform to the Party's demand for stereotyped, hackneyed, embellished reality. When Cherimov and Gene view Fiodor's dazzling canvas "The Skiers," for which they had been the models, the only feature Cherimov comments on is the girl's trousers: "Why are her trousers torn at the knee? Even if our knitted goods today aren't quite up to standard. . . . But I suppose you don't put the duration of the picture at more than five years?" With his master Breughel in mind, Fiodor sorrowfully explains—and Leonov would no doubt agree with him—". . . that apart from the story it tells, every painting must to some extent be subordinate to aims of a purely formal artistic order." The Soviet official critics of literature and art, whom Leonov fiercely satirizes in the novel, look solely for temporal lacquered responses to the "social command" of the Five-Year Plan, whereas Fiodor seeks for the absolutes which are connoted by the indestructible words "spring, winter, love and death, jealousy and delight—those naked stones from which, on the universal shore of the unknown sea, the artist fashions his fantastic forms."

Much more effectively than in his previous three novels, Leonov neatly ties together the various strands of his plot at the conclusion of *Skutarevsky*. Despite the efforts and threats of Petrygin to keep them in line, both Arseny and Herodov crack under the strain of the conspiracy they are involved in. In a haunting scene recalling that in which the guilt-ridden Raskolnikov prowls the streets of St. Petersburg, Arseny wanders at night about the streets of Moscow, his mind a Dantean inferno peopled with horrific shapes and endless torments. Unable to comply with an inner compulsion to confess to the political police, Arseny shoots himself. At the bedside of his dying son, Skutarevsky utters a memorable monologue of mingled shame and pride over the failures and successes of his own life. He regards Arseny as one of his failures. Pathetically he asks: "Who has made you what you are, boy? We have been enemies throughout. Now why? I have never done anything to harm you . . . though I will confess I never had time to be kind to you." He simply cannot understand why this son of his had raised his hand against the Soviet regime, "trying to smash the greatest attempt there has ever been to remake this world—could that be really true?" And sadly he takes his final leave of Arseny with the words: "You've flung a stone at me."

The stone struck home. The head of the conspiracy, Skutarevsky's brother-in-law Petrygin, has been arrested; Skutarevsky's assistant, Herodov, is implicated; his own institute is involved in the plot; and Cherimov knows all. A prominent official cuts Skutarevsky and at once all his intelligentsia friends avoid him. Rumors spread that he is squandering the nation's money on a futile scientific experiment. Here Leonov is reflecting quite realistically the atmosphere of suspicion in which experts like Skutarevsky lived in those painful days of sabotage trials and denunciations against members of the old intelligentsia.

Heedless of all this, Skutarevsky works away feverishly at his great experiment on the wireless transmission of energy. Though he firmly refuses to predict success, his dearest hope is to solve this mystery of nature before death overtakes him, not so much for the sake of socialism as because of "his incomparable pride and his craving to outdo the future generations." However, when the final tests are made, the experiment fails. As he frantically goes over his calculations and formulas again and again, seeking to know the unknowable, Skutarevsky experiences for the first time an utter sense of defeat and a loss of his self-esteem and pride. That night Gene steals into his lonely room, and, sensing the apathy and anguish of his failure, shyly offers him the consolation of her love. But he refuses this way out. Besides, he has already correctly guessed that she and young Cherimov have become deeply interested in each other. Actually, what he is afraid of "was ever seeing himself again, the changed man he was, reflected in her staring and agonizing eyes." As he falls asleep that night he hears the sounds of the love-making of two cats in the moonlight outside his window, and it symbolizes for him, the old and frustrated scientist, that he is still in the world of the living.

After the failure of the experiment, the poison tongue of rumor clacks still more openly and ominously around Skutarevsky, and in a fury of despair and righteous indignation he hands Cherimov his resignation. Into this situation at the end of his novel Leonov introduces the new Party solution, the message of Stalin's 1931 speech. In a heart-to-heart talk the Communist leader of the institute tells Skutarevsky frankly: "But we have never had unconditional faith in you. . . . We have been satisfied throughout with those things which you have achieved. And we are confident that you will go on." The incredulous Skutarevsky explodes, stating that he will need more money, more equipment, and that he will insist that his experiment which has failed at such great cost must remain the central problem of the institute. When Cherimov agrees to all this, the delighted old man blurts out that the pace of the past will have to be speeded up: "That sort of pace won't take us to socialism, if that's where we're going. Socialism is standing upright, full height, it's man completely erect."

The traditions, the way of life, the outmoded thinking of the past have been banished. The adjustment of old Skutarevsky to the new way of life of socialism is almost complete. He sees his artist brother Fiodor off to a new factory whose walls he is going to decorate with scenes of "midday construction, barricades, a procession, spring—in other words, all those epic words with which a class begins its history." Fiodor is happy, for he is going to make a fresh start in his painting, but now in the spirit of socialism. He, too, has made the adjustment. And in the festive atmosphere of May Day eve Skutarevsky timidly walks out on a platform to speak to an assembled multitude of workers in a factory that supplies his institute with equipment. Hundreds of eyes gaze expectantly at the famous scientist who had been only a name to them. "Comrades," he begins, and suddenly a thunder of applause rolls through the auditorium, exploding all his doubts. This magnificent welcome, writes Leonov, "was expressive of much—and in the first place of an invitation to share his temporary failure with millions of others, each little portion then losing its poisonous, destructive bitterness."

By and large Soviet novelists are the official historians of one or another phase of a planned society at a given period of Soviet development; in these novels men and women, like the figures on a chessboard, are shifted hither and yon at the will of the author. But there are exceptions in which the historian, as Fiodor would have it, subordinates the events "to aims of a purely artistic order" that involves living men and women in the process of spiritual and moral growth or decay. This partially defines the superiority of *Skutarevsky* over nearly all other Five-Year-Plan novels. It has serious weaknesses, but most of them are neutralized by the bumbling, erratic, and vital characterization of the old scientist, who never fails to hold the reader's interest. Even his rather swift, propaganda-like conversion at the end seems believable, for it is in keeping with the logic of his nature. And most Soviet critics who hailed *Skutarevsky* as the important fiction event of 1932 thought so too, although they were harsh on several of the other characters.

With this novel the fellow traveler Leonov, like Skutarevsky, appears to have adjusted himself to the new regime and accepted its ideology, though, again like the old scientist, without losing his courage or the will to criticize abuses as he saw them. The success of his two Five-Year-Plan novels had clearly brought Leonov to the attention of high Party officials, for in 1932 he was appointed to the organizing committee for the projected Union of Soviet Writers, which had been set up by decree of the Central Committee.

JOURNEY TO SOVIET UTOPIA. The dynamic movements of Soviet society in the first twenty years of its development exacted from literature an emphasis upon the contemporary which has been clearly reflected in Leonov's novels: the period of War Communism in *The Badgers,* the New Economic Policy in *The Thief,* and the First Five-Year Plan in *Sot* and *Skutarevsky.* His next novel, *Road to the Ocean* (1935), concentrated on the years 1933 and 1934, during which the work was written. These were years of rising hopes in the Soviet Union. The exhausting effort of the First Five-Year Plan was over and its successes in industrialization and argricultural collectivization surprised the world. Food rationing had been discontinued after the excellent harvest of 1933. According to Stalin the corner to socialism had been turned. Official propaganda encouraged the dream, especially among young people, that the Communist Utopia was realizable in the not-too-distant future.

It was in this spirit of present relative well-being and future grandiose hopes that *Road to the Ocean* was created. Leonov, as though conscious of his growing stature and significance as a novelist and now more than ever ideologically identified with the regime, sought the universal not in a microcosm but in the macrocosm of Soviet life. For it is the full-bodied life of the Soviet Union that he grapples with in *Road to the Ocean*. From the vantage point of the end of the First Five-Year Plan with its achievements, its labor heroes and heroines, and its discipline, Leonov looked backward to the prerevolutionary past, though now with a sterner vision of its inadequacies, and forward to the future great destiny of his country which the Soviet present would make possible. As the native critics fully recognized, here was the first attempt to write a large and authentic novel about the age of the new Soviet man.

In Leonov's preceding novels the Communist protagonists had lacked the epic stature of heroes of an epic age. They acted forcefully but they had no philosophy of action capable of articulating adequately the moral pathos of the times in which they lived. Like so many positive Soviet heroes in fiction, they were largely devoid of that humanity and feeling which endow a symbol with the convincingness of life. At the 1934 meeting which organized the Union of Soviet Writers this persistent failure in literature was much deprecated and the demand was made, a demand in which Leonov joined, for the creation of profound and memorable Communist heroes whose lives would faithfully reflect the achievements and optimism of the present, dignify the new Soviet morality, and symbolize the approaching birth of a world as yet only dreamt about. For socialist realism, also formulated at this 1934 meeting,

urged the writer—in fact obligated him—not only to regard
life as an historical process in Marxian terms, but to foresee in
these terms the course of future events.

By creating Kurilov in *Road to the Ocean,* Leonov attempts
to portray the epic hero of the new Soviet age, a character
whose heroic personality will find full expression in a novel
intended to be rich in varied emotional and moral experiences,
in psychological analysis, and in dramatic incident. Kurilov,
however, turns out to be a kind of socialist Don Quixote,
though the author is without any satiric intent in his presentation. Both Don Quixote and Kurilov are cast as morally perfect men though each serves a different system of morality.
The good Knight of the Sorrowful Countenance labored under
the illusion that his own life was being lived in the outmoded
age of chivalry. With a vision scarcely less illusory, Kurilov
firmly believes that the present in which he lives is an inevitable harbinger of a glorious Communist future of which he
constantly dreams. In their illusions both figures, no doubt
contrary to the intentions of their creators, are essentially
tragic.

We are introduced to Kurilov at the start of the novel as a
stern, gray-haired, trusted Bolshevik of fifty, with "the shoulders of a stevedore and the forehead of Socrates." He has just
been made head of the political bureau to reorganize a whole
railroad line, and as we see him at work at his desk, in consul-
tation with his subordinates, or grimly investigating on the
scene the causes of a wreck, we are reminded of the truth of
one character's observation: "Kurilov was a Communist and
these people never did anything without a purpose." His
heroic lineaments, like those of the storied knights of old, have
been acquired through long selfless sacrifice for a sacred
cause—in this case the cause of the Party. The quiet reverence
accorded Kurilov by Party comrades who have shared his
battles and sacrifices is a simple tribute to his leadership
among them.

In this characterization Leonov was mindful of the complaints of the literary critics against atypical, dehumanized Soviet heroes, although he was perhaps not yet sufficiently aware of the aesthetic incompatibility of this familiar but unacceptable dichotomy—the typical versus the official Soviet heroic man, the human versus the official Soviet reality. Nevertheless Leonov strove to neutralize the monumental in the conception of Kurilov. He is "an ordinary human being," protests Leonov. Unlike Uvadiev in *Sot* he is an inveterate pipe smoker; he exults over the beauties of nature, likes wine, reads good books, occasionally goes to the theater, and listens to music. In short, he is represented as a person of wide culture and people enjoy his company and conversation. Children in particular are attracted to him and he has a keen understanding of their natures. Childless himself, he adopted the waif Aliosha Peresypkin during the civil war and Aliosha preserves a fanatical devotion to him. He fascinates Marina's little boy Ziamka, and prefers Ziamka's company to that of grownups. He tries, though unsuccessfully, to reform with kindness the young thief Gavrila. "Under socialism," he declares, "everyone's activity will be a means of proving his right to joy." Leonov even attributes to his hero certain errors of judgment. "Hastiness and oversimplification," he writes, "characterized his deductions."

Unlike that Party hero Cherimov in *Skutarevsky*, who rations love to half an hour a month, Kurilov is allowed to accumulate an imposing record—at least for a Communist celebrity—of affairs of the heart. For in his determination to portray a well-rounded and believable Communist hero, Leonov does not allow sheer labor, that sense-defying *mystique* of so many similar fictional characters in Soviet literature, to dominate the personality and all the waking hours of Kurilov. To be sure, Kurilov has reached middle age and enjoys the security that comes with hard-earned success. As a man who has not had a vacation for seventeen years, he feels entitled to some slight measure of self-indulgence within the severe limits of Communist morality, which adds a touch of mid-Victorianism to his love-making.

At the beginning of the novel we learn that Kurilov's wife Catherine, who had shared all his early struggles, is dying. We gather from Klavdia, Kurilov's sister, who in her own right has become almost a legendary Bolshevik figure (she "had no personal biography; its various stages were marked by social dates"), that Catherine has been a saintly woman of selfless devotion to her husband and his cause. An emotional key to Kurilov's life with her and to the sense of deprivation that he feels now, as she lies on her deathbed, is provided by the novelist: "The sickly and quiet Catherine had never been enough for him. Even the very beginnings of their marital life passed without amorous play, without frolics and excesses, but also without the unleashing of that sinful force which gives the soul primitive satiety. With time he got used to his starveling's love ration, tried to spare his wife's pride and only recently had begun to realize that he remembered all the young women he happened to encounter on the road."

This frank admission bears some promise of a future un-Communist emotional development for Kurilov. He poignantly feels the frustration of his situation and has already begun to regard with envy the embracing young couples he observes beneath his window. Even before Catherine's death he is sure she will not object to the visits of Marina, a pleasant, half-scared girl assigned to write his biography as one of the several instructive life stories of prominent transportation workers. He invites her to his apartment, takes her for a drive into the country, and spends hours playing and talking with her little son Ziamka. Like Desdemona with Othello, Marina, as she listens to Kurilov's story of his career, appears to love him for the dangers he has been through. He blushes in her presence and after her visits he is "tormented by amorous dreams, like

a young boy." Though Marina completes her biography, Kurilov never consummates his amorous dreams. The state of mind
which perhaps contributed to the fecklessness of this whole
affair is suggested by Kurilov's defense of Marina before his
suspicious sister Klavdia: "She's a very nice person. She was
never sentenced, she has never engaged in trade, she has no
record of harmful deviations."

In fact, this affair with Marina has not yet run its course
before Kurilov becomes interested in Liza, an attractive actress.
Despite Leonov's patent ideological intention in this situation
it is developed with realism and deep psychological insight;
as a result Liza is one of his best female portraits. After a
poverty-stricken childhood that drove her into petty thievery
and ugly experiences with a provincial theatrical troupe, she
decides to make her way in the world as an actress. She deliberately sells herself to Zakurdaev, a flamboyant, aging, old-
style actor and head of a small company, in return for his
instruction in acting and influence in getting her started. As
time goes on a lack of talent does not discourage Liza, for she
is convinced that with the proper contacts she will obtain the
lead parts she craves. This is why she marries the distinguished
surgeon Ilya Protoklitov in whose fine apartment she can entertain theatrical bigwigs for her own purpose. Her husband, who
loves her but realizes her lack of talent, wants her to settle
down and have a family. However, she secretly tries to use
his influence to further her career and, unknown to him, has
an abortion performed because she fears that her pregnancy
will interfere with her obtaining the lead in Schiller's *Mary
Stuart*, a part she has always yearned to perform. In a dramatic scene, a mad gathering of theatrical people at Liza's
apartment, which Leonov handles brilliantly and obviously
uses to satirize prevailing abuses in the Soviet theater, Liza's
pretensions and lack of talent are mercilessly exposed before
the company, including her husband, by the drunken Zakur-

daev. Later that evening Liza, in a quarrel with her husband over her thwarted career, spitefully reveals that she has had an abortion.

It is at this point, after Liza has left her husband and lost her job as an actress, that Kurilov comes into her life. He understands the lurking artistic urge within her, "the primitive, imperious greed to dominate the world through creating its image," but he also sees that she has been living selfishly and not for the sake of pure art. Meanwhile the bigness of Kurilov and his moral influence begin to inspire in Liza a sense of humility about both her life and her career. To be happy she now requires not the plaudits of an audience but only a little approval from Kurilov. She accepts an invitation to accompany him to a rest home, for after the death of his wife and the discovery of a serious illness he is finally forced to take a short vacation. Here in long walks amidst the beauties of nature in winter their love for each other grows. On one of these walks, when he confesses his desire for a son, she turns to him and says: "Listen Kurilov . . . I don't need anything from you. I don't need you to be my companion to the end, but . . . look, would you like me to give you a son?" The kiss that seals this offer, however, is never consummated by the embrace of love, for shortly thereafter another attack of illness compels Kurilov to return to Moscow to face an operation.

Leonov fills his novel with other characters and situations often only tangentially related to his hero but designed to enrich this picture of the present in the Soviet Union. One of the most interesting subplots concerns the brother of Ilya Protoklitov, Gleb, who is head of the railroad yard at the Cheremshansk junction on Kurilov's line. Gleb, a former White officer, has so far adroitly concealed his past, joined the Party, and through hard work and his own unusual abilities is on the way to making a very successful career for himself. He has nothing of the counterrevolutionary zeal of that other ex-White officer, Vissarion, in *Sot*. In truth, the Party has no counts against Gleb and he appears to have no interest in life other than to climb higher and higher in his chosen endeavor through industry and application. "I wanted to build railroads, invent engines," he says. He must nevertheless live in a constant state of fear that all he has strived for will be destroyed if his past is revealed. If we did not know that Leonov had moved closer to the ideological position of the Soviet regime, this whole situation would seem to be a trenchant satire on the vindictiveness of the Party and on the fear it inspires in all, both the guilty and the innocent, who were associated with the enemy in the past.

Leonov seems determined to make a sinister character out of Gleb, but he succeeds only in making him one of the most sympathetic and interesting individuals in the novel. It appears to be a clear case of the unconscious triumph of artistic integrity over ideological bias. Thus he imputes to Gleb a harsh and exacting nature in the demands that he makes upon the workers at the railroad yard in the interests of performance, and an unsympathetic attitude toward a group of young Komsomols whose immature enthusiasm for running locomotives is hardly matched by their training and abilities. This latter incident, highly praised by the official critics, is a silly one and a blatant concession to one of the stereotypes of Soviet fiction. A Tatar novice, Sayfullah, is allowed to drive a locomotive in a blizzard and ruins it, as Gleb has feared he would. (One point of the incident is to emphasize the propaganda effort being made at that time to accept members of the minority peoples on the same level with Great Russians.)

Leonov curiously insists that no one should be made to suffer for political sins of the past. That formidable Bolshevik, Kurilov's sister, says as much, and so does Gleb's brother Ilya, whose credo, "Every man accounts for himself by his work for society," which has won him sanctuary from the regime, might easily apply to Gleb but in fact seems inapplicable in his case. For Gleb *is* made to suffer for the political sins of his past.

Perhaps one reason for this, apart from the desire to inject a tense detective-story element into the novel, is to stress another of Kurilov's stern Bolshevik qualities—his eternal vigilance. He correctly suspects that Gleb is the son of one of his persecutors of the past. Gleb's former comrade-in-arms, the drunken and psychopathic Kormilitsin, then begins to blackmail him. At first Gleb actually writes out a confession to the Central Committee of the Party about his past, but he destroys it, apparently unconvinced of the Committee's tender mercy. However, fear of exposure and the desire to preserve what he has worked so many years to achieve drive him to make an unsuccessful attempt on the life of Kormilitsin and to suggest to his brother Ilya, who is to perform an operation on Kurilov, the lover of his wife, that this man should not come out of the operation alive. Ilya denounces his brother and Gleb is arrested. Yet the reader's verdict is that Gleb is more sinned against than sinning and that he is one of the most human and believable characters in the novel. This is often an unpremeditated triumph of the "villains" in Soviet fiction.

The past plays perhaps a disproportionate part in *Road to the Ocean,* but however relevant or irrelevant it is to the main theme—the history of Kurilov—it is cleverly integrated with and motivates the present. Like a somewhat similar structural device in *The Thief,* the mystifying connections between characters and events in the present are clarified only by the record of their interrelations in the past. The device is temporarily confusing and was subjected to much criticism, but it creates drama and suspense and was used effectively by Leonov.

In his earliest fiction Leonov had contemplated the present from the point of view of the past. The comparisons were sometimes favorable to the culture of the past, and victims of the present, such as Professor Likharev in *The End of a Petty Man* and Manyukin in *The Thief,* won from him a certain sympathy. Now he regards the past from his viewpoint in the present, a socialist present in terms of whose achievements the past is made to appear tyrannic, loathsome, and decadent, relieved only by the spirit of rebellion among the masses. In this respect Leonov becomes a typical Soviet propagandist in *Road to the Ocean*. Nevertheless the artist in him responds to this material and the scenes and characters drawn from the past are among the most brilliantly handled in the novel. Much research went into the account of the building, in the 1870s, of the railroad which Kurilov later heads—the fraudulent deals of the interested landed nobility, the stupidity of the tsar's government, and the cruel exploitation of the peasant workers on the road. A vignette of old-fashioned, rapacious merchant capitalism provides a history of the Omelichev family whose members lose all sense of human decency in their relentless efforts to build a financial empire. The products of this era of oppression turn up in the present as fantastic misfits, outmoded relics of a past that will never return: the scabrous scholar Dudnikov and the gargoylish Pokhvisnev, Liza's uncle, both associated with the founder of the railroad; the tattered, embittered Omelichev, bridge-tender and the husband of Kurilov's sister Frosia, with their deaf-mute son, a sad symbol of their family's futility in the new age. These excursions into the past also shed light on the early career of Kurilov, his relations with the Protoklitov family the highborn father of which had sentenced him to Siberia and had obscenely suggested to Catherine, when she asked permission to visit him in prison, that he take her husband's place, an action which years later served to motivate Kurilov's determined tracking down of the son, Gleb Protoklitov. On the whole, it is an unlovely picture of the past but one carefully selected to illuminate and explain the present and to justify Leonov's excursions into the future.

There are three separate excursions into the future in *Road to the Ocean*. They confuse readers and worry critics, some of

whom are inclined to regard them as ill-considered and annoying digressions. They are, however, an integral part of the
total design of the novel; they are extensions not only of time
and space but also of idea. In terms of the new socialist realism, as already indicated, Soviet society in the present must be
regarded as preparation for the future fulfillment of world
Communism. This romantic view into the future to illustrate
deterministic historical development is not considered idealistic and unrealistic. The ideal ceases to be an ideal when it is
realized, and Marxism insists that the realization is inevitable.
Of course, the propaganda element here which sustains the
wavering hopes of a population enduring the difficulties of the
present by the glittering promises of a glorious future should
be obvious.

Unlike the digressive chapters on war and the philosophy
of history in Tolstoy's *War and Peace,* Leonov connects the
three excursions into the future in *Road to the Ocean* with
the action, symbolism, and characterization. Motivation for
the excursions is provided by the tendency to dream of the
Communist future. "A man of his time, Kurilov always tried to
visualize the distant goal toward which his Party was moving."
Leonov himself declares in the novel: "The builder of our
time is formed by dreams; the art of living has always been
essentially the ability to look forward." And typifying this
tendency among the little people, Marina eagerly asserts to
Kurilov on their drive together: "Of course, a beautiful life
will come—I know it better than anyone! I've thought out
everything about it, every corner of it. I visit it every morning,
and touch it. . . . Everything is cheap there, and beautiful
. . . shoes and white bread!"

The form and symbolism of Kurilov's dreams are dictated by
an experience of his childhood. He had read a cheap book
about the various seas on the earth and the fabulous cities on
their shores. The book "left a scar on him, an indelible mark,"

and filled him with a desire to reach the ocean. The recurrent image takes different and confusing forms in his mind. At one point Ocean is the capital of the Communist half of the world and then of the whole world after the total victory of Communism. But the underlying symbol of Ocean is that of a vast free flux into which all past, present, and future streams of socialist thought and action flow.

On occasion Leonov, who represents himself as a friend of the hero, visits Kurilov and together they indulge in these imaginative excursions to Ocean. The first of these journeys takes place during "the next to the last round of world wars," which is begun by the capitalist nations. The struggle centers in the Far East where the people of China arise and proclaim a socialist republic. At the end of the war the principal capital of the various federated socialist republics is placed near Shanghai, "the greatest crossroads of the world," and is called "Ocean." ("Moscow remained now just a Mecca of scientific socialism.") The travelers visit Ocean and Kurilov is curiously represented as disappointed because of the presence among its citizens of faults not unlike those of the people he knew in contemporary life. "But don't you see that you are trying to make a Christian paradise out of your Ocean," comments the more realistic author. "Let them brawl, suffer, mellow . . . after all, that's life!" But Kurilov angrily protests: "You slander the children of the future, scribbler! . . . Furthermore, why do you look for garbage everywhere?" "If only for the reason that it reveals the presence of *living* man!" replies the author, apparently determined to keep the vision of Communism realistic.

The second journey to Ocean takes place on the occasion of a total war between the Old World and the New World. Again the major action is concentrated in the Far East and it is detailed at boring length and with many footnotes. Vast air and naval fleets clash, extensive armed landings are made, and strange new weapons are employed. In the end, however, the forces of the New World, led by a Negro commander, triumph over the forces of the Old World.

On the third journey Ocean now represents the whole planet and it appears that Communism prevails throughout the world. The author and Kurilov visit gigantic hydraulic stations, plants, and "marvelously complex combines where anything could be manufactured out of anything, because matter is one. . . ." And they were happy to see evidence of how the crude socialistic beginnings of their own time had paved the way for a life of abundance. They observe among the inhabitants that people stand more erect and that human nature has improved. "Here man's natural state had at last been attained—he was free, he was not exploited and he rejoiced in the work of hand and brain. But although everything was within reach—bread, work and fate itself—we often saw people with careworn faces . . . they, too, knew tragedy, though of a kind more worthy of man's dignity." And as an example of such tragedy we are told of the heroic deaths of two men on an interplanetary spaceship. A curious reflex of the totalitarian present may be observed in this Communist future: when the fate of the lost men is first ascertained, for unexplained state reasons the newspapers "were forbidden to print obituaries" and "all communication was cut off."

Taken by themselves these three journeys into the future do not possess much merit either as literary exercises or flights of imagination. To be sure, as written in 1933–34 there was something strikingly prophetic in the descriptions of the world wars in the Far East, the nature of military actions, the advanced weapons employed, and the establishment of a Chinese socialist republic. But the final picture of the world Communist Utopia is blurred and unconvincing and must have offered little comfort, even as a propaganda gesture, to Soviet readers. They would most want to know how this future paradise of Communist abundance was organized, but to this the author lamely answers: "I am glad that my ignorance of technology exempts me from the necessity of citing facts and figures."

But these fantasies of Kurilov, these journeys into the future to Ocean, add a final touch of perhaps unintentional irony to his characterization. He hoped to find society in Ocean crowned with the summit of knowledge—freedom from death. For he knew, like any insignificant bourgeois philosopher, that death conquers all. Yet his tragedy was that at the height of his powers he found himself struck down by a cancer, fated to behold only in his dreams the ripened fruit of the tree that was growing before his very eyes. He did not fear death, but true to his notions of Communist service he regretted that he could not end his life "in a more intelligent way," that "he was not fated to screen a great leader with his body, or fall before a firing squad so that his death might serve as an example to others."

Kurilov, however, had to content himself with using his last days to influence for good his friends, the children he came in contact with, and especially Liza. Her association with Kurilov transforms her way of life and deepens her personality with a sense of service to the people before she can serve art. She rejects her husband's humble plea to return to the easy existence he can provide, as well as a priceless offer to join a first-rate theatrical company; instead she elects to instruct an amateur club group in the little railroad town of Cheremshansk. After Kurilov's death following an operation, Liza's "coming of age" is indicated by her dropping and breaking the little toy clown she has treasured, the symbol of her sorry past. The moral change in Liza has seemed to some critics unreal and improperly motivated. A careful study of the characterization, however, indicates that the striking transformation is not inconsistent with the logic of Liza's developing personality.

A meeting of the presidium of the Union of Soviet Writers was devoted to an open discussion of *Road to the Ocean*. This was some measure of the importance attached to the novel as a contribution to Soviet literature. A "magnificent failure" might sum up the consensus of opinion at this discussion. The judgment seems rather harsh, for in the light of what Leonov attempted and actually did accomplish hardly any Soviet novel at this time could be compared favorably to *Road to the Ocean* in complexity of design, comprehensive sweep, and mature artistry. This Soviet reaction was no doubt influenced by the difficulties which the intricate form of the novel presented to the reader, but the basic disappointment was with the characterization of Kurilov, the ideological justification of the work. With this judgment the non-Soviet reader will perhaps agree, but for different reasons. Soviet critics did not find in Kurilov the typical, well-rounded, and, at the same time, monumental positive Communist hero. For them he was too much of an individualist and never succeeded dynamically in identifying his personality with that of the collective.

This is the old dilemma in Soviet literature—the failure to recognize the fundamental incompatibility between the heroic and the collective. The essence of the truly heroic is individualism, and the trouble with Kurilov in the eyes of the non-Soviet reader is that he is not individualistic enough, as was Skutarevsky, in order to become a thoroughly acceptable, believable, monumental hero. As though he realized the unreality implicit in his conception of Kurilov, Leonov has tried to confer the heroic upon him like an award. "Yes, he was like a bridge," Leonov writes, "and people passed over him into the future." There is nothing very heroic about a "bridge," a man whose active great deeds are in the past and who exists largely to influence the lives of people. In fact, in the light of what Kurilov was intended to represent, it was already a confession of failure that Leonov's design called for the death of his hero by cancer at the height of his powers. In this sense Kurilov is a kind of Communist "superfluous man," like Turgenev's hero Bazarov in *Fathers and Sons* who dies from typhus at the point where he might have made a signal contribution to aid mankind. Leonov's failure with Kurilov, however, is some measure of the difficulties he had encountered in identifying his art with the ideology of the Communist Party.

TANK 203. Leonov was present at the meeting of the Union of Soviet Writers which pronounced *Road to the Ocean* a "magnificent failure." The "wisdom" of accepting uncomplainingly such strong official criticism was beginning to make itself apparent to Soviet writers by 1935. Leonov agreed with most of the strictures and defended himself only to the extent of stressing the pioneering difficulties of trying to fill such a large canvas in the spirit of the new socialist realism. However, he must have been deeply disappointed by this official reaction to what he considered a major artistic effort, and one in which he had sincerely tried to fuse ideological correctness with the living reality and complexity of Soviet life. The extent of his disillusion is reflected in the fact that for nine years after the publication of *Road to the Ocean* Leonov turned his back on any extensive attempts at fiction. No doubt the bloody purges that followed the assassination of Kirov in 1934 also contributed to Leonov's discouragement and to the marked diminution of his artistic efforts. Not a few writers were victims of the purges, and silence, especially among prominent authors, was almost the only way of indicating opposition to the excesses of the regime. This despair and revulsion to the ruthlessness of Stalinism, however, were largely submerged in the mighty wave of patriotism that swept the land upon the invasion of the Nazis in June, 1941. Leonov, like so many well-known Soviet writers, plunged into war reporting and patriotic propaganda efforts. There was no time for writing leisurely full-length novels, but poems, sketches, eye-witness accounts, and short stories, all dealing with war themes, appeared in large numbers. Leonov, who had already tried his hand at drama, added distinction to his achievements in this genre by writing two outstanding war plays, *Invasion* (1942) and *Lyonushka*

(1943). Despite his success, any examination of his plays suggests that this confining artistic form is alien to his creative spirit which functions more felicitously in the expansive design of prose fiction, to which he finally returned in his novelette, the *Taking of Velikoshumsk* (1944), translated into English under the title *Chariot of Wrath*. Though only a long short story, it is easily one of the best pieces of war fiction to emerge during the years of strife. (A great many Soviet novels dealing with the war have appeared in the postwar period.)

The ancient dullness that infects so much war fiction is avoided in *Chariot of Wrath* by an unyielding concentration on the main theme and by an unusual restraint in the use of the fictional sinews of war—descriptions and emotions. It is the simple story of a tank and its crew. The thirty-four-tonner 203 has won a reprieve from the scrap heap after having been almost shot to pieces in various engagements. It is returned to the front line with its wounds patched and welded and with a new engine. This iron veteran had accumulated a history of which its reconstructed crew were proud and had acquired a kind of tank personality with its scarred sides, a pin-up beauty torn from an American film magazine pasted in the turret, and a kitten mascot, Kiso, which any member of the crew would have protected with his life. With swift, vivid strokes Leonov quickly draws the contrasting members of this crew of 203. The commander Sobolkov has left his red-headed wife and children behind in the Altai, and one suspects, as he reads over his children's letters, that his wife has already betrayed him. He has a talent for telling wonderful fairy tales, is fond of gardens, and is the kind of man who has won the respect of all his comrades, "which at the front is harder to win than their friendship or even their love." The Pistol-like character of the group is Obriadin, the turretman, a laughable braggart whose vice is vodka and whose vanity is his self-acclaimed genius as a singer and cook extraordinary. A new man on the crew is the driver, little Vasia Litovchenko, half-afraid on this first assignment but filled with a deadly resolve to search the whole front for a particular German soldier who had beaten his mother. (The commander of the tank corp and a peasant woman in the neighborhood also bear the name Litovchenko— a symbolic sign of the unity of the people in the struggle.) On the other hand any German in uniform is the object of the fierce hatred of the uncommunicative radioman, Dybok. Silence had entered his soul when he learned that his young sister in the Kuban region had been torn to pieces by the invaders and that his father had died of grief.

When battle begins we follow the fortunes of 203 until it is left behind on the field, hung up on a German tank trap. As the crew struggle throughout the bitter cold night to release 203 simply because they feel that they must go on, the personalities of these four men unfold in the brevity of bravery, in the quiet heroism of comradely give-and-take. And we realize that their personalities have somehow merged with that of the tank, the beloved instrument by which they will vent their implacable hatred on the invaders of their native land. Freed at last from the trap, the thirty-four-tonner comes up on the German rear on a road before Velikoshumsk filled with Nazi troops and vehicles. The enormous tank charges down the packed road with all guns blazing, causing tremendous havoc and destruction before being riddled by antitank fire. Only Litovchenko and Dybok survive, and one feels that their sorrow for their lost comrades includes also the burnt-out tank which had shared the profound experiences of the whole crew.

Leonov surprises the readers of his previous novels by the simplicity and economy with which he achieves his effects in *Chariot of Wrath* and by the easy symbolism of the tank and its crew representing the unity and qualities of the Soviet armies repelling the invaders. It reveals a new dimension in his fiction which he ought to employ more often. For example, the heroic stature with which he tried so hard to endow Kurilov comes very naturally to a character such as Sobolkov, though otherwise they are hardly to be compared to each other. The difference may be that life and not political ideology dictated the conception of the tank commander.

GENTLE WINDS FROM THE PAST. Despite his wartime writings, an official literary critic in the postwar period charged Leonov with being a "keeper of silence." Indeed, after that first fruitful decade from 1925 to 1935, in the course of which Leonov had contributed five long novels, nothing very substantial in fiction had come from his pen. Vital national developments, which had nourished his inspiration in the past, had not ceased to stir the nation since the disappointing reaction to his last major effort *Road to the Ocean.* Yet only the tremendous event of the war elicited a response from him in fiction and this, as we have seen, was a relatively minor piece. The ideological confusion and fear which adulterated belles-lettres during the purges in the second half of the 1930s was considerably dissipated during the war and led Soviet writers to hope that after victory regimentation in the arts would be mitigated if not eliminated. Instead the decree of the Central Committee on August 14, 1946, made it clear that the Communist Party would control the form and content of literature as never before and would demand from authors a strict ideological adherence to *partiinost'*, or "Party spirit," in all that they wrote. Previous hopes were frustrated and there is reason to believe that the studied silence of a few of the leading Soviet writers during the postwar period, Leonov among them, was intended as a show of opposition to continued and even intensified literary controls. Accordingly, there was much anticipation among critical circles when it was rumored in 1950 that Leonov was again working on a full-length novel. But *Russian Forest* did not appear until the end of 1953, just eighteen years after *Road to the Ocean.*

Polya Vikhrova, a pretty eighteen-year-old girl, arrives one sunny June morning in 1941 in Moscow where she hopes to enter an institute for advanced study. Browned from outdoor

life along the Yenga River in her native northern district of
Russia, Polya is a picture of radiant health, a wide-eyed and
charming young provincial in the great metropolis. Though
her girl friend Varya is not there to meet her, strangers at the
station who are unconsciously drawn to this vision of shining
innocence, willingly reach out for her various bags and bundles
and help her on the bus. No sooner has she settled in at Varya's
apartment than she is off again to wander the city streets, gape
at the shop windows, and buy useless trifles from amused and
excessively helpful clerks. Out of sheer exuberance she sends
a telegram to herself to welcome her arrival in the city. Indeed
the readers, like all the people who meet her in the novel on
this first appearance, fall in love with Polya, captivated by her
breathless joy, her naïveté, and country freshness.

Before this brilliant opening chapter of *Russian Forest* has
ended, the reader is engulfed in a Dostoevskian intrigue which
continues to accumulate mystification to little purpose throughout much of the remainder of the novel. That very first day the
long arm of coincidence, which sticks out annoyingly in the
story, directs Polya to the room of an old woman, Natalya
Sergeevna, who lives in Varya's apartment house. She had
known Polya's father thirty years ago in St. Petersburg and
had been in love with his professional rival in forestry, Gratsiansky. In no time she and Polya are on familiar terms. "You
can talk quite openly," Polya declares to the old woman. "I
hate my father." It develops that fourteen years ago Polya's
mother Elena had for some unexplained reason left her husband Ivan Vikhrov, a professor in a Moscow forestry institute.
Since then Polya had never seen her father, and her mother,
constantly busy and often away from home at her job as a
nurse, had told her daughter nothing of the reasons for this
separation. Thus Polya had grown up nourishing a dislike for
her father which had been intensified by reading certain hostile
articles about him written by Gratsiansky. She now suspects a
betrayal of the mission of Communism which Polya, as a mem-

ber of the Young Communist League, describes to her friend:
"I firmly believe, Varya, that the mission of Communism is to
wipe out pain, evil, untruth, all that is ugly, shapeless and
bare; and that means that Communism, apart from all else, is
the flawless beauty in everything." With such convictions she
has already begun to imagine her father as a bloated pluto-
crat and a concealed enemy of the people.

On that first day in Moscow, however, Polya cannot resist
the temptation to visit her father, but he is away on a trip and
she is received by Taiska, his sister and housekeeper, a wonderful old hunchback peasant character. Polya clutches at the
straws of memory as she tries nostalgically to fit these rooms
into her vague childhood recollection of them. She surveys
closely her father's study. Its faded but comfortable appearance, the heaped-up books and papers, the worn chairs, and
her mother's framed photograph on the desk do not accord
with the distorted image which Polya had concocted of her
father. And Taiska's crude but loyal defense of his views
further serves to upset Polya's preconceived ideas about him.
In a mental and emotional turmoil she runs from the house to
seek the security of Varya's flat. The next day Moscow is
shocked by the news of the Nazi invasion of the Soviet Union.

This effective opening chapter introduces a lengthy novel
which has the scope and even more of the artistic power of
the best of Leonov's earlier works and, like them, is marred by
the same faults. *Russian Forest* is not simply a brief episode
from the endless poem of human destiny; it is also a protest
against the stream of feckless fiction which Soviet authors had
been submissively pouring forth since 1946 in obedience to
the Party's demand for a literature of strict ideological conformity. It is not an overt protest. There is no disloyalty to
Communist ideals in the novel. In fact, lip service is paid to
these ideals and occasionally to Stalin—otherwise the novel
could never have been published at that time in the Soviet

Union. One would have to have a comprehensive knowledge of the stupefying uniformity of theme, plot structure, and motivation and of the stereotyped characters in the bulk of Soviet postwar novels, in order to appreciate the extent to which *Russian Forest* violates the official pattern and dictated conventions in literature. Then there are symbolic overtones in *Russian Forest* which suggest a spirit of deep criticism of things as they are in the Soviet Union.

A major break with these postwar literary conventions is the absence of a positive hero in *Russian Forest*. There is no Kurilov, no "new Soviet man," who, inspired by Communist principles and with the aid of the collective, overcomes insuperable obstacles and in the end wins victory for the greater glory of the socialist fatherland. The real hero of the novel is the Russian forest and Leonov lavishes all his art on it. It is beautifully described, with its surroundings of meadows and streams, as a living, sentient force which helps to form the natures of those who come in contact with it. The good among them draw from the forest a moral philosophy of the eternal renewal of life, of optimism, and human purity. The preservation of the forest as a major timber resource of the country, in a society given to wanton destruction, provides the main theme of the novel. Once again Leonov associated the theme of a novel, although only indirectly in this case, with a national problem—the postwar campaign for soil preservation through afforestation and other means.

With his characteristic fondness for mystification, Leonov introduces at the outset various people whose puzzling relationships to each other can be explained only by excursions into the past. In fact, the structure of the novel involves two related and often intersecting lines of development, one devoted to more than a quarter of a century preceding the 1917 Revolution and the other to the first two years of the Second World War. In no other novel of Leonov is the past with its peasants, landowners, merchants, intellectuals, and revolutionists treated with such authority and convincing realism as in *Russian Forest*.

The account of the childhood and youth of Ivan Vikhrov in prerevolutionary Russia is told in the best tradition of nineteenth-century realism. There are the poverty and misery of his peasant family, but there is also the mysterious forest on the horizon, the magical spring, and the supernatural being who guards the forbidden places which Ivan and his pal Demid Zolotukhin steal away to visit one day. The supernatural being turns out to be the old caretaker Kalina who befriends Ivan and teaches him the wisdom of the forest and the beauty and usefulness of trees. Later this gentle boy with his love of animals and his passion for the forest turns violently on the timber merchant Knyshev in the vividly described vignette of the cutting of the Oblog woods. Knyshev is a striking character who has come up from the lower depths in the old Russia and personifies the spirit of destruction of the forests for the sake of greed. We see him and his henchmen in a brutal scene forcing the sale of the Oblog woods for railroad ties from the bankrupt Sapegin landowners, and next the hundreds of flashing peasant axes leveling these fine trees. As the powerfully built Knyshev himself takes the axe to the huge majestic pine, the mother of the Oblog, which shelters old Kalina's hut, the furious young Ivan Vikhrov strikes him in the face with a slingshot pellet. The boy has already begun to discover in the forest the whole meaning of his life.

The slaying by the police of Ivan's father, whom the village had sent to St. Petersburg to plead the cause of the peasants; the abject poverty that drove the family to the city to seek the aid of a servant uncle there who gives them lodgings in his hole under the stairs of the hotel where he works; the vivid drunken orgy in which the now wealthy Knyshev reappears and is once again defied by Ivan; and the acceptance of the youth in a forestry institute through the efforts of an old professor who has become interested in him—all these and more developments in the early life of Ivan are narrated with a wealth of detail which illuminates a whole area of Russian life that is moving irresistibly toward the explosion of revolution.

Ivan Vikhrov's years of study at the forestry institute in St. Petersburg provide Leonov with an opportunity to dwell upon a different slice of prerevolutionary Russian life. The "three musketeers" of the forestry institute—Ivan Vikhrov, Krainov, and Cheredilov—struggle as much with poverty as with their studies. Krainov is the strong, silent revolutionary type and is already a secret member of the group that later became the Communist Party. It is he who early convinces Vikhrov that the salvation of the Russian forests depends not on the voluntary restraint of the landowners, but on their overthrow by the masses. Having introduced these student friends of Vikhrov at the outset, it is curious that Leonov makes so little of them in the remainder of the novel. Cheredilov appears later, but briefly, as a careerist conspiring against Vikhrov. Krainov eventually becomes an important Bolshevik official who flits in and out of Vikhrov's life on several occasions but to little purpose. Nearly every postwar Soviet novel has a Krainov; he is always like a helpful animal, the omnipresent, all-wise Party official who aids the hero at crucial moments and keeps him ideologically pure. Krainov's comparative insignificance in *Russian Forest* amounts virtually to a satire on the stereotype, and Soviet critics were quick to condemn Leonov's failure to make a fictional mountain out of this Party molehill.

Gratsiansky, another fellow student, does play a significant role in Vikhrov's years at the institute and also throughout the remainder of the novel. He comes from a well-to-do middle-class family, the son of a professor of ecclesiastical law. Why he elects to study in a forestry institute is never made clear, for he is described as an "elegant darling of the drawing room," polished, brilliant, talented, gifted with a remarkable memory,

and capable of succeeding in any profession. He strives to be
accepted by the three musketeers, aids them with money, and
invites them to fastidious evening parties at his home, but
they regard him as a shifty, untrustworthy person and keep
him on the fringe of their companionship. Gratsiansky and the
young men of his social set are involved in a political conspiracy whose perverted idealism and principles of terrorism
recall Dostoevsky's Shigalovism in *The Possessed.* In fact, there
is some reason to believe that the sudden arrest and exiling of
Krainov to Siberia for life and the expulsion of Vikhrov from
St. Petersburg for two years resulted from their betrayal by
Gratsiansky and his followers to the tsar's secret police. The
descriptions of the upper classes of Petersburg society, the conversations and political activities of intellectuals and revolutionists, and the story of Gratsiansky's involved love affair with
Emma, the beautiful wife of the secret police official Chandvetsky, provide a picture of those frenetic years in the capital
leading up to the First World War which is at once socially
authentic and intensely interesting.

Though Ivan Vikhrov does not merit the description "hero,"
he is clearly the central figure in *Russian Forest* and much of
the first half of the novel is devoted to the story of the formation of his character. His nature unfolds in contact with the
forest and is ultimately dominated by it. He spends his two
years of exile in forestry surveys in the far north, returns to
finish his studies at St. Petersburg after the amnesty of 1913,
and is drafted in 1914. A wound in the war leaves him lame.
He is mustered out and spends many months wandering over
the forest regions of Russia. These are among the most remarkable pages of the novel, descriptions filled with the wild beauty
of nature as well as with the wanton desolation visited upon
it by man. More than ever convinced of his sacred mission to
preach the preservation of the forests, this peasant, already
devoted to the cause and theory of the Revolution by virtue
of his experience with life and the influence of Krainov, will-

ingly accepts a position as forester in the regions on the Yenga where he was born. There he conceives his first book as well as his first love—love for Elena, a half-wild orphan of good birth who all her life had been compelled to live as little other than a servant on the estate of distant relatives, the Sapegins. This shy man with black, bushy eyebrows, yellowish skin, big mouth, and drooping mustache, with awkward limping movements, is a most unexciting wooer. "He belonged," wrote Leonov, "to that category of people—the timid, not the tempters in the science of the heart." Though his feeling for Elena is deep and tender, she long evades his patient pursuit. In the end she accepts him; her yearning to exchange her humiliating existence for anything that promises something different seems to have played a part in her decision. With the publication of his book came an appointment to a professorship in the forestry institute in Moscow and the couple moved there in the middle 1920s.

Action in the past alternates regularly with action in the present in the first half of the novel, and throughout the rest of the work the past continues to shadow the present. Though this favorite structural device of Leonov creates mystery and suspense, as in his previous novels, in *Russian Forest* its motivation is often forced—Taiska reminisces at great length about the past on successive visits of Polya to her, or Vikhrov daydreams of his past, or the author simply indulges in a conventional flashback. But Leonov's concern with the prerevolutionary past in most of his fiction, and especially in *Russian Forest*, denotes perhaps more than a deep, personal belief in the historical continuity of Russian life. Like Fedin, he seems to feel artistically more at home in the past, less thwarted by the taboos and interdictions of the Soviet present.

Certainly in the second half of *Russian Forest*, where events of the present (1941–42) predominate, the reader's interest in them flags, largely because the validity of the total pattern of life does not compel belief. The central figure Vikhrov, whose development up to this point has been quite absorbing, now plays the rather passive role of an individual preoccupied with an essentially unreal Soviet doctrinal dispute. And the charming Polya, who like the lovely Anna Karenina had aroused the pleasantest expectations among her readers when she arrived at the Moscow station at the beginning of the novel, after a few more delightful pages dwindles into a stern member of the Komsomol and becomes a victim of the same doctrinal dispute that troubles her father.

There is nothing unique in the essential psychological dilemma of Polya. It is that of the child of separated parents, one of whom is suspected of or has actually committed some shocking crime. The child experiences a strong sense of guilt and while hating the parent who has caused all this suffering, secretly yearns to rehabilitate him and win his love. However, a Soviet twist is added to this fictional formula which renders it singularly incredible to Western readers. The parent's "crime" is that for years he has been publishing and lecturing on the government's need to preserve one of the country's greatest natural resources—its vast timber supplies. Vikhrov counsels a regular system of replacement plantings whenever timber is felled, as well as other scientific methods of conservation. This commonplace, widely accepted position grows not only out of Vikhrov's profound knowledge of forestry in Russia and abroad, but also out of his genuine patriotic feeling for the welfare of his country.

While maintaining a show of friendship for his old student comrade, Gratsiansky has attacked in reviews every book that Vikhrov has published. The reasons for this are buried deep in the strange, distorted personality of Gratsiansky. A professor in the same Moscow institute of forestry, he has really built his fame on these masterpieces of professional invective so that, as Leonov puts it: "Vikhrov's reputation had not had a single unclouded day for a quarter of a century." These reviews are more notable for their brilliance of language and general erudition than for any convincing refutation of Vikhrov's theories, yet by innuendo, deft hints, and half truths Gratsiansky has created a vague impression that Vikhrov is subtly endeavoring to hamper socialist construction.

This implausible situation may well have been intended as a covert satire by Leonov of the widespread Party-inspired smearing of scientific reputations, often on equally implausible grounds, during the postwar nationalistic and anti-cosmopolitan drive. Thus, in trying to offer us a reason for Gratsiansky's unjustified and unscientific attacks, Leonov pointedly declares: "It would be more sensible to search for the explanation in Gratsiansky's extraordinary seismographic sensitivity to all the shifts and changes in the surrounding atmosphere."

Though Leonov carefully explains that this distortion of Vikhrov's reputation is not a part of public knowledge but is restricted to forestry circles, to students in the field, and to readers of the specialized journals, Polya, who has read a few of Gratsiansky's reviews but not her father's books, seems to believe that the whole Soviet world suspects him. She imagines that her mother left him because of the same anti-Soviet offense; she feels unclean, is ashamed of her name Vikhrov and tries to write it illegibly in her school exercise books; she is sure that a passing Moscow policeman looks suspiciously at her. In fact, she even contemplates denouncing her father to the Moscow Party Committee or informing on him to the police!

This absurdity is compounded by another. A talk with her father would have cleared up all of Polya's laboriously constructed doubts and suspicions. After that visit on her first day in Moscow when he was away, her curiosity to hear the whole story of his life from her aunt Taiska draws Polya back on several other occasions. However, she always manages to avoid meeting him. As a matter of fact, though father and daughter live only a short distance from each other in Moscow, the author contrives by a feat of fictional legerdemain to keep them apart for months during two thirds of the whole novel.

Equally improbable is the stubbornness with which Polya clings to the notion of her father's "crime" despite mounting evidence to the contrary. She hears from Taiska a full and truthful account of his life and beliefs. His separation from his wife, which Polya had connected with some offense against the state, turns out to be a sad case of matrimonial incompatibility. Elena had never really loved her husband. An unconventional woodsy creature obsessed with the desire to cast her lot in with the simple Soviet people of her native district, she could not adapt herself to the cultured life of the city or to her husband's busy professional existence. So one day, without any warning, she disappeared with her child, leaving no information by which she could be traced. Shortly thereafter, Vikhrov adopted a five-year-old boy, Sergei, abandoned by his old village friend Demid Zolotukhin. In her inordinately suspicious mind Polya imagines Sergei to be the illegitimate son of a mistress of her father until Taiska straightens this matter out. Finally Polya attends her father's opening lecture that semester at the institute. It is an amazing performance for a novel—a major piece of research complete in thirty-two pages of solid print, containing the story of forests from the dawn of history and illustrated with statistics, numerous references to international legislation on the theme, and quotations from Marx and Engels—a fictional monstrosity which relentlessly dramatizes the social command that Soviet literature must educate as well as entertain. Vikhrov uses the occasion to develop eloquently his theory that a socialist government, which itself owns and thus protects the forests, is to be preferred to a capitalist system that permits exploitation of the forests for private gain. And he concludes patriotically, amidst loud applause, with: "Hail to our people and our army!"

At last this mountain of positive evidence begins to shake Polya's prolonged doubts about her father's loyalty to the regime. Yet in volunteering as a war nurse she strangely imagines that this service for her country will somehow help to redeem the past failings of her father, an aberration in doctrinal purity for a member of the Komsomol which did not go uncriticized in the Soviet reviews. When she is ready to leave for the front Polya finally calls on her father. It is a restrained, well-managed scene, almost Chekhovian in its unattuned dialogue. He insists on his honesty and patriotism and she talks about her ideal of purity to be realized only in a world in which "there will be no war, no mutual recriminations, no slaying of children." And after calming his fear for her well-being she leaves for the front with a light heart, happy at last that she no longer need feel ashamed of her father.

Though the action of the opening chapter of *Russian Forest* coincides with the beginning of the Nazi invasion, surprisingly little of this long novel is devoted to the theme of war. Its artistic purpose in the thematic pattern is the presentation of representatives of a young and entirely Soviet generation who force comparison with those characters who belong to an older generation with its roots buried in the prerevolutionary past. With the possible exception of Polya and Sergei, however, these young Soviet people, such as Morshchikhin the political commander on the armored train, Varya the girl friend and Rodion the lover of Polya, Sapozhkov the Komsomol official, and Osminov a student of Vikhrov, do not grip the imagination. They are predestined heroes, pale allegorical figures in a faded tapestry of Soviet life.

Harsh experiences in the war deepen and mature the characters of Polya and Sergei, Vikhrov's culturally sophisticated, adopted son who longs to identify himself with the proletariat and by heroic deeds on Morshchikhin's armored train to expiate the kulak sins of his real father Demid Zolotukhin. Leonov manipulates events of the war in order to affect the fates of his characters. The campaign in the northern Yenga district overtakes Polya as a nurse there. Her father's student

Osminov also turns up as an officer and enlists this young girl to undertake a very dangerous mission of spying behind the enemy lines on the basis that she will be operating in her native territory. After some dangerous adventures she sets out to return through the forests for a planned pickup only to find herself held down in a bomb crater at night by a violent air battle. There for the first time she meets the wounded Sergei who had left his armored train, which had also entered the northern campaign, to perform a mission. And in this same crater they find the severed arm of Morshchikhin, which Sergei recognizes in the dark by a radium-dialed watch still on the wrist and still ticking! Shortly thereafter in the hospital Vikhrov's daughter and adopted son come across the long-lost lover of Polya, the wounded Rodion, who had also been assigned for combat to the northern area. The three are attended by Polya's mother, for it turns out that she is serving in this hospital! Though there are some striking war scenes in *Russian Forest*, especially the effective descriptions of the night-bombing of Moscow, neither the treatment of war nor its lacerating emotional impact on the human psyche compare favorably with Leonov's artistic achievements in these respects in *The Chariot of Wrath*.

Singularly aloof from the war is the mysterious Gratsiansky, the primary symbol of evil in the novel and one of the most memorable characters Leonov has created. This kind of complex image which requires profound psychological analysis for effective realization is perhaps most congenial to the creative art of the author. It is a simplification to dismiss Gratsiansky, as some Soviet critics do, as a mere "bourgeois survival." He reminds one of those baffling Dostoevskian characters Svidrigailov and Stavrogin, but the compulsion to evil in him is less motivated by what we know of his past. When Polya first meets him in a bomb shelter and, without revealing her name, draws him out about her father and listens to his smooth, friendly, but sly and poisonous innuendoes, she observes that:

"He had a thin ascetic face of brooding grandeur with a touch of contemptuous pride. His skin was dull but sleek, and there were gray streaks in his short beard which was slightly disarranged as if by the winds of inspiration. He wore his hair rather long, and under a high forehead were flickering shadows in the cavities of his eyes. . . . From time to time his eyes in their half-closed lids would shift nervously. . . . It seemed that he was haunted by some constantly recurring memory."

We never learn for certain what this memory is—his youthful involvement in political conspiracy and the tsar's secret police, or his unsuccessful love affair with Emma, or his lingering unfulfilled love for Natalya Sergeevna whose death as an old woman so strangely moves him. The reason for his implacable harrying of Vikhrov is never explained. The author himself admits: "No one could remember what had started the duel." Yet Gratsiansky pursues this malevolent course of ruining the reputation of a man while protesting his deep interest in Vikhrov's welfare and his friendship for him. Perhaps his towering self-esteem may be regarded as a motive— he could not permit a rival, and especially one who had come up from the peasant class, to outshine him in the profession of forestry. It is a curious fact that when Vikhrov finally admits defeat in the long battle and threatens to cease his publications and return to the position of a simple forester, Gratsiansky, aware that his own reputation has been built on his criticism of Vikhrov's works, pleads with him not to do this. Some of the best scenes in the novel grow out of the distorted personality of this absorbing character, such as the splendid one in the institute when Vikhrov is compelled to offer a public defense of his views. Gratsiansky had let it be known that he would not appear because of illness (feigning illness is a part of his personality). But at the opportune moment he makes a dramatic appearance, hair disheveled as though just coming from a sickbed, and in a theatrical speech denounces Vikhrov as a man whose theories on wood-felling have obstructed the five-year plans.

In the struggle between good and evil forces in Gratsiansky's ambivalent nature, the evil prevail and finally dictate his fate. Though he has created a façade of loyalty to the Soviet regime, his dubious political past eventually falls under investigation, and a contact with abroad, forced on him by the old émigré tsarist police official Chandvetsky, dangerously complicates his present existence. In the end it is not the Soviet authorities but Polya who awakens Gratsiansky's long dormant conscience. Steeled by her experiences in the war and now fully convinced of her father's innocence, she seeks an interview with Gratsiansky on one of her leaves. In a gripping scene she confronts him as an innocent victim of his persistent evil, and she terminates the meeting by throwing the contents of a desk inkwell in his face. His "whole being," writes the author, "seemed to have bifurcated, and one half of his soul, as it were, appeared to be asking the other: 'Will you be there soon?'" Shortly after this Gratsiansky commits suicide.

Russian Forest ends on a note of mingled hope and frustration, a marked contrast to most Soviet postwar novels which conclude with the conventional optimistic triumph of Communist principles and the glorification of the positive hero or heroine. The defeat of the Nazis in the northern campaign makes possible the happy reunion, in their native district, of Vikhrov, his wife, Sergei, Polya, and her beloved Rodion. The war has added new stature to the lives of each. The battle-tested Sergei has wiped out his kulak father's debt to Soviet society and won his spurs among the proletarian fighters. A sterner, more mature, but less interesting Polya has found her father, and a future husband in Rodion. But the reconciliation with his wife which Vikhrov had longed for is denied him in the end. Their meeting after years of separation in the familiar surroundings of their childhood is sad and moving. She has changed much over these years; she has found emotional and social stability in hard work as a hospital assistant with her own people along the Yenga, and in courageous activities with their guerrilla bands when the territory is occupied by the Nazis. Though she is frank in admitting her unfairness to Vikhrov, who is still deeply devoted to her, she prefers the happiness of her work to life with a man whom she pities rather than loves. The only consolation Vikhrov receives is a summons back to Moscow to assume a still higher post in laboring for that which he loves—the Russian forest.

Indeed, the majestic forest, an element of continuity between the Russian past and the Soviet present, is the only constant factor in the novel. It stands as a symbol of permanence in an impermanent world where change may be destructive as well as constructive. The eternal forest is Mother Russia embracing all of Russian life, its antiquities, its art and culture. The burden of the symbolism contains Leonov's plea, heard more than once in his novels, to preserve all these things. "What Russian close to his mother does not profit from her?" shouts the forest-destroying Knyshev. "Have no pity, lash her again and again, hew and exhaust her." And not only in the past but in the present—so Leonov clearly implies—is Mother Russia lashed and exhausted.

The texture of *Russian Forest* is enriched by many perceptive observations on a wide variety of political, social, economic, and cultural matters. As usual in Leonov's novels, the characters carry the burden of most of these spoken passages, but in the case of the younger ones it is often Leonov's voice we seem to hear rather than that of Polya or Sergei or Morshchikhin. The intellection involved would seem to be beyond the capacities of eighteen-year-olds. Such, for example, is Sergei's extraordinary indictment of the art of the past, especially the Western European past—a curious, anachronistic, satiric echo before the war of the Party's vigorous postwar anti-

Western campaign. And Morshchikhin's crushing answer, based on the authority of Lenin, is likewise Leonov's—that Communist culture must build on the best of the past.

As the first long novel by Leonov in many years, *Russian Forest* may be regarded as something less than the anticipated artistic fulfillment of a superb literary talent. *The Thief,* written twenty-five years earlier, is in some respects a deeper, more emotionally disturbing, and certainly a more challenging novel. On the other hand, there are many things in *Russian Forest,* some of them already singled out, which artistically are unequaled and unsurpassed by any other Soviet writer. It is almost oppressively apparent that these fine things, with few exceptions, belong to that large part of the novel dealing with Russia before the 1917 Revolution. It has been said that a man can know intimately only the span of his own lifetime, but Leonov seems much more at home in the past. He evokes it with sympathy and understanding, and his most interesting and convincing characters are nearly always figures from the past who either adjust themselves happily to the Soviet present or become its victims. These gentle winds from the past murmuring through the ancient Russian forests bring with them a message from old, forgotten things which constitutes the principal charm of Leonov's latest novel.

THE DOSTOEVSKY OF THE SOVIET UNION. The fact that Leonov's creative life has spanned virtually the whole existence of the Soviet Union could be regarded, in the history of that country's literature, as either an accidental triumph or an artistic defeat. The evidence indicates that Leonov has endeavored— though not with full success—to preserve his intellectual and artistic integrity while gradually accepting over the years the developing ideology of the Communist Party. Like so many of the young fellow travelers in the early days of the regime, Leonov welcomed the Revolution as a tremendous elemental force that would arouse the long dormant energies and creative powers of the masses of Russian people and inspire them to great achievements. And though he admired the Bolsheviks as the leaders of this movement, he was critical of their ruthlessness toward the culture of the past and the old intelligentsia. He also distrusted the rational approach of Communism in solving the purely human problems of individuals. These were the concerns on which Leonov focused his art in the first novels, *The Badgers* and *The Thief*. However current and topical the basic situations of his novels may be, Leonov attempts to transcend them in working out the fates of his characters in terms of the more universal problems of human behavior.

Leonov moved toward a less critical acceptance of the Party position in his Five-Year-Plan novels *Sot* and *Skutarevsky*. It was the doctrine of socialist work rather than the extreme methods employed by the government to achieve results that won his support. In fact, Leonov has never written unadulterated propaganda novels however much he may have bowed to Party enthusiasm for particular themes. There is criticism of Five-Year-Plan bureaucracy in *Sot* and of the Party's unjust persecution of scientists in *Skutarevsky*. As always, however, the center of his interest is the psychological problem of human adjustment confronting men and women who find themselves living in a planned society evolving toward socialism.

Though Leonov appears to have identified himself more fully with the ideology of the Party in *Road to the Ocean* and in *Russian Forest*, he still clings to his convictions of the autonomy of art and to his belief that the life of today "serves only as material for the creation of a lasting picture of man on earth." If the goal of the novel is to reveal the direction in which society is moving, there seems little reason to doubt that Leonov believes that it is moving in the direction of Communism. But he asks for the right to describe that movement in his own terms. In his last two novels, no less than in his earlier ones, he has not failed to criticize abuses and satirize the foibles of the regime, especially the ugliness, insincerity, and banality that are the products of a government-controlled art.

In the end, however, Leonov has become an ambivalent victim of the circumstances under which he has been compelled to create. His works give the impression that he has intellectually accepted the Soviet scheme of things without ever having been able to identify himself with it emotionally and artistically. After *The Thief* the reader senses Leonov's lack of inner involvement with the Soviet way of life in his succeeding novels. It is there to be sure, but always overshadowed by the vivid, living presentation of the past. No Soviet-born hero or heroine is attempted—the young Soviet characters in his later novels are never central and for the most part seem contrived and politically doctrinaire. On the other hand, all the truly central figures—Mitya Vekshin, Uvadiev, Skutarevsky, Kurilov, and Vikhrov—have their roots deep in the prerevolutionary past and in one way or another this fact influences their lives in the Soviet present. These lonely men are the triumphant victims, so to speak, of the struggle between the past and the present, and in their struggle they must suffer for the sins of the past in achieving the victory of the present. "The victory in the struggle between the old and the new," says Varya in *Russian Forest*, "will be achieved without the present suffering only under Communism."

Again and again do we find Leonov withdrawing to the past, withdrawing with obvious relish and a sure sense of authority and artistic fulfillment. His head is abundantly stored with knowledge of the past and his finest character creations belong to it in spirit if not always in actuality. And it is in the great scenes and descriptions dealing with the past that one of Leonov's most brilliant contributions is at its best—his extraordinary language. His style is unusually complex, often rich in metaphor and symbolically ornate in descriptive passages, yet in dialogue uncannily adapted to the nature, personality, and mood of the speaker. On this superb gift of language rests his clearest title to originality.

Of course no novelist can remain untouched by his times, but in the Soviet Union the writer is required to observe both the past and the future through the prism of the political ideology of the present. Leonov is no exception to this rule, although he tries to keep the powerful sense of the present, with its richness in tragic suggestion, from deteriorating into the fictionized official news so common in the Soviet novel. However, the felt need to subscribe to dogma, to become, in effect, a propagandist, deprives Leonov of that imaginative freedom in treating the present which he employs so impressively in recreating the past. This is the creative tragedy of Leonov, a writer whose great gifts freely exercised on the present would have enabled him to become the Dostoevsky of the Soviet Union, the artist of its spiritual agony, of all its doubts and all its sufferings.

Mikhail Alexandrovich Sholokhov, 1905-

Mikhail Sholokhov

Not until Mikhail Sholokhov was seven, in 1912, did his father, a cattletrader and storekeeper, bethink himself to legitimize the boy's birth by marrying his mother. Something of the same casualness attended his early upbringing in his native village of Veshenskaya in the Don Cossack Military District. He was subsequently shunted around to various provincial schools in surrounding towns and his contact with home was maintained only through correspondence with his parents. Though his father had some slight education, his half-peasant, half-Cossack mother had to learn to write in order to answer her son's letters. When civil war broke out on the Don, after the 1917 Revolution, life took on a stern and bloody direction for young Sholokhov, who later joined a food-requisitioning detachment of the Red Army. With that appalling brevity which Soviet celebrities seem to consider an order of merit in their fugitive autobiographical notes, all that Sholokhov tells us of this formative and stirring period of his life is: "We hunted down the bandits who overran the Don in 1922, and the bandits hunted us. All went as could be expected. I was in many a tight spot, but nowadays all this is forgotten."

By the time of his fiftieth birthday, in 1955, Sholokhov was regarded as the most renowned author in the Soviet Union. For the second time he was given the government's top award, the Order of Lenin, and celebrations in his honor were held all over the country. Up to 1955 his works had been reprinted 421 times in 55 languages, totaling almost 21 million copies, a staggering figure when it is realized that the bulk of it is accounted for by the only two novels Sholokhov has published—*The Silent Don* and *Virgin Soil Upturned*. Operas, films, and a play have been based on his works, and literally hundreds of articles and several books have already been published on his life and writings. In 1941 he received a First Stalin Prize in literature, and in 1945 he was awarded the Order of the Fatherland War, First Degree, for his war work. He has been elected Deputy from his district to the Supreme Soviet, a member of the Academy of Sciences, and serves on the Presidium of the Union of Soviet Writers. Despite these many high honors and national fame, no prominent Soviet author has kept himself more remote from the centers of Party struggle and literary politics or has acquired a greater international reputation for artistic integrity than Sholokhov.

In contrast to the older Fedin and Leonov, Sholokhov is an indubitably *Soviet* writer. He was only twelve years old when the Revolution came and twenty-five when he joined the Communist Party. No memories of the fine culture of the old intelligentsia troubled his spirit, and he has never heeded the siren call of the culture of the West. (He once abruptly terminated one of his very few trips abroad out of homesickness for his beloved Veshenskaya.) What he has learned from the great Russian novelists of the past, and he has learned much, has been their literary art and not their democratic faith and hatred for oppression. The struggle between the old and the new has been fought on a battlefield of his own choosing, with victory for the new predetermined by Soviet power. Unlike Fedin and Leonov in their early years, lurking doubts never cast Sholokhov in the role of a fellow traveler of the Revolution. From the outset of his career he was a convinced partisan of the new regime. Yet the devotion to the Communist cause of this singular, isolated author has never ceased to be conditioned by his devotion to the independence of art.

Sholokhov's isolation and artistic independence were evident in his first literary experience. In 1923, when the civil war on the Don was over, he came to Moscow as a lonely youth of eighteen to obtain more education and to seek his fortune. Though he began to contribute humorous sketches and short stories at this time to Komsomol newspapers and magazines, he had to work as a common laborer in order to support himself. The bubbling literary ferment of Moscow, filled with the yeast of early revolutionary idealism, did not concern him. He appears to have been uninterested in the credo and the writings of the Serapion Brothers, the literary movement then most in vogue, and the startling Formalists with their provocative "new criticism" contributed nothing to the development of his artistic values. These were all fellow travelers at heart. But neither did Sholokhov identify himself with any of the several groupings of left-wing proletarian writers then very active in the capital. He became friendly only with the old writer, A. S. Serafimovich, who favored the Soviet regime. In short Sholokhov's independent instinct, so unusual in Soviet authors motivated by collectivism, manifested itself at the outset of his career.

CREATIVE BEGINNINGS. *Don Tales,* Sholokhov's first thin volume of collected stories, appeared in 1925. A second small collection, *The Azure Steppe,* appeared the following year and was reissued in augmented form in 1931, containing nearly all the short stories which Sholokhov had written between 1923 and 1925. This collection was published in an edition of 5,500 copies and it has long since become a collector's item. In a fragmentary introduction to the opening tale, Sholokhov writes with asperity of the popularly entertained clichés about the Don region and its Cossacks, such as the "gray feather grass . . . which has its own special fragrance," and how "the Red warriors died on the Don and Kuban steppes, choking with high-flown words." In fact, he drily remarks, the gray feather grass is "a foul, colorless weed without any smell," and on the cattle roads to the villages may still be seen the old trenches, "the silent witnesses of recent fighting which could tell how the people in them died hideously and simply." Sholokhov wanted to present a true picture of the life of the Don Cossacks during the civil war, not a romanticized or idealized one.

Only part of the truth is told in *The Azure Steppe,* and it is a stark, cruel part which is relieved occasionally by characters, situations, and passages of tenderness, humor, and warm humanity. Each of these tales is about an unusual incident and in many of them the hero is a young member of the Komsomol. Though the author understands that the essence of this kind of short story is "news," he is rarely content with a simple communication of incident; he tries, not always successfully, to humanize the narrative of events by a curious combination of his own ideological empathy and psychological realism in the delineation of characters. The Komsomol member Styopka is mercilessly killed by his anti-Soviet father ("Wormholes"); the young Mitka slays his father who heads a military tribunal condemning Reds to execution ("The Melon-Patch Worker"); the returning Red Army soldier Yefim is murdered by the rich Cossack Ignat ("The Mortal Enemy"). In fact, a number of the tales deal with the tragic conclusions of such political enmities in families. The events leading up to these brutal denouements are striking and the principal characters are realistically projected, but in this fierce fratricidal strife on the Don during the civil war, moral justification is somehow always on the side of the Reds. The young author had not yet learned (nor did he ever entirely learn it) that art is impartial, that it favors neither the victor nor the vanquished.

A few of the tales, however, do suggest a dawning awareness of the impartiality of art. Life is grasped at its moments of
tender weakness; the proverbial cruelty of the Cossacks fades
into legend. In "The Foal" Trofim sacrifices his life for the
sake of a beloved horse, and in "Alien Blood" the old father
Gabriel, heartbroken over the death of his son in the White
cause, transfers his affection to a badly wounded Red Army
youth and nurses him back to health. Such stories were condemned by early Soviet Party critics. Sholokhov, they said,
was lubricating the class relations of his characters with ideas
of humanism and with love for mankind in general. The
humanism of Sholokhov continued to trouble such critics until they learned how to transform it into a variant of "Soviet
humanism."

Nowhere is the mark of the budding artist more in evidence
than in the language of these stories. Sholokhov is essentially
a novelist of action, but the medium is a carefully orches-
trated language. Thus speech is a major factor in the individ-
ualization of his characters; the intonation in each case is
not so much an imitation of life as it is a divination. Such
efforts in these early tales are striking even in their imperfections, as is the entirely natural speech of the eight-
year-old Mishka, who is disconsolate when he discovers that
his dream-vision of a tall, heroic Lenin, inspired by the
rhapsodic descriptions he has heard from his Red sailor
father, has nothing at all in common with the plain, stubby
figure of Lenin which he sees on a picture postcard ("The
Impudent Brat"). Or language will be used as the medium of
humor. Hard foreign words that came in with the Revolution
collide with the natural speech of these simple Cossacks. Such
words are amusingly mispronounced and give rise to howling
malapropisms. Or the meaning comically evades the user:
"Our republic," a character solemnly declares, "is not especially enormous—in all about a hundred households and it
extends about forty versts from the village up to the swampy

ravine." When the Whites threaten to attack this "republic"
the same specialist in hard words shouts: "Comrades, let us
go to the aid of our Soviet rule and engage this band in
battle to the last drop of blood, because it is a hydra right to
the very roots, a blood-sucker that sucks away at world-wide
socialism!" ("The Chairman of the Revolutionary War Council
of the Republic.") And the language of the landscape descriptions in the tales is suffused with that quality of poetic observation of nature which Sholokhov later developed and enriched in numerous passages of stylistic brilliance.

These early tales are obviously the efforts of a youthful
writer who was already a conscious literary artist. Sholokhov
deliberately confines himself to people, situations, and locale
which he knows from first-hand experience and he is never
tempted to stray beyond the circumference of his own knowledge. Though in his treatment of the Don Cossacks he ad-
mittedly wishes to correct mistaken popular notions about
this unusual people, he does not overtly plead a cause. If his
sympathies are with the Reds, he does not portray them un-
realistically—their failings as well as their virtues are revealed. There is little basis for the insistence of some recent
Soviet critics that in these tales Sholokhov was already aware
of all the implications of the class struggle on the Don.
He seems aware solely of a tragic civil war in which the
Communists, who were a minority, were trying to force their
rule over a people who for generations had exercised considerable democratic freedom in managing their own local
affairs. The political niceties of Marxian explanations of the
reasons for the struggle had not as yet occurred to the young
Sholokhov. Fedin, in *Transvaal,* saw only the apathy and
sluggishness of the old which opposed the new in the story
of civil war in the village; Leonov, in *The Badgers,* studied
the struggle as reflected in the dark psychological relations
between two brothers, Semyon and Pavel; for Sholokhov,
in *The Azure Steppe,* the simple cleavages of rich and poor,

exploited and exploiters, and Reds and anti-Reds define more correctly the motivation of strife during the civil war in the village.

There is immaturity in these early tales, but surprisingly little. One may well doubt whether Sholokhov is a natural short-story writer. The form seems too confining for an author who plainly relishes action and sets much store in long descriptive passages to provide atmosphere. The art of selection for the novelist becomes the art of omission for the short-story writer for whom no addition can ever be as important as a deletion. Restraint was plainly difficult for the beginner. The accumulation of heroic events sometimes clutters the narrative and distracts the reader's attention from the central incident. Worse still, Sholokhov's excessive preoccupation with action within the narrow scope of a short story often prevents him from revealing with sufficient depth the inner world of his heroes.

For the student of the development of Sholokhov's creative art, however, *The Azure Steppe* has considerable importance. We see in embryo in these early tales the future powerful psychological realist as he creates characters and bold, dramatic situations. Further, there is more than a suggestion of his future narrative skill, his humor, his remarkable descriptive powers, and his impressive use of language. A careful reader may also discern in the tales whole incidents and narrative sequences, as well as certain characters, which were taken over for further development in the novels. With *The Azure Steppe* Sholokhov had unobtrusively but firmly launched himself on a great career.

THE BIRTH OF A CLASSIC. There is no evidence that Sholokhov was inclined to be complacent with his first effort, for young as he was he had already begun to dream about a novel of epic proportions. But he had to get back to his beloved Don, to the region and scenes and people that were crowding his imagination. He returned in 1925, married a peasant girl, and settled down to family life and to the fulfillment of his great artistic design. Two years later the editors of the Moscow left-wing journal *October* received a discouragingly long mishmash of a manuscript—there were often no spaces between the typed words or intervals between the sentences; words were copied over and letters illegible. From what the editors could make of it, they decided that it was a story about the prewar Cossacks and hence of little political interest in those harsh days of rugged Communism. That might have ended the matter if the manuscript had not been brought to the attention of Sholokhov's friend, the old writer A. S. Serafimovich, an honored member of the editorial board and a descendant of Cossacks. With much effort he made his way through the manuscript, pronounced it a masterpiece, and ordered it printed. It began to appear in the January number of *October*, 1928. The work was the first volume of *Tikhii Don*, translated into English as *The Silent Don*, although a more precise rendering of the Russian title would be "Quiet Don."

Left-wing Soviet critics were somewhat baffled by this first volume of the novel which concerned life on the Don between 1912 and the early part of the First World War. Events of national importance were taking place so swiftly then in the Soviet Union that tsarist Russia and even the recent war seemed like ancient history to critics who were demanding that fiction treat the life of the throbbing present. Of the few notices only Serafimovich's in *Pravda* seemed aware of the birth of a classic in this brilliant beginning. Other reviewers restricted their comments largely to praising Sholokhov's creative ability and narrative technique and to rather poor guesses about the future ideological development of the hero.

The speed with which the second volume appeared, in 1929, was owing to the fact that Sholokhov had originally begun his huge novel with this part which covers events from 1916 to 1918. After he had got well into it, a surer grasp of the expanding design of the whole work convinced him of the necessity of laying a firmer foundation for the future development of the Cossack people and the character of his hero in a revolutionary period by returning to the events of a still earlier period. It was a creative experience that Tolstoy had also gone through in beginning *War and Peace*. In both cases the artistic results justified these second thoughts.

The second volume of *The Silent Don* provoked much more and much sharper criticism than the first. Revolution and civil war were dangerous subjects and in his treatment of them Sholokhov seemed to the literary politicians something less than "objective" from the official Soviet point of view. The hero was denounced by some critics as a reactionary and embittered Cossack, and Sholokhov was described as a man for whom the Whites were enemies but still heroes. He was charged with being a petty-bourgeois fellow traveler devoid of any sense of class consciousness. A nasty rumor went the rounds in literary circles that the novel was actually the work of a White Guard officer and that Sholokhov was merely an intermediary for purposes of publication.

No doubt this opposition contributed to delaying the publication of the third volume, for Sholokhov wrote to Gorky in 1931, obviously seeking his intercession, to complain that certain leaders of the Russian Association of Proletarian Writers, who had read his manuscript, had objected to so many passages that three fourths of this volume would have to be discarded if they had their way. They accused him, he wrote, "of trying to justify the Cossack uprising in 1919." The description, he declared, is historically correct. "Without concealing the colors, I have described the stern reality preceding the uprising." Here Sholokhov is being faithful to his own conviction that the literary artist must tell the truth as he understands it. He apparently persisted in this conviction, if one may judge by the contents of the third volume, which appeared, through the aid of Gorky, in serial form in 1932 and as a book the next year. "It is more important than the second volume and better done," Gorky wrote the editor.

Impatient readers, however, had to wait eight years between the third and last volume of *The Silent Don,* the first part of which appeared in 1938 and the second in 1940. To be sure, Sholokhov was by now a celebrated writer, harassed by endless visitors and a huge correspondence, and as a Communist he took part in the local cultural activities of the Don region. But as in the case of Leonov's silence, one reason for the delay may have been the enormities committed during the purge years in the middle thirties. Sholokhov may have found these terrible years unpropitious for the continued publication of his novel, or his silence may have been intended as a public sign of personal condemnation of Stalin's bloody course of action. (Twice in 1937, for example, Sholokhov refused to join well-known writers in official statements in the press excoriating victims of the purge—a courageous action in those days.) However, there may also have been still another reason for the delay: the artistic and ideological difficulties involved in the resolution of his hero's fate in the last volume.

Thus *The Silent Don* is a novel in four volumes of some fifteen hundred pages, and the writing of it occupied Sholokhov over the greater part of fifteen years. In essence it is an historical novel of a tragic decade (1912–22) in the life of the Don Cossacks. Native critics, who now fondly compare it to Leo Tolstoy's *War and Peace,* which certainly deeply influenced it, acclaim the work as the foremost Soviet literary classic.

Many years before, Tolstoy, in his fascinating tale *The Cossacks,* contrasted the Cossack natural man to his hero, a Russian of refinement and culture, to the disadvantage of the latter. Tolstoy's Cossacks are a bit idealized. Sholokhov was the first in Russian literature to reveal this unusual people fully and realistically and at a time when the combined circumstances of world war, revolution, and civil war had cruelly uprooted the Cossacks and ultimately brought them under the power of the Soviets. To tell this absorbing story compellingly and truthfully—within the limitations of historical fiction—is the conscious artistic purpose of Sholokhov and the grand design of the novel.

With an understandable concern for the strange impression his picture of the Cossacks would make on foreign readers, Sholokhov wrote in an unpublished foreword intended for the first English edition: "The possibility that the novel may be regarded in England as an 'exotic' production troubles me somewhat. In an account of Don Cossack life alien to Europeans, I would be happy if the English reader would take into consideration the tremendous dislocation of existence, of life, and of human psychology which is caused by war and revolution."

Indeed, even for the Russian the popular image of the Cossacks was a combination of myth and bitter experience; for the foreigner it was mostly myth, best summed up, perhaps, by the old Barnum and Bailey Circus posters of exotic, daredevil, hard-riding, sabre-wielding horsemen, garbed in wide-skirted coats and rakishly worn sheepskin hats. However, the men and women who emerge from the pages of *The Silent Don* are the real descendants of those adventurers, fugitive serfs, and outlaws who early in Russian history sought refuge along the Dnieper and spread to areas of the Don, Kuban, Terek, and beyond. Over the centuries they developed into a proud, warlike, freedom-loving, and homogeneous people, uniting in bloody struggles against the tsars under such leaders as Pugachov and Stenka Razin. Though basically Russian in origin, they came to regard all non-Cossacks as

foreigners and they held the Russian peasantry and proletariat in contempt. Eventually a discerning autocratic government learned how to exploit these rebellious people and their
fighting qualities. In return for long obligatory army service
to the tsar they were organized into military colonies under
their own leaders, allowed to hold their land by military
tenure, and were exempt from taxes. From marauders they
developed into an agricultural people settled in villages
where the land was worked on a commune basis. But the Cossacks' allotments of land were larger than those of the
ordinary peasant, and they ran their local affairs as free
men and in a democratic spirit. However, the social and
economic cohesion of the Cossacks was broken by the
Statute of 1869 which enabled officers and civil servants to
become wealthy proprietors of extensive lands, thus creating
a class structure which many years later the Soviets exploited
for their own purposes.

To Russians everywhere, however, the Cossack became the
hated symbol of oppression. Their valiant deeds in war
could not efface from the minds of the people an image of
the fierce horseman with the knout running down recalcitrant
peasants, lashing striking workers, or breaking up student
demonstrations. Their traditional feeling of apartness from
the common herd was deliberately fostered by government
officials in order that they might better trust these mercenaries
of the tsar in police actions against rebellious subjects.
Mothers in peasant huts and worker hovels hushed their
crying children with warnings that the Cossacks would "get
them," and in the minds of the revolutionists of 1917 the
Cossacks were identified with everything opposed to their
movement.

As in *The Azure Steppe,* Sholokhov wished to correct this
distortion in *The Silent Don,* to present the real Cossack, to
take his readers into the Cossack homestead, the village, the

whole Don Military Region, into the hearts of his people. The Melekhov family in the village of Tatarsk on the bank of the Don is the novelist's focal point in a large canvas of expanding action that extends over much of western and southern Russia. Though the story begins in 1912, there is a striking flashback to grandfather Prokoffey Melekhov who introduced an alien strain into this typical Cossack family. Returning from the Russo-Turkish War, he brought back with him a frail Turkish captive girl whom he married. The village women gossiped so much over this stranger in their midst that "they had no time to hunt for their fleas." And they told tales of the strong husband tenderly carrying his sick wife in his arms to the Tatar mound at the end of day to watch sunset over the steppes. Then one summer when the cattle began to die from a disease the ignorant and superstitious villagers laid the blame on the pregnant "witch of a Turkish wife." A crowd of them descended upon Prokoffey's hut:

"Drag the bitch into the yard!" came a roar from the steps. A regimental comrade of Prokoffey's wound the Turkish woman's hair around one hand, pressed his other over her screaming mouth, dragged her at a run through the porch, and flung her beneath the feet of the crowd. A thin shriek arose above the howl of voices. Prokoffey sent half a dozen Cossacks flying, burst into the hut and snatched a sabre from the wall. Jostling against one another the Cossacks rushed from the porch. Swinging the gleaming, whistling sabre around his head, Prokoffey ran down the steps. The crowd shuddered and scattered over the yard. By the threshing-floor he caught up with the slow-moving artilleryman Lushnia and with a diagonal sweep down the left shoulder from behind he split the Cossack's body to the belt. . . . About a half hour later the crowd ventured to approach Prokoffey's farm again. Two of them crept cautiously on to the porch. Prokoffey's wife lay on the kitchen threshold in a pool of blood, her head flung back awkwardly. Her lips writhed tormentedly back from her teeth, her bitten tongue protruded. Prokoffey, with shaking head and glassy stare, was wrapping in a sheepskin a squealing, crimson, slippery little ball—the prematurely born infant.

When Prokoffey returned from penal servitude he brought up his child, Pantaleimon, and eventually married him off to the daughter of a Cossack neighbor, who then bore two sons, Piotra and Gregor, and a daughter, Dunia. The Melekhovs, father and children, were nicknamed "Turks." In truth, the swarthy, hook-nosed face of Pantaleimon and his ungovernable temper seemed to set him apart from his Cossack neighbors. Neither Piotra nor Dunia resembled the father, but the tall, dark, hooked-nose Gregor, with his slightly oblique eyes and the savage quality of his smile, was the image of his father. Gregor is the unforgettable hero of *The Silent Don.*

Like Tolstoy in *War and Peace,* Sholokhov fills his canvas with a series of families whose activities and interrelationships reveal the social existence not only of Tatarsk, a village of some three hundred households, but of the whole Cossack population of the Don. In addition to the father and three children in the Melekhov family, which belonged to the social milieu of middle Cossacks, there is the wonderful old mother Ilinichna, and Daria, wife of the eldest son Piotra, a handsome Moll Flanders of a woman. Their neighbors are the Astakhovs—Stepan the strong, cruel, and gloomy husband, and his beautiful young wife Aksinia, the heroine of the novel. Then there are the well-to-do Korshunovs: father and mother; grandfather Grishatka, the picturesque ancient warrior with his medals; Mitka, the slimy sadistic son with the cat's eyes; and the attractive marriageable daughter Natalia. The poor Cossack family of Koshevois consists of the mother and her son Misha, friend of Gregor Melekhov. There is the prosperous village merchant Mokhov with his silly son Vladimir and his daughter Elizabieta; and at near-by Yagodnoe is the rich officers' family of Listnitsky, the old retired general and his son Eugene, a young lieutenant.

Scores of other characters supplement these central families and provide a picture of Cossack society in the early twentieth century which seems unbelievably medieval in its backward agricultural economy, in its manners and customs and age-old superstitions. In the winter the animals of the barnyard compete with humans for living space in the tiny thatched huts with their earthen floors. Meat is fished out of the common family stew bowl and greasy hands are wiped on the hair. Village gossip and derision are merciless to all, especially to women who offend the strict moral code. For it is a cruel patriarchal society in which the father of the household is absolute master and beats his wife and children at will. Though reactionary and deeply prejudiced in the matter of "foreign" ideas, customs, and people, the Cossacks are patriotic, devoted to the land and to the beauties of nature, free in their movements, fun-loving in their play, filled with a strong sense of honor; they are inheritors of a glorious past ennobled in poetic song and story. These are the people whom Sholokhov vividly portrays with love and sympathy, but he reveals all their evils and cruelty as well as their sterling virtues and spiritual strength.

GREGOR MELEKHOV. As the novel opens Gregor Melekhov is a lad of nineteen, half a head taller than his father and a favorite with the village girls. He is an accomplished young Cossack in riding, hunting, and fishing, but is also a hard worker in the fields. Life seems good to him, free from care; a light, pleasant void is in his heart. The void is soon filled by his passionate love for Aksinia, the beautiful young wife of the Melekhovs' neighbor Stepan Astakhov. Gregor's behavior creates a turmoil in the Melekhov household, for it is his first major act of rebellion against parental authority and the mores of the village. The star-crossed destinies of Aksinia and Gregor compose one of the great love stories of Russian literature, a story that is the very core of *The Silent Don* and a spiritual anodyne to its pages of blood and strife.

The irate parents hasten a match with Natalia, the pretty but old-fashioned daughter of the well-to-do Korshunovs, and the immature, carefree Gregor thoughtlessly falls in with their plans. The matchmaking is a raucous scene rich in crude country humor which might easily have come out of one of Gogol's early tales—the two fathers, reeking with the smell of vodka and pickled cucumbers, their heads so close together that their greasy beards intertwined, tearfully haggling over the dowry; the two old mothers, flushed with liquor, locked in an embrace, deafening each other with praise of their children; and the bride-to-be, Natalia, alone in a farther room, quietly weeping and fearful of the new life opening before her.

Not long after their marriage, however, Gregor begins to realize with vexation and anxiety that he cannot dismiss Aksinia from his thoughts. Soon they resume their former relations and eventually run off to near-by Yagodnoe to live as cook and coachman in the household of the highborn Listnitskys. The guilty passion that has joined their lives has at last begun a maturing process in the gay, irresponsible Gregor.

This process is quickened by Gregor's first experience with war in 1914 when he serves with the Cossacks at the front fighting the Germans and Austrians. Sholokhov is unsurpassed in his handling of war scenes—descriptions of slashing Cossack cavalry attacks, of individual combat, and pictures of carnage and destruction. The selection of detail is unerring and the sense of violent action conveyed has a thrilling immediacy about it. Strangely enough, however, the abiding pathos of war, in which the living go on dying and the dead are forever dead, is also reflected in his pages. He understands the false heroics, the terror of the brave, and that death comes to all alike, to those who pray and those who blaspheme. Gregor likewise comes to learn these things.

Qualities begin to appear in Gregor's nature which set him apart from his Cossack comrades. He protests forcefully the hideous collective rape of the coquettish servant girl Frania by the soldiers in his troop. After he sabres his first enemy a "loathing and perplexity crushed his spirit," and the horrible bloody face of the dead man continues to torment his imagination. Yet he hardens himself and learns to kill and to fight with great bravery.

But as the war stumbles on in a triumph of boredom and human idiocy, the latent feeling of rebellion in Gregor mounts. He tells his older brother Piotra, who has been drawn into the later stages of the conflict along with other Tatarsk reservists, that he feels dead in spirit, like a man all but killed. He yearns for home, for his native fields, for Aksinia. A feebly dawning political sense sets him to wondering about the causes of war. "They've set us to fighting one another," he protests cryptically to Piotra, "but they don't come themselves."

Gregor's awakening political consciousness is suddenly transformed into a set of convictions by the Ukrainian blacksmith Garanzha whom he meets in a Moscow hospital where both are recovering from wounds. In days and nights of earnest discussions, Garanzha impresses his revolutionary views on the puzzled, intently questing Gregor. Sholokhov sums up the results of this first significant exercise in political thinking by his hero: "Gregor realized with horror that the intelligent and milicious Ukrainian was gradually and surely destroying all his former ideas of the tsar, the country, and his own military duty as a Cossack. Within a month after Garanzha's arrival the whole foundation on which Gregor's views of life rested was a smoking ruin. The foundation had already been rotten, eaten up with the canker of the monstrous stupidity of the war, and it needed only a jolt. That jolt was given and his mind awoke."

When he returns home unexpectedly on a furlough after

more than two years' absence, Gregor's awakened mind is
crushed by the discovery that Aksinia has become the mistress
of Eugene Listnitsky. Gregor beats the young officer within
an inch of his life, lashes Aksinia with his knout, and returns
to his home at Tatarsk. The patient Natalia stands there
pallid and with a tortured smile. That night the irrepressible
father Pantaleimon, in bed with his wife, gives her a dig in
the ribs and whispers to her to peek and see if the young
couple are lying together. "Well, God be praised! God be
praised!" he whimpers and crosses himself when Ilinichna
brings him the longed-for news.

Once again in the bosom of his family, surrounded by scenes
of his childhood and comforted by Natalia's love, Gregor
reverts to his old gods. Psychologically his break with Aksinia
no doubt has helped to quell the spirit of rebellion in him.
And what is left of the revolutionary enthusiasm which he
imbibed in the hospital is erased by the flattery and admiration of the Tatarsk villagers for a war hero wearing the St.
George Cross. Gregor easily falls back into the traditional
martial pattern glorified by the Cossacks. He returns to the
front after his furlough to fight with renewed vigor for the
sake of Cossack honor, accumulating more wounds and medals
for his bravery.

Sholokhov conveys well the emotional and intellectual turmoil, the shattering of conventional loyalties, the sudden advance and recoil among a population staggered by the tremendous impact of national revolution when it came in 1917.
The contradictory views and reactions of his people at this
time of violent change also plague the half-educated and sensitive mind of Gregor Melekhov. Indeed, he symbolizes the
groping, confusion, and wavering of the Cossacks in a troubled
time of desperate choices. But for Gregor the difference is
that there can be no compromise with truth; yet the search for
political truth in a world of shifting values seems beyond his

limited comprehension. He has to feel rather than think his way, and his feelings are often guided by elemental distinctions between right and wrong, by appearances rather than actuality.

After the February Revolution, when Gregor is promoted to company commander in the regular army for heroic action in the field, he is much influenced by a well-educated Cossack officer, Izvarin, who convincingly argues the Cossack separationist position for complete autonomy of the Don region. Gregor compares these views with those of Garanzha and asks Izvarin what he thinks of the Bolsheviks. They have only peace in common with the Cossacks at present, Izvarin indicates, but the minute the Bolsheviks attempt to touch the Cossack possessions, their roads will part. "It's hard for me to make head or tail of it," mumbles Gregor. "I'm all over the place, like drifting snow in the steppe."

In truth, drifting rather than firm convictions leads Gregor into the camp of the Reds in the autumn of 1917. Instead of making his way to Tatarsk when the Russian front disintegrates, he remains at Kamenska where a revolutionary spirit prevails among the deserting troops. There he meets Podtielkov, an historical figure in the Bolshevik movement in southern Russia. When Gregor confronts this former sergeant-major with Izvarin's conception of an autonomous Cossack state, the burly Podtielkov counters that it would make no difference; the atamans and officers would run things as of old and would continue to oppress the people. And to Gregor's despairing query: "Then what are we to do?" Podtielkov answers that the Cossacks must become part of a people's government which, he blithely explains to the anxious Gregor, would allow the Cossacks to govern themselves, to take the landowners' estates for their own use, and prevent the peasants from getting any additional land.

This kind of Bolshevik double-talk appeals both to Gregor's

traditional middle Cossack instincts and to his slumbering
resentment of the Cossack overlords. When the civil war
breaks out in 1918 he takes up the cause of the Reds and sees
some fighting as commander of a "division" of a few hundred
troops. At the conclusion of a battle, however, his feelings are
outraged at the sight of Podtielkov cutting down with his
sabre a captured White officer and then commanding his men
to massacre the remaining disarmed captives, which they do.
But Gregor's hysterical protest, as he lies wounded, only
arouse Podtielkov's suspicion of his loyalty to the Red cause.

The incident leaves a spiritual scar on Gregor and provokes
doubts about the sincerity of a cause which he has barely begun to understand. Indeed, as he is being driven home by
his father to recover from his wound, Gregor thinks that what
he most wants is to turn his back on this hate-filled, hostile,
and incomprehensible world. He yearns only to grip the plow
handles and breathe in the scent of freshly turned earth. "He
wanted peace and quietness," Sholokhov writes, "and so his
harsh eyes nursed a constrained gladness as they gazed at the
steppe, at the horse, at his father's back. Everything reminded
him of his half-forgotten former life. . . ."

What Gregor could not understand was that revolution and
civil war had put an end to this former life. When a small
detachment of the Red Army crosses over into Don Cossack
territory for the first time, raping and looting in the villages,
all of which Sholokhov describes quite realistically, Gregor
resists the appeals of a few youthful Tatarsk friends with
Communist leanings to steal off and join the Red forces. On
the other hand, he surlily refuses the request of the village
elders to lead a Tatarsk contingent against the Bolsheviks.
However, he allows himself to be mobilized when it is learned
that Podtielkov and a band of Reds have invaded Cossack
territory. The invading band is surrounded and wheedled into
surrendering their arms without a fight on the promise of fair

treatment. Then they are harshly abused and condemned to execution. Sholokhov describes this historical scene with harrowing detail. Podtielkov singles out Gregor from among the witnesses at the execution and taunts him with being a turncoat. In a fury Gregor reminds him of how the White officers had been murdered by his order, and then rides off to get away from this scene of death. With this, Gregor's renunciation of his brief Bolshevik past seems complete.

Though Gregor's decisions in the trials that now await him spring from the fatal ambivalence of his nature, Sholokhov also insists that historical events were the matrix enveloping his destiny. Historical necessity may be defied but not overcome. When the Reds finally occupy part of the Don region, the proud, quick-tempered Gregor is again compelled by events to struggle between two opposing elements, both of which his deepest instincts urge him to reject. He scornfully tells his former boyhood friends, Ivan Kotliarov and Misha Koshevoi, who have become Soviet officials at Tatarsk, that the "liberty" and "equality" of the new government are deceptions and that the Cossacks want none of them. "What did you fight for?" demands Kotliarov. "For the generals?" And Gregor replies: "I fought for myself, not for the generals. . . . The Communists and the generals are all alike; they're all yokes on our neck."

Gregor had correctly sensed the feelings of his people toward the Bolsheviks and after some months of occupation the accumulated fury aroused by harsh requisitioning, imprisonments, and the arbitrary executions of so-called prosperous Cossacks bursts into revolt which spreads like wildfire throughout the Upper Don province. When he hears the news Gregor, whose arrest has long since been ordered, is in hiding. He experiences a tremendous gladness. Gregor's thoughts on this occasion are extremely important for a psychological understanding of his lacerated, dualistic nature. In them he identifies himself with the historical mission of the Cossacks from which he has been alienated by what now seems to him a false faith:

It was as though those days of search for the truth had been lifted from his shoulders, those stumblings, transitions, and painful inner struggles. Those days had passed like the shadow of a cloud and now his searchings seemed aimless and empty. What had there been to think about? Why had his spirit twisted and turned, like a hunted wolf seeking to escape, in search of a resolution of his contradictions? Life seemed absurdly, wisely simple. Now he believed that there never had been any such truth beneath whose wings all might shelter; now he believed each had his own truth, his own furrow. For a piece of bread, for a strip of earth, for the right to live, men always had fought and would fight so long as the sun shone on them, so long as their blood flowed warmly through their veins. Those who wanted to deprive him of his life, of his right to live, must be fought resolutely and with no wavering, but steeled in hatred.

Gregor was a simple man of action and his feelings were the truest image of his nature. Now in action he finds relief from the political doubts that have obsessed him. As a commander of several thousand Cossacks he is proudly conscious of his power, and he leads his troops against the Reds well and often victoriously. But as the months of savage fighting wear on into 1919, his spirits fall as he begins to realize the hopelessness of the task in the face of the seemingly endless waves of Bolshevik reinforcements. Then the old doubts begin to stab his mind again. He admires the courage of these Red proletarian soldiers. Against whom is he leading his men— "Against the people?" he queries. "Who is right?" His growing discouragement was aggravated by dark suspicions of the real forces behind the Cossacks' revolt. Is he fighting to restore the rule of swaggering, oppressing officers over the Don? He expresses his despair in rash acts of bravery, but finally the moral fabric of his nature is torn badly by the pressures of endless fighting and consuming doubts as to the rightness of his cause. He seeks escape in drinking bouts and nightly carousals with loose women in the villages. In the morning after one of these debauches, lying beside his companion of the night, a flood of memories fills his mind. He recalls his "beloved steppe, and suddenly, blindingly, it opened its expanse before him. He saw the summer cartload, a bullock-wagon with his father sitting on the cross-tree, the ploughed land and the golden brush of harvested grain, a black sprinkle of ravens on the road. As his mind wanders among memories of the irrevocable past, it stumbled against Aksinia. 'My love, my unforgettable love!' he thought, and contemptuously shifted away from the woman sleeping at his side."

Perhaps these thoughts have something to do with his quarrel with Natalia when Gregor returns for a brief furlough to Tatarsk. Rumors of his drinking and loose living have already circulated in the village. Natalia harshly criticizes his faults and he frankly admits them, but in a pitiless self-examination of the futility of his life he declares that he has dabbled so much in men's blood that he has no pity left for anyone. The quarrel seems to snap again the tenuous emotional thread that has bound him to Natalia. On the last day of his leave he meets Aksinia at the watering place on the Don where their love began years before. She left Listnitsky when he returned from the wars with a wife and has gone back to her husband at Tatarsk. The awkward restraint of former lovers inhibits conversation at first, then the welling feelings in Gregor finally burst forth: "But I can't tear you out of my heart anyhow, Aksinia. Here I've got children growing up, and I'm myself half gray, and how many years lie like an abyss between us! But I still think of you. In my sleep I see you and I love you still." She replies simply: "I too. . . . But I must go . . . we're standing talking. . . ." That night Aksinia sends a message to Gregor by Daria, and the two lovers steal out together onto the steppe.

Shortly thereafter the Soviet government sends a large force to crush the revolt on the Don and the Cossacks begin a retreat across the river. Gregor sees clearly that all is lost. It seems that the only thing left in life for him is his passion for Aksinia. Without hesitation he decides to take her secretly with him on the retreat and to leave his mother and wife with his two children at Tatarsk. After two days on the road with his adoring Aksinia, he tells her admiringly: "You're diseased with love."

It would be a mistake to demand from Gregor the sophistication of thought and values of the individualistic heroes of modern fiction. He is an epic hero as *The Silent Don* is an epic novel. Action and sensuous perceptions are not for him a proving ground for ideas as they are, for example, among Tolstoy's heroes. To have made a deeply reflective, philosophical person of Gregor would have been foreign to the total logic of the nature with which Sholokhov endows him. Yet the tragedy that breaks over his head is no less compelling or deeply moving as an experience of life than the tragedy that breaks over the heads of the mighty of the earth.

THE RIVALS—AKSINIA AND NATALIA. No remedy or incantation can cure Aksinia's "disease of love." It was not the passion of a Juliet, but the earthy poetry distilled from its tragic course fills the mind and imagination with as much wonderment and deep human sympathy. Aksinia is the natural woman, almost primitive in her instincts, but capable of infinite sacrifice for the object of her love. Beautiful and proud in her bearing, she is contemptuous of the envious and the gossipers who censure her actions. However imperfect her sense of moral values, she is not devoid of strong feelings of loyalty and constancy although these qualities are sorely tried in her unhappy life.

If Aksinia violated her marriage vows, she did not do it lightly but only under extreme provocation. Raped at the age of sixteen by her own father, she was married off within a year to the strong, stiff-necked Stepan. The morning after the marriage Stepan, having discovered that she was not a virgin, "took his young wife into the barn and beat her deliberately and terribly. He beat her on the belly, the breast and the back, taking care that the marks should not be visible to others. After that he neglected her, kept company with flighty grass-widows, and went out almost every night, first locking Aksinia into the barn or the room."

Though embittered by Stepan's calculated sadism as well as by the loss of her first child and endless toil in the fields while her husband loafs with his cronies, Aksinia at first resists the impetuous and persistent attentions of the attractive, swarthy young Gregor. She then realizes with terror that she cannot resist them any longer. Anguished over his thoughtless marriage to Natalia, Aksinia nevertheless preserves his image in her heart while she submits to the unwanted attentions and beatings of her gloating husband. And finally, when Gregor, determined to leave his wife, asks Aksinia if she will go away with him, she instantly replies: "I'll sleep with the cattle to be with you, Grisha. Anything to be with you."

Their life together as workers on the Listnitsky estate at Yagodnoe, before Gregor is called up for army service, is the glorious summer of their love. Never again is the wayward fate that cankers their existence to be so kind to them. Critics have compared this love story to that of Anna and Vronsky in Tolstoy's *Anna Karenina*. Whatever similarity there may be in the intense and enduring passion that compels Anna and Aksinia to desert their husbands and flout the condemnation of all, the social chasm dividing the two sets of characters makes the comparison peculiarly inept. Love for the sophisticated Anna and Vronsky is a secret thing expansive only in hidden ways; Aksinia and Gregor love openly and unashamedly. The difference is between members of a cultured class who mask their feelings and control their behavior in public, and very simple people who express their emotions and live their illicit lives together for all to see. On another level the difference is more sharply seen by comparing the furtive account of the birth of Anna's son with the shockingly detailed description of the birth of Aksinia's daughter by Gregor in a peasant cart. This is not mere sensationalism on Sholokhov's part. Both he and Tolstoy, with whom he has so often been compared, are always faithful to the immanent demands in artistic expression of the different social strata they describe.

As the months of waiting for Gregor to return from the front wear into years, Aksinia sobs night after night out of longing for him and out of anxiety for his life. She pours out all her love for him on their daughter, naively believing that he will feel through his child how much she yearns for him. This only support in her loneliness is snatched from her when the child dies from diphtheria. The tragic event coincides with the return of the young officer Eugene Listnitsky on a furlough. One night he enters her room to express his sympathy to the inconsolable Aksinia and ends by seducing her. "Burdened by her despair," writes Sholokhov, "not realizing what she was doing, Aksinia yielded herself to him with all her strong, long dormant passion."

This one flaw in Aksinia's imperishable love for Gregor is perhaps psychologically understandable in terms of the syndrome of events connected with the lapse and the emotional imperatives of her nature. Sholokhov, however, wisely attempts no explanation other than the simple statement: "Life dictates its own unwritten laws to man."

Three years pass before this rupture is healed in the love of Gregor and Aksinia. Events and distance are the only obstacles in the way of reconciliation, for the passion of each smolders like live embers that will burst into flame whenever brought together. Stepan and Listnitsky are merely unhappy incidents in Aksinia's life; Gregor is a timeless, unforgettable image of love. But she fears and is intensely jealous of his wife, Natalia.

Though a worthy rival, Natalia is in nearly every respect a striking contrast to Aksinia. Attractive in appearance, shy, secretive, excessively modest, she nevertheless possesses strength of will and inner beauty. But the forces of her nature are destructive rather than creative, unharmonious rather than attuned to the mixed demands of life. She is religious and devoted to the rigid moral proprieties of her more affluent social circle in the village. Though the marriage was arranged by her parents, the good-looking Gregor had long fascinated Natalia and as his wife she deeply loves him. However, it is a love more of the spirit than of the body. "Your father must have made you of ice," the frustrated Gregor once told her.

Driven to despair by Gregor's desertion of her and the lewd, ribald gossip of the villagers, Natalia attempts unsuccessfully to commit suicide. All the members of the Melekhov family love and sympathize with Natalia, except for the uninhibited sister-in-law of Gregor, Daria, who is annoyed by her patient suffering and moral rectitude. Gregor's regards to Natalia in a letter to his parents during his early experience at the front inspire his wife to visit Aksinia to plead that she release her husband. This confrontation of the lawful wife and the paramour with Gregor's child in her arms is a powerful but painful scene. One's sympathy goes out to Natalia, the crushed, abandoned wife, but one cannot fail to admire the elemental, eternal woman in Aksinia who proclaims boldly her right to the man she loves. Pouring withering scorn on Natalia, Aksinia accuses her of having tried to take Gregor away from her by marrying him. And when Natalia reminds her that she has a husband of her own, Aksinia shouts: "Except for Grishka I haven't any husband. No one nowhere in the whole world."

Gregor's resumption of relations with Natalia is not motivated by love or pity for his wife or even resentment over

Aksinia's betrayal of him with Listnitsky. She is simply there, his lawful wife, still living with the Melekhovs and patiently waiting for him. He has no place to go after rejecting Aksinia and Yagodnoe. There are also the prayerful wishes and pressures of his parents for a reconciliation with his wife. In becoming a member of the family again, participating in its daily labors on the farm, it seems entirely natural that he resume his life with Natalia who has also become very much a part of this family. As time passes and his rebellious feelings and search for political truth lessen, Gregor accepts this situation with equanimity. Natalia bears him twins, a boy and a girl, and the pleasure he takes in his offspring seemed to bring him closer to their mother.

However, Aksinia still appears in his dreams. He sees the perfect oval of her face and smells the aroma of her hair. And as tension on the Don mounts and he becomes involved in the civil war, Natalia is inevitably drawn into the orbit of his growing dissatisfaction with himself and his life. At this crucial time he again sees Aksinia in a dream and he realizes that he still loves her "with all his old, exhausting love; he felt that he loved her with all his body, with every beat of his heart." Only Aksinia's physical presence is needed to cause him to abandon Natalia again for the one love that he cannot tear out of his thoughts.

MISHA KOSHEVOI—THE IDEOLOGICAL FOIL. Soviet critics regard Misha Koshevoi as the secondary hero of *The Silent Don,* as the Cossack who finds his way to Communism and remains its staunch defender in the face of numerous obstacles. Whatever one may think of his "heroic qualities," he appears to represent the ideological foil of Gregor, his boyhood friend at Tatarsk. A poor, barely literate young Cossack of stocky build and genial disposition, Misha and his worker friends Ivan Kotliarov and Valet are introduced to Marxian ideas of the inequalities of life by the shadowy professional agitator Stockman, who seems as much out of place as a forerunner of the Bolsheviks in this Cossack village at the beginning of the novel as he is unconvincing as a character.

Stockman's teaching, however, falls on fertile soil, for we catch fleeting glimpses of Misha Koshevoi playing the part of a Red propagandist in the second volume of the novel, which is devoted to the events of the war with Germany and the outbreak of the 1917 Revolution. The inchoate mind of this rather primitive young Cossack has been prodded into thinking by Bolshevik doctrine and his impoverished world of desires has suddenly been grossly enlarged by the utopian promises of the Revolution. As a propagandist he is often inept, whether in preaching the cause of Communism or in trying to overcome the traditional Russian dislike of Cossacks as the mercenaries of the tsar. For example, he philosophizes to an army comrade at the front on the subject of Muscovite misconceptions about Cossacks: "They believe the Cossacks think of nothing except knouts; they think the Cossack is a savage, and that instead of a soul he's got bottle glass. And yet we're men like them and we're just as fond of women and girls; we weep over our sorrows, but don't rejoice over others' gladness."

Misha's Communist sympathies almost cost him his life on the occasion of the first invasion of the Don region by the Reds. But instead of being shot down by his fellow Cossacks, he is given a public beating on his bare buttocks. "It isn't right," he said, all but weeping, to the Cossack who birches him: "It was the head that thought of it, and my arse has had to pay for it. I'm shamed for the rest of my life."

Only the pleas of Misha's mother save him from being sent to the front to fight the Reds. Instead he is assigned as the district drover of Cossack horses. This unusual section of the novel is a jewel-like inset of peace in a narrative of violence and war. The beautiful lyric descriptions of nature and outdoor life, and the expert account of the semiwild existence of herds of grazing horses in a remote steppe have a fascination all their own. These idyllic scenes influence Misha and set him to wondering whether he ought not to forget the Reds and be content with the life of a drover in the immensity and quietude of the steppes. But political factionalism has penetrated even to this distant region. His reputation as a Bolshevik leads to a fight with another drover and brings Misha back to the reality of the Revolution.

When the Reds overrun the Don, Misha Koshevoi and Ivan Kotliarov turn up as the Bolshevik bosses of Tatarsk where only a short time before they had been among its lowliest inhabitants. It is at this point in the novel that one detects a sudden doctrinaire hardening in Misha Koshevoi's nature which seems out of keeping with his geniality and the earlier development of his personality. He comments to Kotliarov, after a bitter political argument with Gregor: "It was as though he were taking something from me, robbing me! And I could have killed him as we talked. There are no brothers or cousins in this war. You just draw a line and follow it." And when Stockman mysteriously reappears at Tatarsk as an important Bolshevik commissar, he so fires Misha's enthusiasm for the Red cause that Misha unhesitatingly approves an order for the arrest of Gregor and his father. In the fighting that ensues after the Cossack revolt Misha and a group of Red Guards cut off a few of Piotra Melekhov's troops in a ravine, and in a scene of blood-curdling horror the captive Cossacks are executed on the spot. Misha personally shoots his old friend Piotra.

Misha's inhuman loyalty to a political faith was alien to Gregor's nature. If failure to achieve it in a time of civil war contributed to the futility of his search for political certainty, it also served to humanize him and to render him believable as a character. In this respect as well as in many others, Misha Koshevoi is repulsive and never gains our sympathy. If Sholokhov intended him to be the shining and acceptable Communist counterpart to the vacillating and defeated Gregor, which is to be doubted, then he failed badly. Gregor could never learn to murder as an act of political vengeance, nor could he divest himself of elementary human pity for the helpless, the insulted, and the injured.

For example, when Gregor learns that a small group of local Cossacks, including Ivan Kotliarov and Misha Koshevoi (it turns out that the latter was not actually one of them), have been singled out from a defected Red regiment to be marched as punishment through the Cossack villages, he immediately gallops off, thinking: "I must see Misha and Ivan alive. . . . I must save Ivan and Misha from death. . . . There's bad blood between us, but after all there's our old friendship."

Not a vestige of this kind of ordinary humanity remains in Misha Koshevoi by the time his character is fully delineated, and it is inconceivable that Sholokhov expected his readers, even within the Soviet Union, to prefer this Bolshevik monster to the tragic Gregor Melekhov.

After the Reds finally conquer the Don, Misha returns to Tatarsk. Now a Communist fanatic in his fury over the slaying of his comrades Stockman and Kotliarov, he orders all his Cossack prisoners to be executed, burns down the houses of former well-to-do Cossacks in the village, and shoots in cold blood the harmless, ancient, Bible-reading, addled-brain Grishatka Korshunov.

For two years Misha has been in love with Gregor's sister Dunia, who was sent away across the Don as an attractive young girl who might fall victim to predatory Reds. Misha, now the chief Soviet official in Tatarsk, pays her mother a visit, tells Ilinichna of his love, and peremptorily warns her not to let Dunia marry anyone else. Then he concludes his visit by informing Ilinichna that his first business will be to catch and hang her son Gregor. This is the character about whom the outstanding Soviet student of Sholokhov writes:

"The behavior of Koshevoi is justified on the whole both politically and psychologically. The very image of Koshevoi is conceived with great sensitivity and in places achieves beauty and the perfection of pure poetry." *

LIFE AT TATARSK. Though the story of Gregor and his love for Aksinia dominates the pages of *The Silent Don,* it is skillfully woven into the extraordinarily rich and variegated tapestry of life at Tatarsk and the whole Don region. The quiet, meandering river, the beauties of nature along its banks, and the delightful country scenes of fishing and mowing contrast vividly with far-flung actions of war, brutal bloody scenes of fratricidal strife, and detailed pictures of important historical events. And crowding this fabric are numerous secondary characters, many of them memorably portrayed and contributing significantly to one of Sholokhov's main objectives in the novel—a revelation of the Cossack ethos.

The Melekhov household is a turbulent, noisy, quarrelsome lot but has a strong family loyalty: the older brother Piotra, a hard-working, conservative, tradition-bound Cossack; his lusty, wayward wife Daria who lives "in the world like a red-barked switch of dogwood, flexible, beautiful, and accessible"; the sprouting, attractive sister Dunia who, angry over Gregor's admonition to keep away from Misha Koshevoi, pointedly reminds him: 'Don't you know brother? You can't command the heart"; the uncontrollable father Pantaleimon roaring threats at all of them, taking a stick to the disobedient Gregor, and then rejoicing when this son, as a "general," offers to dismiss him from the armed service into which he has been drafted despite his age; and the old mother Ilinichna moving quietly among them all and gently composing their quarrels.

The merchant Mokhov and his family represent typical exceptions in the Cossack society of Tatarsk. Sholokhov pursues their fortunes, especially in the person of the daughter Eliza-

* I. Lezhnëv, *Mikhail Sholokhov* (Moscow, 1948), p. 222.

bieta. After being seduced by the sadist Mitka Korshunov, she leaves the village to go to Moscow to study medicine. There her tawdry love affair with Timofei, a young intellectual, is told in his diary for the amusement of a friend. Ironically enough, the diary amuses instead a group of soldiers, for Gregor Melekhov takes it from the body of Timofei, slain in battle, and hands it over to the company clerk. The wretched, spoiled lives of Elizabieta and Timofei are vividly etched in the jottings of the diary, and Sholokhov manifestly introduces this unusual incident to criticize the merchant and intellectual classes through these two representatives of them.

In one sense Eugene Listnitsky is also something of an intellectual whose total character and well-developed feelings of class consciousness have been designed by Sholokhov to contrast with those of Gregor. A Cossack officer and a gentleman, Listnitsky finds the bourgeoisie distasteful and the Bolsheviks positively dangerous. His own officer class, devoted to the tsarist fatherland, he regards as superior people and the destined rulers of the country. On the other hand, he fears that the "simple and primitive Cossacks," who have "more of the animal in them" and lack the strong, moral consciousness of "duty and responsibility to their fatherland," will provide a favorable soil for Bolshevik propaganda.

Though obviously one of the "enemy" in Sholokhov's eyes, Listnitsky is portrayed with commendable objectivity. After fighting through the war against Germany, he joins the embattled White generals in southern Russia in their struggle against the Red Army. There he loses an arm in combat and gains a wife in Olga, the young widow of one of his officer friends. In the treatment of Olga and Listnitsky we have the only concentration in this long novel on the social feelings, conversation, and actions of members of a sophisticated layer of society. Sholokhov admirably meets the challenge, so different from that presented by the lowly characters who abound in *The Silent Don.* Indeed, the complex emotional relations of

Olga and Listnitsky are handled with as much authority, even though briefly, as the simpler, more direct relations of Gregor and Aksinia.

The contrast of the simple and the sophisticated is revealed in a tragicomic manner when Listnitsky brings home his new bride to Yagodnoe where his mistress Aksinia still lives as the family cook. Upon the advice of his father, Listnitsky delivers a self-conscious little lecture to Aksinia: "I am married now and as an honest man I can't do anything shameful. My conscience won't allow it." And he concludes by offering her a small sum of money with her dismissal. Aksinia has been expecting this, but an uncontrollable desire seizes her to prove to this gentleman the sham of his professions of honesty and conscience as a married man. At this rendezvous, after quietly agreeing to leave Yagodnoe, she draws the unprotesting Listnitsky to her in the bushes. Later, as he rubs his trouser knees, green with grass stains, he sees Aksinia in the window of the servants' quarters, a smile playing on her lips, and is puzzled.

Early in the novel, on the German front, Sholokhov briefly introduces a new character, a Russianized Cossack volunteer who has lived among workers in Moscow. This is Bunchuk, a sturdy thickset figure whose hard glance reveals an inflexible will. He makes no secret of his desire to learn everything possible about machine-gun fighting in order to be more useful in the coming revolution. Unlike Misha Koshevoi who acquires Communism, or the several historical Communists in the novel, Bunchuk seems to have been born a Communist. And the long digression from the main theme in the second volume, which contains the story of Bunchuk and his sweetheart Anna Pogoodko, is a Red revolutionary episode that may have seemed necessary to Sholokhov as a counterbalance to his major concentration on non-Bolshevik characters and actions. But Bunchuk is an idealized Communist whose personality, if not his activities, seems contrived. One can understand his accepting the grisly job of executioner for the Red military tribunal, but there is nothing in his nature that explains why his conscience should have been tormented by this role. The Jewess Anna Pogoodko is more believable as a Communist and a human being perhaps because she appears to have been born with a conscience. Their love for each other, however, is beautifully and movingly told, as is Anna's tragic, self-sacrificing death. After it, the inconsolable Bunchuk willingly goes to his end with Podtielkov's band.

The Silent Don is studded with magnificent scenes, often written with great dramatic power and narrated with Sholokhov's consummate mastery of realistic detail. Their effect is pictorial and sensuous and their elements are either pathos or humor or sometimes a combination of both. Physical horror also plays its part in some of these scenes, and though they nearly always advance the action of the novel, the author rarely draws any philosophical implications from them.

There is the humorous description of the marriage of Gregor and Natalia and the mad wedding feast that follows at the Melekhovs, with its Cossack customs, superstition, singing and wild dancing and drinking, all capped by the hilarious sparring of the two Cossack grandfathers as they drunkenly relive the cavalry charges of battles long ago.

Or there is the colorful scene of the Tatarsk villagers anxiously assembling at the news of the overthrow of the autocracy. The red haired, cross-eyed ataman is crushed by the announcement. And when the merchant Mokhov tells the gathering they must now live without the tsar, all the old men begin shouting at once: "But how without the tsar?" "Our fathers and grandfathers lived under the tsars. And now isn't a tsar necessary?" "Take off the head, and the legs won't go on living!"

The intensely harrowing scene of the execution of Podtielkov and his band is surpassed in sheer physical horror by the description of the death march of twenty-five Red-infected Cossacks, in the heat of the day, mile after mile, through

village after village, with the enraged populace beating them
mercilessly with every conceivable instrument of destruction.
It is one of the most gripping yet repulsive scenes in all literature. No detail of bestiality perpetrated on helpless human
beings by people aroused to a primitive pitch of animal
fiendishness is left unrecorded. The brutality of the account
is almost too excruciating to be borne by the reader. When
the bloody mass finally reaches Tatarsk, Daria Melekhov
finishes off the half-dead Ivan Kotliarov with a bullet, more as
a stupid gesture of public self-glorification than out of
vengeance, as she declares, for the Red execution of her husband Piotra whom she betrayed as a wife at every opportunity.
Her dramatic shot acts as a signal for the villagers to fall upon
the rest of the bleeding band and kill them off.

An entirely different scene, and certainly one of the finest
pieces of writing in the novel, is the brilliant description of
the first retreat of the Cossacks across the Don in the face of
the overwhelming force of the Red Army. The picture is one
of infinite confusion, of thousands of civilians and their household goods piled high on carts mingled with Cossack troops
fleeing before the Reds. It is a scene filled with high tragedy
and low comedy, especially in the person and the antics of
that glorious, garrulous, drunken character, Prokhor Zykov,
the orderly of Gregor.

THE CONCLUSION OF *The Silent Don.* For years a large and enthusiastic reading public eagerly anticipated the last volume
of *The Silent Don.* It is reported that Sholokhov received many
anxious letters from readers and critics who speculated on the
ultimate fate of the hero and even offered their advice. There
were pleas for a happy ending or, if Gregor had to die, that
it would be while leading a glorious attack of Budyonny's
Red cavalry. At the least there was general expectation in
Russia that the hero would somehow or other find his way to
an uncompromising acceptance of Communism at the end.

Though Sholokhov appears to have been fully aware of the difficult aesthetic and ideological problems that confronted him in concluding his long novel, especially in resolving his hero's fate, there is no indication that he made any concessions to either public or Party opinion in this final volume. The inexorable logic of life seems to dictate the final solution of his characters and the conclusion of the majestic course of his narrative.

At the end of the third volume Sholokhov had left his hero with Aksinia in the retreat across the Don. As the last volume opens we learn that by June, 1919, the White Guard cavalry had broken through the Red Army lines and relieved the hard-pressed Cossack insurgents. With this victory civilians were able to return to their homes on the other side of the river. Gregor's reunion with his family at Tatarsk is sensitively described. His eyes "momentarily, unexpectedly, moistened" as he embraced Natalia, who had been ill with typhus. A flood of tenderness swept over him and he wanted to say something warm and kindly to her, but he could not find the words and simply kissed her on the forehead.

The tenderest scenes are reserved for Gregor and his children. His "eyes were filmed with a mist of tears, his lips quivered," when he first greeted them, seated them on his knees, and listened to their merry chatter. Gregor adored his little son and daughter, and some of the most charming pages of the novel are devoted to the expression of his affection for them, as in the present instance when Gregor, leaving for the front again, bids farewell to his son. The child bravely tries to hold back his tears (it was a terrible shame for Cossacks to cry, his grandfather had told him), and then, noticing that his father's eyelashes are wet, he bursts out crying and bellows: "Let Grand-dad go and fight! What has he come back to us for? I don't want you to. . . ."

Gregor's unaccustomed show of sensibility and sadness on this occasion seems to be prompted by a premonition that

there will be no more such family reunions. He is convinced
that the victory of the White Guard is only temporary and
that the Reds will return with redoubled force, and that if this
does not happen, then these conquering officers will lord it
over the Don Cossacks as of old, a possibility that was as
hateful to his democratic spirit as the efforts of the Reds to
impose their rule on the Don.

Gregor's summons to the White General Fitzhelaurov leads
Sholokhov, in the early part of the fourth volume, to offer a
penetrating insight into an important aspect of his hero's
nature. Gregor is accompanied by his chief of staff, Captain
Kopylov, a former Cossack schoolteacher. Though critical of
Gregor's failings, Kopylov is devoted to him because of his
bravery, skill in battle, and his just behavior to both his own
troops and the enemy. On the way Gregor delivers himself of
a furious tirade against professional army officers whose dress,
polished manners, and punctilio make him feel uncomfortable.
In friendly fashion Kopylov tells Gregor that he is a bit of a
Bolshevik, that he is offended because these officers look down
on him and do not treat him as an equal. And from their point
of view, Kopylov insists, they are right for he is a boorish
Cossack, who has received his officer's rank through special
circumstances, is poorly educated, speaks awkwardly, and has
atrocious manners. With some temerity Kopylov lists a few
of Gregor's bad habits: blowing his nose in his hand, biting
his nails or paring them with the edge of his sword, buttoning
up his fly in front of a woman of the intelligentsia class while
questioning her. Gregor at first laughs good-naturedly at this
dressing down, but then replies firmly that he does not want
to learn the manners and customs of the educated, that they
would be of no use to him if he ever got back to driving bullocks.

When they arrive at General Fitzhelaurov's headquarters
Gregor is announced as Melekhov, commander of the First
Insurgent Division. After a studied delay over the remains

of his breakfast, the general, an aged, massive, puffy, and very tall man, rises slowly and sharply demands to know why Gregor has disobeyed his orders to go into an attack. Gregor's explanations displease the general who in a loud, angry voice berates the insurgent division as a rabble and Gregor as fit only to be an orderly. Gregor, dropping his voice almost to a whisper, says: "If you, Your Excellency, attempt to lay even a little finger on me, I shall sabre you on the spot!"

The astounded general resumes some measure of calm and invites Gregor to sit and talk over business. But to the end Gregor refuses to take any orders from him, and on the way back to their men the horrified Captain Kopylov lapses into silence.

Gregor is soon demoted to captain and his division is broken up among the White Guards. The Cossacks grumble and deeply resent the "Russian officers" placed over them. Before he has time to become accustomed to his lower status, a tragedy summoned Gregor home from the front. Daria, who "loved as a dog loves," has contracted syphilis (which eventually leads her to commit suicide). In a spirit of revenge for her own moral suffering, and perhaps because she has always despised the purity of Natalia, she tells her of the night she took Aksinia's message to Gregor. Natalia loses no time in confronting Aksinia again; this second poignant scene is cast in a calmer atmosphere of restrained bitterness on the part of both women. She has had children, Natalia asserts, and she knows how to stand up for them and for herself. And when Aksinia admits she has taken up with Gregor again, Natalia scornfully reproaches her, demanding how she ever could have loved him and played the wanton with Listnitsky. Aksinia replies with a simple dignity: "I'm not your Daria. In all my life I have never played about where such things are concerned. You have got children but all the same he's . . . all I care for in the whole world. He's my first and last. But let's not talk about him any more. If he comes through alive, if the Queen of Heaven saves him from death and he comes back, then he'll choose for himself."

The next day, while working in the field with old Ilinichna, all Natalia's pent-up emotions burst forth in a fit of hysterical weeping. In a vindictive prayer she pleads with the Lord to strike Gregor dead for the torment he has caused her. It is a powerful scene accompanied by crashing thunder and a downpour of rain over the steppe, while the superstitious old lady, terrified by the concurrence of the storm and Natalia's invocation of the Lord to punish her son, tries gruffly to comfort her by the pitiful story of her own early married life. Natalia's only reply is that she is three months pregnant and will not bear Gregor's child. In an attempted abortion she dies, an account in which Sholokhov spares neither detail nor human pity. This is the sad news that brings Gregor back from the fighting.

Grief takes possession of the Melekhov household. Gregor also deeply mourns the passing of his wife, for in his own way he has come to love her and he now feels responsible for her death. He realizes that the children have been the chief reason for his altered attitude toward Natalia, and he now takes comfort in the thought that he never would have deserted her again despite his renewed love for Aksinia. Though Natalia's death fills him with a mute anger against Aksinia for betraying their relations, he still loves her and gropes in his conscience for the eternal male's justification for a simultaneous love for two women. In his sorrow he seeks relief by lavishing all his affection on his children.

In the following months the waning resistance to the Reds infects the Cossacks with despair. Gregor is invalided home with typhus, and he has barely recovered when the order comes from the regional ataman for all Cossacks to retreat. Though he has not had any relations with Aksinia for a long time—with wise feminine intuition she has kept away from him since Natalia's death—he now asks her once again to go away with him. And as before her answer is unhesitating: "You remember I told you a long time ago that I'd go with you to the very edge of the world? And I'm just the same now."

Sholokhov's description of this last retreat of the Don Cossacks before the Red forces is again a piece of powerful and effective writing. The winter roads clogged with refugees, the overburdened villages on the way, and the mingled bickering, cowardice, and bravery of despairing men frantically struggling for shelter, a crust of bread, and safety—all is told with a wealth of detail and bitter realism. In anguish Gregor is compelled to leave Aksinia behind in a peasant hut, desperately ill with typhus. With this parting he loses all interest in everything. On the road he comes across some Tatarsk folk who tell him of his father's death on the retreat. Then Gregor himself contracts typhus again. Only the impatient devotion of his former faithful orderly, the inimitable Prokhor, keeps him alive.

Sholokhov describes a deeply touching scene on the retreat. As a Cossack cavalry column passes the barely crawling refugee carts on the road, suddenly a voice among the troops begins an old Cossack song. Many hundreds of voices take up the refrain, accompanied by a tenor of astonishing power and beauty. The long train of refugees falls silent. Gregor, half delirious in a sleigh, chokes back his tears and soundlessly whispers after the solo singer the words he has known since childhood—the simple story of how long ago his Cossack ancestors shattered the Russians invading the Don.

By springtime Gregor has recovered. He finds himself in Novorossisk amid hordes of Cossacks and White Guard officers desperately crowding the few evacuation boats under the guns of British warships. Gregor refuses to take this way out; he cannot plead for a place on one of these boats. And the first part of the last volume ends with a group of Red cavalrymen riding down a street of the town, with Gregor and a few of his old comrades-in-arms facing them.

Tatarsk is the scene of the opening of the last part of *The Silent Don*. Aksinia, recovered from her illness, has made her way back to the village, and so has Misha Koshevoi with the Red forces which have now come to stay. Over the bitter objections of Ilinichna, Koshevoi and Dunia marry and remain in the Melekhov house. Soon thereafter the old mother begins to fade. She is no longer head of her own household. Eventually her strong, unrelenting nature grows reconciled to much, even to the marriage of her daughter with the man who has killed her son Piotra, and to Aksinia, the "hussy" who poisoned Gregor's marriage. She longs only to see Gregor, the last of her menfolk, before she dies. A letter from him fills her with joy, and she asks Aksinia to read it to her again and again. Her long life has been very hard and full of sorrow, but this proud, great-hearted old lady passes away serenely before Gregor's return.

Gregor turns up at Tatarsk only after he has been demobilized from the Red Army. For in the end, he went over to them and fought with distinction in Budyonny's cavalry against the Poles. He understands this service as a purging of his offenses against the Reds, and now, after seven long years of fighting, his only hope is to settle down with Aksinia and his children and farm the land. But after his first serious conversation with his new brother-in-law, Misha Koshevoi, who has become chairman of the Revolutionary Committee of Tatarsk, he realizes that he can expect no mercy. Koshevoi is convinced that Gregor has been demobilized from the Red Army because they distrusted him. Gregor frankly explains his position: "I've served my time. I don't want to serve anybody any more. I've fought more than enough for my age. I'm fed up with everything, with the Revolution and the counter-revolution. Let all that—let it all go to hell! I want to live the rest of my life with my children, to return to the farm, that's all." The fanatical Communist Koshevoi, however, insists that he must report to the revolutionary military tribunal, and he confides to his wife that Gregor will probably be tried and shot.

Gregor finally understands that his faithful service in the Red Army will not atone for his political sins of the past. He is alone now and time has passed him by. The White officers have never really accepted him, a half-literate farmer's son, nor did the Reds because they suspected him as a former enemy. He told his old orderly Prokhor that he always felt envious of the Red, Koshevoi, and the White, Listnitsky, who committed suicide on the great retreat. "Everything was clear to them from the very beginning," Gregor reflected, "but nothing is clear to me even now. Both of them saw straight roads before them, and saw the ends of them; but since 1917 I've been going round and round in a circle, reeling like a drunken man."

One night, shortly after his return, Gregor is at the hut of Aksinia (her husband vanished in the fighting), who is now taking care of his children. Suddenly Dunia, who has already begun to quarrel with her husband because of his aggressive Communism, rushes in to warn her brother that Koshevoi, with four men, is coming to arrest him. The vision of a prison or of being led into a dirty cellar with bound arms and a revolver at his head, has been haunting Gregor's mind. He bids Aksinia a hasty farewell, says she will hear from him, and disappears into the night.

A life of hiding out is peculiarly alien to Gregor's freedom-loving nature. For days he avoids detection, but then one night he is set upon by three armed horsemen and brought before their leader, Fomin, an unscrupulous Cossack known to Gregor. Earlier Fomin conveniently accepted the Red cause and occupied a position of authority at Vieshenska. Recently, however, he thought it to his advantage to lead a revolt

against them and is now scouring the villages to raise a force
large enough to drive the Reds out of the Don region. Fomin
is delighted with the capture of Gregor and promptly offers
him a high position in his enterprise. Presumably the alternative, among these desperate men, is death, though Sholokhov
does not make this entirely clear. Either because he fears
the alternative or because there is nowhere else to turn in
his hopeless situation, Gregor accepts, although he is under no
illusions about the futility of this cause or the shady character
of the men he is joining.

For months Gregor leads this wretched, dangerous existence,
always one jump ahead of pursuing Red Guards and becoming more and more ashamed of his association with these marauders as he sees their last shred of decency and idealism
vanish. His many wounds over years of fighting have begun
to take their toll on his health and he longs for Aksinia and
his children. Finally, he can stand it no longer and after much
careful planning he escapes from the band.

Gregor's secret reunion with Aksinia and the children at
Tatarsk is a scene of simple, unrestrained tenderness. All the
months of anxious waiting and longing are given vent in her
prolonged sobbing as she drops to her knees, puts her arms
around his legs, and presses her face to his wet greatcoat.
They will go to the Kuban or farther, he explains when she
grows quiet. "We'll manage to live and get our food somehow or other. I shan't be ashamed to do any work." And she
tearfully agrees: "I can't live without you. . . . Kill me, but
don't leave me again." After making arrangements for Dunia
to take charge of the children, the two of them ride off in
the night. A rapturous joy fills Aksinia at the thought that
her Gregor is again at her side.

When dawn breaks they hide in a glade. Worn out with
fatigue Gregor sleeps while Aksinia watches. The homely
thoughts that run through her mind as she dwells lovingly
on his motionless features and recalls the few joys and many

sorrows of their life together reveal the charmingly naive and passionate soul of this natural woman. Now the sorrows are all behind her and the world seems exultant and bright. "We too will find our life," she thinks, and she weaves a garland of varicolored wild flowers and places it on the head of the sleeping Gregor. When it grows dark they set out again. Suddenly they are halted by the guards of a grain-requisitioning detachment. Gregor brings his whip down hard on Aksinia's horse and they both gallop off in the darkness. Shots ring out. Some distance away he notices that Aksinia has sagged in her saddle. He catches her and they ride on. In a ravine he dismounts and quickly ascertains that the wound is fatal. "And, going numb with horror, he realized that it was all over, that the most terrible thing that could happen in his life had already happened."

Aksinia dies in his arms, without recovering consciousness. He silently kisses her on the lips. In the early morning he digs a grave with his sabre in the soft earth. And the novelist writes:

Gregor buried his Aksinia by the brilliant morning light. As she lay in the grave he folded her deathly pale, yet swarthy arms across her chest and covered her face with her kerchief, so that the earth should not fill her glazing, half-open eyes as they gazed unmovably at the sky. Then he took his farewell of her, firmly believing that they would not be separated for long.

With his palms he diligently pressed down the damp yellow clay over the mound and remained long on his knees beside the grave, his head bowed, his body swaying a little.

Now he had nothing to hurry for. Everything was finished.

The sun rose above the ravine through the smoky haze of the burning wind from the east. Its rays silvered the mass of gray hair on Gregor's head and slipped over his pale and terribly immobile face. As though awakening from an oppressive sleep, he raised his head and saw above him the black sky and the blindingly glittering, black disc of the sun.

Gregor wanders about the steppes after Aksinia's death and finally takes refuge in a deep forest, a known haven of deserters. Through the long nights he dreams of his children, Aksinia, his mother, of all the dear ones no longer among the living. "Just to see the old spots once more, to feast my eyes on the children; and then I can die," he often thinks. This longing finally prevails. One March morning he approaches Tatarsk, crosses the Don over the blue, half-thawed ice, and catches sight of his son at the landing stage on the bank near the house. The meeting is movingly narrated, and Sholokhov closes his novel with the sadly ominous words: "And now that little thing of which Gregor had dreamed during so many sleepless nights had come to pass. He stood at the gate of his own home, holding his son by the hand. This was all life had left to him, all that for a little longer gave him kinship with the earth and with the spacious world which lay glittering under the chilly sun."

ARTISTIC FULFILLMENT. Sholokhov's long task was over, and with the publication of the last volume of *The Silent Don* his reputation as the greatest Soviet novelist was secure. At that time many critics, while hailing the total accomplishment, sharply attacked the author's resolution of his hero's struggle with life. To the very end Gregor never frees himself of the political doubts that obsess his mind, never accepts the Soviet system, and he is drawn back to his home and his children because he cannot do otherwise, although he can expect only punishment—prison or even death—from Soviet authorities.

The enormous popular success of *The Silent Don* (almost eight million copies have been printed) eventually obliged official Soviet critics to propound a Marxian rationalization of the novel and of the fate of its hero. A class struggle—the argument runs—had been going on among the Don Cossacks for generations, in which the well-to-do Cossack and the officer class, aided by the tsar's government, economically and socially oppressed the poor Cossacks. The middle Cossacks, with their ancient traditions, privileges, and prejudices, assiduously cultivated as minions of the tsar, remained either neutral in this struggle or sided with constituted authority. The October Revolution, these critics maintain, brought this class struggle to a head by inspiring and assisting the poorer Cossacks to revolt, to liquidate their overlords, and to achieve their freedom. In the class war it was essential to win over the large numbers of middle Cossacks to the Revolution and to the side of the poor Cossacks. This is the historical situation, the critics insist, which Sholokhov depicted in his novel. Gregor, who belonged to the middle Cossacks, could not escape from the determinants of his class. All his doubt and hesitancy, his tormented search for truth, for a way out of the impasse, were simply a reflection of the similar turmoil which prevented many of the middle Cossacks from giving their whole-hearted allegiance to one or the other side in this struggle. Thus the fate that overtook Gregor was predetermined by the class struggle. At a time when "objective" political reasoning should have told him that his future destiny, as well as that of the mass of his people, was bound up with the success of the Soviet Revolution, Gregor, caught in the web of contradictions of his own class, persisted in his individualistic reactions and hence had to pay the penalty. Gregor's tragedy, then, in the eyes of these apologists, is that of the individualist in an epoch of socialism.

An impartial reader does not perceive any such Marxian pattern in the march of events or in the lives and deaths of the many characters in *The Silent Don.* Even granting the historical factors and some elements of class struggle, choices were made not on the basis of political convictions or class consciousness, but through force, fear, or the urgent desire for security. The novel does not appear to serve any social purpose that is understandable in terms of the usual Soviet demands on art in this respect. In fact, for a Soviet novel its emphasis is curiously removed from the center and surge of Soviet activity and Communist ideology. The Don Cossacks

and their life, the White Guards, and a fierce struggle of
armies treated almost entirely from the point of view of the
opponents of the Reds—these are the warp and woof of the
novel. Even the hero is spiritually if not always actively alien
to the Soviets. It is significant that apart from the brief account of Gregor's first association with the Reds, his later
penitential service with Budyonny's cavalry is only mentioned in passing—the one period in Gregor's life which
Sholokhov fails to chronicle fully. And the few active Bolshevik
characters—Stockman, Koshevoi, Kotliarov, Valet, Bunchuk,
and Anna Pogoodko—are hardly to be included among the
superior creative achievements of the novel.

In short, the greatest Soviet novel has somehow managed
to escape the tyranny of strict ideological conformity and the
literary flatulence that comes from imposed Party stereotypes
of form and content. Instead of attributing the tremendous
success of *The Silent Don* to its adherence to Marxian principles and socialist realism, Soviet critics would do well to
recognize, on the strength of this example, that an avoidance
of such prescriptions is an important condition for the creation
of any worth while literary art in the Soviet Union.

Without denying Sholokhov's awareness, from the Communist point of view, of the political significance of the struggle
that took place on the Don, his major interest as a literary
artist was in the human beings who were the victims of war,
revolution, and civil war. And his hero Gregor was one of
these, a lonely, sensitive being who was swept into the mael-
strom of violent historical events over which he had no effective control. His tragedy was not that of an individualist in
an epoch of socialism, but of an individual for whom the
times were out of joint. He was a "Hamlet of the steppes,"
capable of swift decisions in moments of danger, yet incapable
of deciding between the conflicting political ideologies with
which new, distressing events confronted him. Like most of

the Cossacks, he regarded the invading Reds as "foreign enemies," not as revolutionary apostles of light in the darkness
of a bitter class struggle, the existence of which he had never
heard until he listened to Bolshevik propaganda. All the heritage of the Cossack past swayed him to preserve things as
they were. Yet an innate pride, dignity, and democratic spirit
led him to resent the overbearing attitude of Cossack rulers
and officers, a resentment which made him vulnerable to the
Red appeal of social equalitarianism although he doubted the
sincerity of this appeal. Perplexed in the extreme, he drifted,
until he began to suspect that there was no final Red or White
truth under whose wings all might shelter. Each man has his
own truth, he discovered, and for Gregor it was home, the
farm, work, and most of all, his eternal love for Aksinia. For
these he fought the Red invaders as men had always fought
"for a piece of bread, for a strip of earth, for the right to
live."

It is impossible to accept the judgment of many Soviet
critics that Gregor's tragic failure was an inability to find
his way, along with the mass of Don Cossack people, to the
side of the Reds. Only a minority of Don Cossacks voluntarily
joined forces with the Bolsheviks during the years of civil
war, and no doubt their reasons often had little relation to
sincere ideological ones. The simple fact is that the majority
of Don Cossacks were conquered by the Red Army which
then imposed the rule of the Soviet government on them.
Gregor was one of the many thousands of defeated Cossacks,
and because he had been an officer, not even his service in
the Red Army could win him forgiveness. In a real sense, his
tragedy was that of all of the Don Cossacks in the civil war.
It is a striking fact, however, that perhaps the greatest hero
created by a Communist author, certainly one of the most
human and appealing characters in the whole range of Soviet
literature, is not the iron-willed, positive Soviet hero devoted

to Communism, the type continually called for by the Party, but an intensely tragic Gregor Melekhov, an enemy of the Soviet regime.

In the last analysis, nothing could be more irrelevant than the attempts of Party-minded critics to use *The Silent Don* as a text out of which to expound the political aims of art. What political implications it may have are really incidental to the dominant human interest theme of the novel—the narration of a great and moving love story, almost the only great love story in Soviet literature. And Sholokhov casts this story in a rich and varied setting of Cossack life, in the course of which he creates a series of extraordinarily memorable and typical characters. The lively humanity of the author is reflected in these intensely realized characterizations, even in the humorous secondary ones such as those of old father Melekhov, Prokhor Zykov, Christonia, and Sasha, the stableman of the Listnitskys. The earthy quality of Don Cossack life, its stark incongruities, and epic sense of fun which appear in the incidents and speech of these characters have made the relevant passages in the novel favorite readings in public recitations.

The degree of artistic control over language which Sholokhov had early revealed in the tales of *The Azure Steppe* is everywhere evident in *The Silent Don*. One observes the development of this control from volume to volume, from the lush language, the strained and sometimes absurd metaphors and similes of the early writing, to the perfected restraint and often beautiful figures of speech in the last volume. The language pattern is extremely varied in the novel. Despite the social homogeneity of the central figures, the speech of each is brilliantly individualized, corresponding to the character's mental, emotional, and spiritual nature. The author's own speech in reflective and descriptive passages is amazingly close to what might be designated as a norm of the speech of his Cossacks. Similarly Sholokhov skillfully adapts his language to the dialogue of non-Cossacks and characters drawn from the upper classes, and to the commentary, both in the text and in footnotes, which he provides to the historical documents quoted in the novel. In an effort to assimilate completely the special flavor of native speech, Sholokhov employs a profusion of dialect words and phrases, local turns of speech, and profanity—to such an extent that a glossary of obscure words is essential even for the Russian reader.

Apart from the characteristic native speech, the local color of the novel is variously enriched by a wealth of Cossack lore. Peculiar manners and customs, superstitions, proverbs, charming songs, and many motifs and observations drawn from the folklore of the Don are used in abundance. These devices are often employed to achieve poetic effects. In fact, no Soviet novelist has so much of the stuff of poetry in him as Sholokhov.

This poetic trait in his artistic personality comes out most strongly in his unusual concentration on nature. He describes it for its own sake in all its manifestations, for he obviously loves the region of his story, its birds and beasts, flowers and waving grain, forest and steppe, its storms and its sunshine, the line of the sky and the majestically flowing Don. He describes it with exact detail and as it affects all the senses, especially the sense of smell. (Sholokhov is inordinately partial to the sense of smell, which accounts for some of his least attractive observations on humans and animals.) But he also describes nature in a subtle, antiphonal manner, recording its responses to the joys and sorrows, to the lives and deaths of his characters. Often the lyric beauty of these descriptions needs only meter and rime to turn them into sheer poetry.

Sholokhov seems also to be preoccupied with the subject of death in *The Silent Don*. The novel covers a decade of death in war, revolution, and civil war, and no historical record of that time, especially one involving the kind of story

that Sholokhov elects to tell, could possibly avoid this theme
without being unfaithful to reality. In the hero's own household six deaths occur in the course of the novel. But realism
spills over into offensive naturalism in Sholokhov's pronounced
tendency to linger longingly and often over every last con-
vulsion of the dying person, or to dwell with nauseating detail
on the fatal effects of violence on the human body. Nor is any
corpse on the roadside passed by without a vivid description
of the gruesome appearance of man or woman in the posture
of death. Here we have an artistic lack of measure. To be
sure, the cumulative effect of these many scenes may have
been designed to achieve a realistic purpose in keeping with
the period of bloody strife which forms the background of
the novel. However, there are other more selective and less
offensive artistic ways of achieving such an end. This unnatural concentration is all the more surprising in that there
is no evidence of morbidity in Sholokhov. On the contrary,
his temperament appears to be an optimistic one, and the
novel, despite its tragic theme, is full of a zest for life. One
suspects that the frequency and naturalistic detail of these
scenes of death were part of a misguided notion of the
artistic function of realism in the young author, since most
of these scenes occur in the earlier volumes of the novel.
The good taste of which Sholokhov is capable in such scenes
is to be observed in the exquisitely restrained description
of Aksinia's death at the end of the novel, with its inspired
symbolic and poetic fusion of Gregor's terrible grief with the
aspects of nature.

The Silent Don is directly in the tradition of nineteenth-century Russian realism and much has been said about the
influence of this realism on the novel. Sholokhov has modestly
remarked that he is indebted to all the great Russian writers
of the past, but more specifically he owes most to Leo
Tolstoy and to some extent Gogol, although lesser authors
may also have influenced him. Though the form of *The Silent*

Don is not original, the novel is filled with an innovating power which derives from the impact of the author's creative personality on a subject matter all but unique in Russian or Soviet literature. There have been many Soviet fictional treatments of the Revolution and the civil war, but none that involves so thorough and effective a revelation of the life of the Cossacks. In this sense, as well as in its artistic fulfillment, *The Silent Don* stands alone.

Though the presentation of life and character of the decade covered by *The Silent Don* amounts to an amazing achievement in objective realism for a Soviet novelist writing on so controversial a subject, the work is not free of the tendentiousness of an author who perceives a Communist political purpose in the historical forces which dominate the action of his story. The purpose, however, does not intrude upon the grand rhythm and breath of destiny surging through Sholokhov's masterpiece. With artistic honesty he unhesitatingly reveals the cruelty, deception, ugliness, and occasionally the nobility of participants on both sides. The freedom ordinarily granted a creative writer in the use he makes of historical material is not exercised as license to manipulate history overtly in order to make it conform to a political ideology. The behavior of Whites and Reds at the political gatherings and conferences which Sholokhov describes, and the crude, puzzled, and disbelieving reactions of simple Cossacks to Bolshevik propaganda in these early years of the Revolution ring true because they are consistent with the historical events at that time. The novel gains both in stature and moral grandeur from this faithfulness to reality.*

* Readers of the English translation of *The Silent Don* may miss the degree of Communist tendentiousness and also obtain a somewhat distorted notion of Sholokhov's objectivity in treating the struggle between the Whites and the Reds. About a hundred pages of the original have been omitted in the English version, and most of these involve severely critical handling of the White leaders. The deletions seem to be made for the usual editorial reason in making such a foreign work available in English: to shorten a very long novel by omitting what seems unim-

Though a great novel was born in 1940, when Sholokhov published the final volume of *The Silent Don,* it had still to live through a savage ideological "maturing" process before it could be granted the title "Soviet classic." In successive editions Sholokhov has altered the text more or less in answer to the objections of Party critics, among whom must be included Stalin. These changes, relatively slight before the war, have culminated in extensive revisions, which must have cost Sholokhov enormous labor in the 1953 edition. Whether he has been the editor making the changes in all these instances, and especially in the last one mentioned, is not entirely clear. It may be assumed that he is, since introductions to the editions and reviews of them ascribe the alterations to him.

The pattern of revisions in the 1953 edition of *The Silent Don* clearly conforms to the rigid Party demands made upon literature, history, and all intellectual endeavor in the postwar period under the initial cultural directives of the late Andrei Zhdanov, member of the Politburo. Soviet history in particular, which has always troubled the consciences of Communist leaders, had to be brought up to date, as it were, to accord with the latest postwar insistence on how historical events in the past must have taken place if the Party's rela-

portant, dull, or difficult for the non-Russian reader to comprehend. However, some artistically important passages are omitted, especially those concerning the characterization of Listnitsky, which are intended to emphasize the contrast between him and Gregor Melekhov, and other details such as the diary of the dead Timofei, which has important bearing on the further story of Elizabieta Mokhov. Finally, the divisions of the parts and the chapters of the original have been altered in the English translation. It should be added that when the work was first translated into English (1934–40), it had not then achieved the position it now occupies as a great Soviet classic. For a discussion of this whole matter, see David H. Stewart, *"The Silent Don* in English," *The American Slavic and East European Review,* April, 1956, pp. 265–75. In the present study full use has been made of the first complete one-volume Russian edition (*Tikhii Don,* Moscow, 1941). The quotations have been taken from the English translation, but checked with the Russian original and in several places altered.

tion to them was always to be ideologically correct. Communist heroes in literature were now required to be Party supermen without fault or stain, morally above reproach and politically dedicated saints.

The plain intent of virtually all the substantive changes in the 1953 edition is to bring the Communist Party and Communist characters much more fully and favorably into the action of *The Silent Don*, and, on the other hand, to disparage the Whites still more and to emphasize their "wicked crimes" against the people of Russia. On the historical level no opportunity is lost to bring out the positive and astute direction of the Party in every significant action that led to the Sovietization of the Don region. One addition tells of a Cossack delegation to Lenin in Petrograd to obtain his encouragement and advice, and another is a quotation of a note from Stalin to Lenin concerning activities on the southern front. In fact, the credit the edition accords Stalin for the strategic success of the Red Army in the south may well require a further revision, for since its appearance in 1953, Stalin's reputation as a military genius is no longer tolerated in Party circles.* The characters of Kornilov and of other White generals were further blackened, and a more sinister direction was attributed to the anti-Communist movement by describing it as inspired by the Triple Entente and imperialistic America.

In keeping with these revisions, the characterizations in the novel of the historical Party figures Krivoshlikov and Podtielkov, to which Stalin had objected in a letter in 1929, were considerably altered. The political immaturity, vanity, haughtiness, and moral failings of Podtielkov, as well as some of

---

* Since this was written, a new Soviet 1956–57 edition of Sholokhov's works has come to the attention of the author, though up to July 1957 only two of the four volumes of *The Silent Don* were available for checking in this country. These indicate, as suggested above, that certain passages added in the 1953 edition have been deleted in this most recent edition, and that some omitted passages have been or will be restored. No doubt one reason for the alterations is the changed Party line since Stalin's death.

his important and influential remarks to Gregor Melekhov, were effaced. In short, in the 1953 edition Podtielkov emerged as a modern version of the idealized Communist leader. And the imaginary Communist characters Stockman, Kotliarov, Bunchuk, and Anna Pogoodko were transformed into more perfect and hence less human servants of the Party. Sholokhov had nibbled away at the moving and thoroughly realistic love story of Anna and Bunchuk in earlier editions; in the 1953 edition it became a pale reflection of the original story. Public display in literature of a Communist indulging in the strong emotion of love had come to be regarded as an offense almost tantamount to political deviation. Finally, in the 1953 version, Sholokhov gave more space to the activities of the Red Army and toned down both its lapses from good behavior and the hostile attitude of the Cossack population to it.*

As a literary artist who obviously cares very deeply for the perfection of his writing, it was to be expected that Sholokhov would avail himself of the opportunity of successive editions to eliminate faults in *The Silent Don*. And the constantly growing fame of the work, as well as the knowledge that it was being assigned as reading matter in the schools, undoubtedly encouraged him to take infinite pains with any imperfections. In fact, most of the revisions concern language and style. (Criticisms of the language and style of the novel have been the only ones which Sholokhov has ever publicly acknowledged as deserving.) He has made literally hundreds of changes in these respects in an effort to remove difficult dialect words, excessive profanity, vulgarisms, extreme naturalistic descriptions, and the ornate figures of speech and stylistic ineptitudes which occur particularly

---

* For an excellent study of the revisions in the various editions see David H. Stewart's unpublished study: "Sholokhov and the Soviet Critics since 1947," Master's Essay, Columbia University, 1954. The 1953 Soviet edition of *The Silent Don* was not available for use in this investigation.

in the first two volumes. For some tastes, however, he has gone too far in this kind of pruning.

On the other hand, it is not easy to understand how a writer of Sholokhov's integrity could have submitted to the demands—and there have been many—of the Party critics that he make extensive ideological changes in *The Silent Don* in substantive matters. In the postwar period such revisions of new editions of well-known novels of the past have not been uncommon. Since the government ultimately controls all publication, it is unlikely that authors would be permitted to issue these new editions of older works without some effort to bring them into conformity with the latest ideological line. In an historical novel written soon after the events described, it is possible that errors of fact which subsequent studies have revealed, as Soviet critics maintain, might have been included in the abundant documentary material supplied by Sholokhov. But the revision of Soviet historical accounts in order to adapt them to new ideological positions has become a commonplace of Party misrepresentation, a process implicit in the frank admission of "errors" in the history of the past in the present efforts to depreciate Stalin. Needless to say, the same process dictates the revisions of historical matter in *The Silent Don*, where it is now maintained that there was no real difference between Kerensky and Kornilov, and that Kornilov's efforts were in full accord with the designs of the Provisional Government!

An historical novel is not an historical chronicle. Historical events are only the frame of a canvas on which the novelist depicts a story of life. In the original version of *The Silent Don* historical events are described as the characters saw them happening in those days, and their understanding of and reactions to them have the vital immediacy and convincingness of participants. The historical events bearing on the Revolution and the civil war in the 1953 revised edition of the novel reek of the political propaganda of today, and the Bolshevik characters of 1917–22 now react to these events as would similar idealized Communists in Soviet fiction of 1953. A pronounced tendentious purpose very much obtrudes in this edition of *The Silent Don* and seriously compromises the artistic integrity of the novel.

However, the best features of the work remain relatively unchanged in this revision—the total picture of Cossack life, the characterization of the hero, and his love for Aksinia. One must assume that Sholokhov, as a sincere Communist, believes that all art should serve the needs of the Party, whatever they may be. But he is also a sincere artist of superb ability, and faced with this struggle between his Communist conscience and his artistic conscience, he has apparently taken the way out of sacrificing the minimum to Party demands in order to preserve the finest artistic achievements of his masterpiece.

ART AND AGRICULTURAL COLLECTIVIZATION. While he was working on the third volume of *The Silent Don*, Sholokhov turned his attention to the creation of another novel. "I wrote *Virgin Soil Upturned*," he relates, "following a hot scent, in 1930, when there were still fresh memories of the events taking place in the village and turning it upside down in a radical way: the liquidation of the kulaks as a class, collectivization everywhere, and the mass movement of the peasantry towards the kolkhoz." He finished the first volume in 1931 but, as in the case of the third volume of *The Silent Don*, he encountered difficulties in getting the work published. The editors of the magazine to which he submitted the manuscript insisted upon deleting many passages which they regarded as politically harmful. According to a recent Soviet account, which offers no documentation, the Central Committee of the Communist Party interceded on behalf of Sholokhov and

Virgin Soil Upturned appeared serially at the beginning of 1932 in the pages of the journal *New World.*

The intercession of the Central Committee, if true, would be understandable. Though *Virgin Soil Upturned* has been regarded abroad, in translation, as a remarkably objective treatment of the theme of agricultural collectivization, in reality it is subtle Soviet propaganda embodied in the compelling, artistic form of fiction. Soviet critics of Sholokhov took a much more favorable attitude toward him after the appearance of this work, which is sometimes regarded by them, incredible as it may seem, as superior to *The Silent Don. Virgin Soil Upturned* has appeared on the book lists of Soviet schools as "required reading," whereas his masterpiece has fallen under the more cautious designation of "recommended reading." Perhaps the fact that Sholokhov joined the Communist Party in 1930 had something to do with his desire to write this novel, as well as with the theme and the manner in which he handled it.

Like Leonov's *Sot* and *Skutarevsky, Virgin Soil Upturned* was written in response to the demands made upon writers to advance the cause of the First Five-Year Plan in literature. Of the novels devoted to the agricultural phase of the Plan, *Virgin Soil Upturned* is easily the most distinguished artistically. The theme, however, presented more ideological pitfalls for the unwary novelist than that other major phase of the Plan so frequently celebrated in belles-lettres—industrial reconstruction. Though not the initiator, Stalin was the architect, the theoretician, and the unyielding taskmaster of this vast effort to collectivize the peasant masses. In the class struggle that existed among the peasantry, according to Stalin, the kulaks, the wealthiest stratum, were the exploiting "bloodsuckers" of the rest and hence had to be liquidated as a class. At the bottom of the heap were the poor peasants, exploited semiproletarians, who, Stalin assumed, would flock to the cause of collectivization. The greatest task was to win over the middle peasants, the majority, whom Stalin placed "at the crossroads between capitalism and socialism," emulating the kulak on one hand and being exploited by him on the other. Stalin insisted that the collective farm was needed to secure for agriculture a technical base comparable to that of industry, and as "the principal base for remolding the peasant, for reworking his psychology in the spirit of proletarian socialism." By 1929 this far-reaching and fateful drive to transform the whole face of agricultural Russia was well under way. At first it was conducted like a military campaign with its "fronts," "brigades," and "shock troops." There was something both appropriate and sinister in Stalin's admission to Churchill years later that the struggle with the peasants during the period of agricultural collectivization was a greater undertaking than the battle of Stalingrad. In short, it was war in the countryside.

Sholokhov's contribution to winning this struggle for agricultural collectivization is all the more effective in that his novel appears to be faithful to the harsh realities of a situation which must have been frequently repeated all over the Soviet Union during this period. Life is not lacquered with a veneer of evasions. The literary artist is not subordinated to the propagandist, for here the "social command" is regarded as a Party directive and not as the inspiration to create.

Virgin Soil Upturned is the story of the struggle to set up a collective farm in the Cossack village of Gremyachy Log in 1930. The theme would appear to be an unlikely one for a novel, but Sholokhov invests it with all the excitement, tension, and anxiety which a compact rural community undergoes at a time of extreme social change. Here he is again among the familiar scenes and characters he knows to perfection. These are the same Cossack people he described in the village of Tatarsk in *The Silent Don,* only they are seven years older and Soviet rule is supreme in Gremyachy Log. And now the leading characters are Communists and the whole ideological direction of the novel is for and not against the Soviet government. Sholokhov brought to the story his own experiences as a worker in the collectivization drive in the Don region, and he tried out factual sections of the novel by reading them in manuscript to Cossack collective farmers in his neighborhood.

In January, 1930, Davidov arrived in Gremyachy Log under Party orders to organize the Cossacks into a collective farm. On the way he had given the district Party secretary, his local superior, the back of his hand in a sharp argument over policy. The secretary was too cautious, not severe enough with the kulaks; Davidov quoted a Stalin speech to support his views. Thus we learn at the outset that this stocky, thickset, gap-toothed man of about forty is a dedicated Communist, direct and fearless in his approach, and entirely devoid of political subtlety. Davidov was a sailor in the Red Fleet and after the civil war worked in the Leningrad Red Putilov Factory as a locksmith. He knows nothing of agriculture, yet this is the man the Party has sent to organize a collective farm in a remote village inhabited by freedom-loving Cossacks who for generations have lived on the soil and knew only individual farming. Davidov, in fact, is one of the famous "twenty-five thousanders," the selected body of proletarians whom the Party directed to the far-flung agricultural front for propaganda and organizing work when the drive for collectivization was going badly in 1929–30.

Davidov at once discovered that he could count immediately on only two supporters, the ex-Red partisans Makar Nagulnov, secretary of the tiny Gremyachy Party nucleus, and Andrei Razmiotnov, chairman of the village Soviet. A Gremyachy Association for joint working of the land, consisting of eighteen of the poorest farms, had been stumbling along for some time and was now at the point of complete disintegration. Davidov's rough plan was to use this loose Association as the basis for organizing Gremyachy Log into one hundred-percent collectivization.

At a meeting of the Association Davidov addressed its members. He was neither an orator nor a logician, but he understood that he was talking to simple, uneducated, poor peasants and that he must appeal to their prejudices, their needs, and even their greed. They must all join together in a collective farm, he exhorted them, socialize the land and their implements and cattle. Why must they do so? Because it was impossible to go on living as they did. The kulaks were the cause of it all and they must be deprived of their property which would then be taken over for the use of all in the collective farm. So went the argument and Sholokhov adds nothing to palliate its unreasonableness.

Sholokhov is at his best in a scene of this sort. Davidov had hardly begun his talk in the hot, smelly room before the vigorous audience began interrupting and making speeches. A cross section of the village is quickly revealed in these salty, pungent interpolations. Petty animosities, jealousies, and long-standing quarrels are aired. Shockheaded, squint-eyed Diemka Ushakov blamed Arkashka, chairman of the Association, for being a snotty-nosed trader. "You're lying like a counterrevolutionary element!" screams Arkashka in his tenor cock-crow. "Did you exchange the bull for a motorcycle without asking permission? You did!" shouted Diemka. And the huge Pavel Liubishkin caps a long speech, in which he demands tractors for the collective farm (Davidov had boldly spoken of tractors though the Soviet government had none to give at this time), by going up in front of the room, dropping his ragged trousers, exposing the terrible scars which pucker the skin on his belly and thigh, and exclaiming: "What did I get these souvenirs of Cadet hospitality for?" Widow Anisya calls at him in a shrill, indignant voice: "You shameless devil! Why don't you let your trousers drop altogether?" "And you'd like him to, wouldn't you?" Diemka squints contemptuously at her.

After many such interruptions and calls for order, Davidov manages to get all these poor peasants of the Association to agree to join a collective farm, and to agree on the dispossession of a list of village kulaks, which Davidov, with the aid of Nagulnov and Razmiotnov, thoughtfully drew up before the meeting.

The dispossession of the several kulak families is described with unsparing realism. Though only briefly portrayed, some of them, such as Damaskov, Borodin, and Lapshinov, emerge as striking individuals. Their chief offense, it appears, is their success at farming. They had abided by the government regulations and contributed their quota of grain to the state, yet they and their families are evicted from their homes with only the clothes on their backs and are ultimately packed off to Siberia. One of them, Borodin, had even been a loyal soldier in the Red Army and had built up his property only by the hardest kind of work. Though Sholokhov blackens their characters a bit by attributing unpleasant practices to them, such as hoarding, sharp bargaining, and underpaying hired labor, he does not attempt to conceal the undercurrent of sympathy among the villagers, especially the women, for the sad plight of the evicted kulaks. "He's saved and saved, and now it's out into the steppe with him," mutters one of the onlookers at the dispossession of Lapshinov.

Indeed, realism verges dangerously on counterrevolution when the Communist Razmiotnov most un-Communistically rebels against this cruel treatment of the kulak families. The curly-headed Razmiotnov, whose wife has committed suicide after being defiled by Whites because of her husband's service with the Reds, cries out to Davidov and Nagulnov after another eviction job: "I've not been trained! . . . Do you call it right? What am I, an executioner?" But the resourceful Davidov calms Razmiotnov by telling him the story of his childhood, how his father was sent to Siberia for joining a strike at a factory and his mother had been forced to sell herself on the streets to buy bread for her starving children. Through some legerdemain of logic, Davidov's suffering childhood is supposed to justify the present suffering of the kulak children. "We're clearing them out," he concludes, "so they shan't prevent our organizing a life without any of those . . . so it shan't happen again in the future."

Something of this same realism of dissent, which contributes so much to the convincingness of *Virgin Soil Upturned,* is present at the meeting of the whole village Soviet on the question of a collective farm in Gremyachy. Much doubt, hesitation, and even outright opposition against so extreme a change in their way of living is voiced from the floor by these Cossacks. The doubt is well summed up by one speaker who points out, with homely illustrations drawn from farming, that human nature cannot be changed, that some loaf and others work, and that if you throw them all into a heap in a collective farm, "you'll get such a muddle as we won't ever be able to get out of." But the meeting is swayed by a middle peasant, Kondrat Maidannikov, who, encouraged by the roaring Liubishkin's "Give it to the sons of bitches, Kondrat!" makes an impassioned plea on behalf of the collective and the new life that the Communist Party was trying to build for the people. However, out of the representatives of 217 households, only 67 raise their hands in favor of the collective farm.

Soviet critics place Maidannikov next to Davidov as the most acceptable character creation in the novel, though he is hardly on the scene long enough to convey a well-rounded image or a meaningful personality. He is the first to join the collective, is its most steadfast defender, and because of his indefatigable labor he is the first to win the title of "shock worker." From the point of view of the Soviet critic, however, Maidannikov is the perfect ideological symbol of the middle peasant with a "dual soul" who struggles manfully against his kulak tendencies and in the end finds his way to a complete acceptance of Party doctrine. Born into a life of poverty, he returned to Gremyachy after the civil war, in which he fought on the side of the Reds, and by dint of the most back-breaking labor he builds up a wretched farm above the subsistence level. Now he is faced with turning over his land, livestock, and agricultural implements to the collective. Even after he has made his painful decision the "cankerous yearning for his property" keeps him awake at night. As manager of the collective farm stables, Maidannikov understands very well why the peasants keep dropping in to see that their horses, which they no longer own, are being well tended, for he cannot resist the temptation to give his own horse sweeter, finer grass than the others. "When will you leave me, accursed yearning?" he laments to himself. Even at the end of the novel, by which time he has proved himself an exemplary collective farmer, he rejects for the time being Nagulnov's invitation to join the Party because he still has not rid himself of this longing for property: "I'm sick at heart for my bullocks, and I'm sorry for them. . . . They don't get the care they ought to get." And the literal-minded, fanatical Communist Nagulnov agrees: "If you see your own bullocks in your sleep, then you can't be in the Party." Sholokhov realized that the property instinct was the "root of all evil" among these Cossack farmers, but he did not seem to recognize it as a universal instinct which Communism would never be able to extirpate.

Organized opposition to the collective farm at Gremyachy is provided by a White Guard conspiracy which has more of the *opéra bouffe* about it than political plausibility. Yet it is supposed to be based upon an historical anti-Soviet plot in the Don region in 1930. Perhaps the rather unrealistic melodramatic impression is due to the strained effort to adapt a widespread conspiratorial movement to a purely local situ-

ation in the village of Gremyachy. Captain Polovtsiev, a
former Cossack officer who had been in hiding for years,
appears one night at the Gremyachy farmhouse of Yakov
Ostrovnov, who had been one of his devoted soldiers in the
war against Germany. A huge man, memory-haunted, with
prematurely white hair and a great rock-hewn lower jaw,
Polovtsiev is distinguished more for his passionate hatred
of everything Soviet than for resemblance to anything human. He easily signs up Ostrovnov in the Alliance for the
Emancipation of the Native Don, lives secretly in his house
undetected for months, receives mysterious visitors, and rides
out over the countryside in the dead of night on his great
black charger organizing kulaks and middle peasants for a
rebellion which he promises will come soon with the aid of
support from abroad.

Ostrovnov, however, is one of the most interesting characters in the novel, another of those villains in Soviet fiction
whose individual personalities and human qualities compensate for the unreality of the artificial heroes. The total effect
in the case of Ostrovnov was hardly intentional on Sholokhov's
part, though his creative mind has an obvious affinity for the
human personality in conflict with itself. There is a good deal
of the dualism of Gregor Melekhov in the nature of Ostrovnov,
who is similarly forced into a desperate struggle of hard
choices in the labyrinth of life.

Ostrovnov had returned to till the soil after the civil war.
He worked hard but intelligently, increasing his plantings year
by year and adding to his livestock at the urgings of Razmiotnov, head of the local Soviet, because the government needed
grain and cattle. The government requisitioned much of his
grain and often taxed him hard, but he bore it stolidly and
constantly forged ahead. It was not difficult to surpass his
neighbors, for he read scientific literature on agriculture and
put into practice what he read. The District Agricultural De-
partment praised him as a scientific farmer.

In short, Ostrovnov was ambitious. He wanted only to be let alone, to expand his holdings by hard work and thrift, and eventually to become rich. He had dreams of great future success, of even one day driving his own car! But now he was classed among the middling-to-rich peasants. If he wished to escape the designation of "kulak," which would cause him to lose all he had worked so hard to accumulate, he would have to join the collective farm and turn over to it all his substance.

Polovtsiev had arrived at a strategic moment in the crucial situation of Ostrovnov, whose quick acceptance of the conspiracy was based on something more than Polovtsiev's picture of how hopeless life in the future would be under the Soviets. Faced with the loss of all his property and the leveling process of the collective farm that would reduce him once more to the status of a poor peasant, Ostrovnov clutched at the hope that successful rebellion would enable him to fulfill his ambitious desires to amass wealth.

From this point on Ostrovnov leads a double life. He joins the collective farm and even becomes its manager at the request of Davidov, who is impressed with his reputation as a scientific farmer, but he also carries out Polovtsiev's directives to sow dissent among the peasants, to sabotage, and to play the part of an accomplice in the murder of Khoprov, a prospective informer, and his wife—a nightmarish scene of violence which Sholokhov describes in haunting detail.

It soon becomes plain that the constructive elements in Ostrovnov's nature predominate over the destructive ones. As manager of the collective farm he has larger scope than ever for his abilities as an agricultural expert and he simply cannot resist the temptation to exploit them fully. Gradually the collective farm absorbs all his efforts and his promotion of dissension lessens. Davidov and the peasants respectfully accept his innovating ideas and Ostrovnov, almost against his will, begins to take pleasure in the successes of the collective farm. As his powerful ambitions are redirected, his regrets over what appears to be the prospective failure of the conspiracy are tempered by a tranquilizing joy and satisfaction in his new work. Yet he cannot always still a sense of fear for his own future or the conviction that the hated Soviet government has deprived him of his rightful opportunity as a free man to live his own life. These mixed feelings are well reflected in a poetic passage toward the end of the novel. Ostrovnov is marking trees to be cut for a dam which he has proposed to aid the collective farm. After marking a particularly majestic oak, a painful feeling of incomprehensible anxiety and alarm seizes him and he quickly erases the mark with a sense of joyous relief: "Live and grow on!" he declares. "Show off your beauty! There are things life doesn't mean to you. No taxes for you, no self-taxation, no need to join collective farms! Live as the Lord ordained you!"

As the first non-Cossack proletarian hero Sholokhov has portrayed in a novel, Davidov merits close attention. If Sholokhov largely ignored Party nostrums in the creation of Gregor Melekhov, he was clearly not insensitive to them in Davidov. In a sense Davidov may be considered as a kind of apologia for the ideological waywardness of Gregor, and native critics have consistently held him up as an early, outstanding example of the positive Soviet hero. It is a tribute to Sholokhov's artistic talents that he was able to infuse life into a political formula, to create a Communist hero who is something more than a model of ideological rectitude.

Davidov is just as dedicated to the Party as Uvadiev in *Sot* and Kurilov in *Road to the Ocean,* but with him the sense of dedication is a living thing and not a static worship of dogma. At times he acts like a testy tar from the Baltic blundering among the cabbage patches of the Don. Sholokhov has obvious difficulties with the language of this sailor turned proletarian; he has no evocative substitute for the racy naturalness of the speech of his native Cossacks. Indeed, the character of Davidov is conveyed more through his actions and what the other characters say about him than it is by his own discourse.

If circumstances had deprived Davidov of formal education, the reading of Stalin's speeches and Party reports seemed adequate compensation to him. Andreev's report to the Rostov Party active members, he tells Razmiotnov, is "worth a dozen novels, my boy! Fact! I started to read and then forgot my grub." To be sure, he committed political errors: he illegally exiles the kulaks, socializes the village fowls in the collective farm, and he allows himsef to be deceived by Ostrovnov despite various warnings. But like a good Bolshevik, he corrects his errors and unhesitatingly follows the line of the Party. Socializing the fowls, he declares, after some study of the matter, is a left-wing deviation, a step in the direction of a commune and not of a cooperative association.

Yet Davidov is always naively puzzled by the stubborn reluctance of the majority of the middle peasants, and more so by a few of the poor peasants, to join the collective farm despite what he considered its obvious advantages. And when many in the village indulge in an orgy of slaughtering their cattle rather than turn them over to the collective farm, a practice anticipated by the Central Committee of the Party in the stern punishment it decreed against such offenses, Davidov's reaction of hurt amazement suggests his lack of knowledge of peasant psychology.

The fortitude with which Davidov faced every discouragement has become a hallmark of the Soviet positive hero in fiction. When the news reaches Gremyachy Log, in March, 1930, of Stalin's famous "Dizzy from Success" speech, in which he castigated Communist organizers who used forceful tactics to compel peasants to join collective farms, Davidov sees his own hard-won gains dissipated. The speech is represented as undermining Polovtsiev's political conspiracy in the region, for the Cossacks, now permitted to leave the collectives

if they wish to—and many do—inform Polovtsiev and Ostrovnov that they no longer regard the Soviet government as an
enemy. The obedient Communist Davidov promptly accepts
this new shift in the Party line, the consequences of which a
representative of the district committee frankly explains to
him: "Altogether, things are difficult. We've got to pay for the
distortions, brother, and someone will have to be made a
scapegoat. That's the system." In keeping with the new emphasis on persuasion, Davidov argues patiently with the
peasants who desert the farm, and he stoically, even jokingly,
endures a terrible beating from the village women who mistakenly believe that their seed grain, deposited in the granary
of the collective farm, is to be given away to a neighboring
village. Then, at a meeting of the peasants in which he mildly
reproves them for their acts of violence, he quite wins them
over by assuring them that they will not be punished. "Davidov, you're a great lad!" shouts one of the audience. "Dear
old Davidov! Because you don't bear malice in your heart
and don't remember the evil. . . . The people here are
touched." These were the first words of affection he had received during months of effort with these recalcitrant villagers, and they marked a turning point in the good fortunes
of the collective farm.

However, one cannot be sure whether this lack of vindictiveness and severity is a real trait of Davidov's nature or
merely a tactic derived from the altered Party line on collective-farm organizing, which Sholokhov is patently concerned
with justifying. At any rate, Davidov now has recourse to
persuasion and example rather than coercion in proving to
the peasants the positive virtues of agricultural collectivization. When reports come in that certain peasants are shirking
in the plowing, he goes out into the fields to lend inspiration.
Though he has never handled a plow and bullocks, he under-
takes this physically difficult task in order to stimulate a com-
petitive spirit in the brigade: "I'll die at the plow," he thinks,

"but I'll do it! I'll plow at night by the light of a lantern, but I'll plow three acres. I mustn't do less! It would be a disgrace to the whole working class." Sholokhov makes of this work in the fields a colorful scene of activity, a stirring picture of hard physical but self-satisfying labor as he expertly describes the slow rhythm of plowing, the crumbling virgin soil upturned, cut by the coulter and share, in furrow after furrow.

The characterization of Davidov takes on another dimension as we are allowed glimpses into his personal life. As a rule a Soviet positive hero has no personal life worth chronicling; the individual is supposed to be merged with the collective. Sholokhov's deviation in this respect is a humanizing factor in the portrayal of Davidov. The deviation is love, a rare emotion among Soviet positive heroes, usually perfunctorily treated when mentioned at all, a minor aberration in the hero's progress toward surpassing a work norm or organizing a collective farm or building a factory. It is possible indeed that Sholokhov, in emphasizing Davidov's weaknesses of the flesh, was deliberately trying to indicate that a positive Soviet hero was no less heroic or Communistic by virtue of being more human.

At the outset Davidov appears to be quite invulnerable to an affair of the heart. He lives with Nagulnov and Nagulnov's attractive young wife. The girlishly slender Lukeria, who has "an alluring and unclean beauty in her coal-black eyes," has already estranged her husband by carrying on with Timofei, the son of a kulak. Davidov sternly takes Nagulnov to task for permitting this: "She's discrediting you in the eyes of the masses and you say nothing"; and he threatens to raise the matter at a meeting of the Party nucleus. Nagulnov, however, finds it hard to break with Lukeria. He asks Davidov if he's married. "No," he declares, "and after seeing your family life I never shall be married to my dying day!"

Yet it is precisely this wanton Lukeria, the wife of his friend, who is secretary of the Party nucleus of Gremyachy,

with whom Davidov falls in love and whom he ultimately
thinks of marrying. The path to love is not an easy one for
him. He keeps nagging her husband to get rid of Lukeria,
and Nagulnov finally sends her packing after she disgraces
him, "in front of all the class-conscious people," in a tearful
farewell with Timofei when he is exiled with his kulak father.
Then Lukeria, who had observed the hunger in Davidov's
eyes when he looked at her supple form, coquettes with him.
She laughs when he suggests that she take a job on the collective farm, and brazenly counters by offering to be his wife.
In embarrassment he passes it all off as a jest, but as she leaves
Lukeria smilingly taunts him: "I don't need such as you. I
need a fiery love, and what have you got? Your blood's gone
rusty with work, and the heart freezes in a poor body."

Lukeria senses Davidov's weakness and continues to stalk
him. She agrees to work on the farm, calls at his office and
home, borrows propaganda reading material, and listens patiently to his endless talk on agricultural matters. In turn he
worries about possible gossip in the village, what the district
committee may think, whether he is sacrificing his work to
this personal folly. He convinces himself, however, that he
is fulfilling a Communist duty in reforming Lukeria and even
offers her the headship of the collective-farm dairy. Finally,
with her woman's intuition, she knows that the moment has
come. On a walk in the moonlight along a country road, she
places her face close to his and sweetly says: "Enough of the
grain and the collective farm! This isn't the time to talk about
them. Can you smell the scent of the young leaves on the
poplars?" Davidov's vacillation ends. When they arise, she
asks him with a smile: "I'm nice-looking, am I not?" "What do
you expect me to say?" he replies, embracing her slender
shoulders.

The transformation of this dry, exacting, consecrated Communist into the carnal lover of another Communist's wife
curiously raises his stature as a human being while it lowers

it as a positive Soviet hero. And it makes more palatable his passionate ambition: to live to see the day when machinery will do all the heavy work of man. He senses that this is a vain hope, however, and in his unmarried state he clings to still another: "But you'll die, Brother Davidov, as sure as you're alive! Instead of descendants you'll leave behind the Gremyachy collective farm. The farm will become a commune, and then, you see, they'll call it by the name of the Putilov locksmith Simion Davidov."

It is Makar Nagulnov, rather than Davidov, who represents that extreme degree of militant Communist saintliness which disfigures so many positive heroes in Soviet fiction. Since Nagulnov symbolizes left-wing deviationism in the novel, he emerges as something of a comic figure, a deliberate caricature of Bolshevik fatuity. Yet there is about him the aspect of the inspired fool, a man whose Communist virtues transcend his defects of deviation and thus suggest ultimate rehabilitation.

Long and distinguished service in the war and afterwards as a Red cavalryman, in the course of which he has been gassed, often wounded, and decorated with the Order of the Red Banner, have left the broad-chested, bandy-legged Nagulnov with a nostalgia for those romantic days of fighting and with an irritating conviction that most problems can be solved by violence. He goes about constantly with a revolver and does not hesitate to threaten with it or to beat defiant kulaks over the head with the butt of it. The slaughter of the cattle in the village enrages him to the point where he seriously proposes to Davidov that they shoot a few of the offending peasants as an example to the others: "He thinks he's killing a bullock," Nagulnov argues, "but in reality he's stabbing the world revolution in the back."

The Communist Party is Nagulnov's church and the world revolution its *mystique*. The son of a former kulak, he turned against his family with loathing, eagerly gave away his small property, and sought to identify himself completely with the working class. Obsessed by his monolithic Communist faith, he sorts all the forces of society into two eternally irreconcilable divisions—those that impede the world revolution and those that advance it. All the bourgeois, kulaks, and even the middle peasants are "reptiles" and "scum" opposing the world revolution; all workers and poor peasants he loves as soldiers of the world revolution. He ardently and impatiently aids the organization of the collective farm because he believes that agricultural collectivization will hasten the coming of world revolution. He has painfully begun to study English in the hope that when the world revolution comes he can tell English proletarians in their own language about the secret enemies of the movement whom they must shoot. Nagulnov has even come to the conclusion through his own experience with his wife Lukeria that marriage should be forbidden to Communists. He warns Razmiotnov, who longs to marry: "But now you're in the Party, you must leave all stupidities behind. After the world revolution you can die on a woman for all I care, but now you must be entirely concentrated on work for that revolution."

Of course, these extreme views and this monomania contribute comic flavor to the characterization of this knight of world revolution. But along with satire of the type, a political lesson was also intended by Sholokhov in the portrayal of Nagulnov. "Makar's head got dizzy with success," Davidov pointedly remarks after the appearance of Stalin's speech, for Nagulnov's forceful tactics on behalf of the collective clearly identify him with the left-wing deviation stigmatized by Stalin. To the consternation of Davidov and the other members of the nucleus, Nagulnov insists that Stalin's speech is wrong, that you have to knock the kulaks and middle peasants on the head if they oppose collectivization. Out of consideration for Nagulnov's past services, his illness, and his drunken state when the incident occurs, the shocked Davidov lets him off with a stern reprimand and the admonition that the Party has broken better men than he.

The district Party committee, however, is not so lenient in its search for scapegoats after Stalin's speech. Nagulnov is called up before it and in a frank scene of charge and counter-charge, illuminating this kind of official Communist delibera-tion and maneuver, he is read out of the Party for violating its line in the collective farm movement. The decision is re-flected in his deathly pallor, trembling hands, and the tears that trickle down his cheeks as he mumbles: "Where am I to go outside the Party? And why am I to go? No, I won't give up my Party card. I've given all my life. . . ." On the way home he thinks seriously of committing suicide but finally decides to work for the good of the collective farm while outside the Party.

In the end the leadership of the district committee is changed—apparently some right-wing deviationists had crept into power there—and as a result Nagulnov is taken back into the Party on the ground that his errors deserved only a repri-mand and not expulsion. In short, once he was made to see the peculiar defects of his virtues, his hallowed dedication to the Party was bound to be recognized. Such Communist faith and virtues were not expendable and they inspired this strange but interesting character to perform further deeds on behalf of his beloved Party.

The element of humor is more pervasive in this second novel than in *The Silent Don* and it imparts an abundant vitality and naturalness to a subject matter in which these qualities are not often implicit. Sholokhov combines language, incident, and character to achieve humorous effects which have the flavor of picaresque exaggeration and caricature. The humor resembles the swashbuckling variety of Fielding's fiction rather than anything in the Russian classics, though there is a touch of the early Gogol in it. Daddy Shchukar surpasses even Gregor Melekhov's orderly, Prokhor Zykov, as a figure of fun. A Cossack Munchhausen, he is laughably pathetic in his anxiety to be accepted as an equal by the village leaders, a foible accentuated not only by his incapacities but also by the sadly whimsical story he tells of the misfortunes of his early life. The superb yarn of how the gypsy cheated him in the sale of a horse and the wonderful account of his misadventure in preparing a chicken meal for the workers into which he unsuspectingly introduced frogs would not be out of place in *Lazarillo de Tormes* or *Gil Blas*. When Shchukar is off-stage there are many humorous compensations, in the speech and behavior of the peasants at the various meetings, in such minor characters as Diemid the Silent, or in such scenes as the argument between Liubishkin, Razmiotnov, and his Amazon-like mistress Marina, which loses nothing in effectiveness because of its physiological frankness. The Russians love humor and Sholokhov is a master of it, but at a time when laughter seems to have been frightened out of the pages of fiction, he has been one of the few Soviet writers with the will to introduce it into his novels in a warm-blooded, carefree spirit.

THE SECOND VOLUME OF *Virgin Soil Upturned*. The first volume of *Virgin Soil Upturned* ended with Ostrovnov's discovery that Timofei, the lover of Lukeria, has escaped from his place of exile in the far north and was in hiding near Gremyachy Log, waiting to take his revenge on those who exiled him and his kulak father. When Ostrovnov returns home after this disturbing news, he is still more upset to find Polovtsiev waiting for him, which means that the political conspiracy will be resumed. Such startling developments at the terminating point of this volume leave the reader as much concerned with what is to follow as is Ostrovnov. However, twenty-three years passed before the second volume of *Virgin Soil Upturned* began to appear in print in 1955, which perhaps establishes something of a record in the publication of a fictional sequel. So far only eight chapters have appeared, which cannot be more than a small part of what is apparently intended to be the final volume.

Some idea of the lofty position Sholokhov now occupies in Soviet literature may be gathered from the fact that the resumption of this novel was regarded as such a significant national event that these early chapters appeared at about the same time in three national publications: *Pravda, Ogonyok,* and *Oktiabr.* A parallel situation, if it could be envisaged at all, would be the simultaneous publication of, let us say, a few chapters from the beginning of a new novel by Hemingway in the New York *Times, Life,* and the *Atlantic Monthly.*

In this continuation of *Virgin Soil Upturned* one naturally searches for indications of the possible changes which time and the many important events in the Soviet Union since 1932 may have worked in the mind and art of Sholokhov. Unfortunately the sample is too limited to permit any substantial conclusions. One is surprised at the similarity to the first volume in narrative style and pattern which suggests that these opening chapters of the continuation may have been drafted only a few years at most after the first volume (as early as 1934 Sholokhov mentioned in a letter that his work on the second volume was "almost finished"). However, there is a mellowness and lightness of tone in the continuation and a greater tendency toward diffusion and digression, such as in the drawn-out concern of Nagulnov and Shchukar over the crowing roosters in the village, and in what amounts almost to interpolated short stories in the accounts of the lives of the blacksmith Shaly and of Arzhanov, a new character.

The most striking change is in the continued development of Davidov who now moves still further away from the conventional image of the stereotyped Soviet positive hero. In the first volume Davidov had only begun intimacy with Lukeria; in the continuation he is deeply in love with this woman who is essentially an enemy of Communism. He grows thin

in the pursuit, worries about her indiscreet behavior undermining his authority in the collective farm, and struggles with
his conscience in a desire to make a clean breast of it to her
husband, Nagulnov, and to marry her. What he does not
realize is that Nagulnov and the whole village are already
gossiping about the affair. In fact, Nagulnov is deeply concerned over the thought that his friend might marry Lukeria,
who, he remarks, ought to be driven out of the village to the
frozen north. "Wenches for us revolutionists, brother, are pure
opium for the people!" he characteristically declares to Razmiotnov.

Worse still, Davidov does not seem to realize that he is
being made a fool of by Lukeria, although she rarely misses
an opportunity to throw it in his face. His hesitating, worried
courting annoys her. During a feckless rendezvous on the
steppe one night she throws off her skirt and orders him to
undress—she will wear the pants and he the skirt, she scornfully indicates. In the midst of another altercation, she turns
on him: "I thought you were a real man, but you are like my
Makar: the only thing in his mind is world revolution, and
with you it is your authority. Life with the likes of you two
would bore any wench to death!"

Davidov seeks relief from Lukeria and his painful thoughts
in hard physical labor among the collective farmers in the
fields. Here he meets a charming seventeen-year-old girl, Varia
Kharlamova, who hero-worships him. Sholokhov handles this
idyl of rustic affection with sensitivity and deep insight into
the burgeoning emotion of a young girl struggling between
adulation and dawning love for a man old enough to be her
father. Davidov's vanity is flattered by Varia's attentions and
the experience focuses his thoughts on the difference between
a loose woman like Lukeria and this pure young girl, which
leads him to reflect self-pityingly again on his unmarried,
childless state.

The startling news that Nagulnov had been shot at while sitting by his window one night takes Davidov back from the fields to Gremyachy. Through Andrei Razmiotnov, Sholokhov provides a hilarious account of this incident. Hearing the shot, Razmiotnov dashes into the hut and finds Daddy Shchukar, who was staying with Nagulnov, on the floor. A pine splinter, chipped off the window frame by the bullet, has nicked the old man on the forehead. "For God's sake, Andriushka, tell me, am I alive or dead?" Shchukar demands of Razmiotnov. Nor will he be persuaded by Razmiotnov that the cut is only a superficial one. "Go, for Christ's sake," he says, "and call my old lady; I want to say farewell to her before death." And then he begins to wonder whether the bullet ought not to be preserved as a precious keepsake. Razmiotnov humorously enters into the spirit of the old man's wishful thinking, suggests that the bullet should be sent to a museum as a relic, and ceremoniously presents Shchukar with the pine splinter.

The resolution of the conspiracy elaborated in the first volume gets rapidly underway in the continuation of *Virgin Soil Upturned*. The hopelessness of the proposed uprising is foreshadowed by the growing despair and drunkenness of its would-be leader Polovtsiev and the bitter quarrels with Liatevsky, the co-conspirator he has brought with him to Ostrovnov's home. Ostrovnov himself has begun to lose faith. He is offended by the shabby way these former tsarist officers and gentlemen treat him, and he guesses that if they succeed the old regime will return with its oppression. All his dreams of future wealth and affluence seem vain. Then suddenly his worry turns into positive alarm when he learns that his aged mother, half-demented and deeply religious, has gossiped to old cronies at church that officers are staying at her house. He convinces Polovtsiev to leave, locks his mother up in her room, and slowly starves her to death. Sholokhov brings out the anguish and heartless inhumanity of this terrible scene, em-

phasizing the evil-begetting power of evil which grips the
clever Ostrovnov in his ambitious desire to get ahead in the
world of the Soviet Union.

The net closes about Ostrovnov. Davidov, in a long conversation with the blacksmith Shaly, who was only briefly
touched upon in the first volume of the novel, learns much of
Ostrovnov's shady past, of the smith's suspicions of his com-
plicity in the murder of Khoprov and his wife, and in acts
of sabotage in the collective farm. Shaly does not hesitate to
tell Davidov that by working in the fields and chasing after
Lukeria he has been deserting the real business of running the
farm and that Ostrovnov has taken advantage of this for his
own ends. Finally, he supplies Davidov with the important
information that he has seen Lukeria and the kulak's son
Timofei together in the fields, and he suggests that Timofei
was probably responsible for the shot at Nagulnov.

This continuation of *Virgin Soil Upturned* ends when Nagulnov shoots Timofei as he comes to call on Lukeria. He tells
his wife where she can find her dead lover if she cares to say
farewell to him and then orders her to leave the village forever. Nagulnov still loves Lukeria and her betrayal of him
with Timofei has been at the root of much of his misery and
strange behavior.

Final judgment on *Virgin Soil Upturned* as a work of art
must be postponed until the novel is finished. These opening
chapters of the second volume enhance, if anything, the high
quality of the first and give promise of a superb achievement
when the work is finally completed. On one level the novel is
a remarkable social document of the initial stages of perhaps
one of the most fateful experiments ever undertaken by the
Soviet government—agricultural collectivization. Official accounts, documents, and statistics of the movement seem like
an abstract painting compared to Sholokhov's Breughel-like
canvas of vivid, realistic detail and bright, living colors. The
personal anguish of dispossessed kulaks and their families, the

refusal of anxious peasants, torn by the property instinct, to surrender their land, cattle, and implements to the collective farm, the illogical and often lying reasoning of Communist organizers, the slaughtering of cattle and the hiding of grain by peasants reluctant to hand them over, the bungling and coercion of Party officials—these and many other human factors enter into Sholokhov's picture and point up the vast imperfections of the official propaganda version of the introduction of agricultural collectivization. It is clear, of course, that Sholokhov has accepted the Party's objective in his treatment of collectivization, and to this extent he is a propagandist himself. But it is equally clear that he has not allowed his belief in the wisdom of the Party to deter him from presenting a picture of the collectivization of a village which is extraordinarily faithful to the realities of those days.

In considering *Virgin Soil Upturned* as a work of art, it must be remembered that it was initially conceived in 1930 as a response to the "social command" of the First Five-Year Plan, a kind of fictional handbook on how and how not to organize a collective farm. It has nothing of the scope, the design, or the concentration on the tragic significance of universal human conflict which we find in *The Silent Don.* Yet it seems likely that the original limited theme of the birth of a collective farm at Gremyachy Log expanded as Sholokhov worked and an intended single volume lengthened into two volumes.

In any event the mature artistry which he developed in writing his masterpiece has transformed a documentary propaganda novel into a living slice of Cossack Russian life. There are no great characters such as Gregor Melekhov and Aksinia in *Virgin Soil Upturned,* but there is a group of thoroughly interesting characters, several of whom may acquire a more memorable significance if the novel is ever finished. Nor are there the varied nature descriptions of *The Silent Don* or the intimate, often symbolic, fusions of the aspects of nature with the emotions and actions of individuals, though there are enough of these qualities to provide Sholokhov's lesser novel with more than ordinary stature. However, the social pattern of Gremyachy Log and the lives of its striking personalities are as vividly and entertainingly revealed as are those in the village of Tatarsk, and this is perhaps the major artistic achievement of the novel.

In the 1953 edition of *Virgin Soil Upturned* Sholokhov has done as much violence to the original version of this novel as he did in the case of the 1953 revised edition of *The Silent Don*, and probably for the same reasons. If anything, the results are more concentrated and hence more deplorable in the shorter work, for a novel in which the initial propaganda elements were rather well assimilated and diffused throughout a narrative of genuine human interest is now transformed into what is essentially a propaganda instrument. Most of the claimed twelve hundred changes are in language and style, and many of them go far toward emasculating the naturalness and virility of the original language, thus weakening its artistic effectiveness. Most of the substantive alterations, as was true in the case of the revision of *The Silent Don*, concern the Communist characters, but since they are the major figures in *Virgin Soil Upturned* the artistic harm done to the novel is much greater. Again the main intent of the revision is to purify these characters in language and behavior, to make them conform to the devitalized and idealized Communist moral prigs in postwar Soviet literature. Free and sometimes vulgar expressions by Nagulnov and Razmiotnov about sex, marriage, and the beating of women are eliminated. Davidov's relations with Lukeria are toned down, the description of his first sexual lapse with her is omitted and a pretty passage about nightingales is substituted. In short, Davidov emerges from this wringer washed clean, drier than ever, and as a consequence much less human. It may be said of the 1953 revised edition of *Virgin Soil Upturned* that it is now,

in the eyes of the Party, more suitable reading for the school-
boys and schoolgirls of the Soviet Union, but that in the
process it has lost a large part of its original artistic appeal.
In this instance Sholokhov seems to have sacrificed too much
in adjusting his Communist conscience to his artistic conscience.*

SHOLOKHOV—A TRAGICALLY SOLITARY FIGURE. The year after
the last volume of *The Silent Don* appeared, the Nazis invaded
the Soviet Union. Like other prominent Soviet writers, Sholokhov became a war correspondent. He wrote newspaper dis-
patches and several short stories, such as the bitter and
highly effective propaganda tale, "The Science of Hate." The
news soon got around, however, that he was working on a
novel, and a few of the early chapters were printed in
Pravda (between May 5, 1943 and February 15, 1944). These
fragments are from the first volume of a trilogy on the Patriotic War, tentatively entitled "They Fought for Their Country." In an interview in May, 1950, Sholokhov announced that
the first volume was completed, but no more of it has been
published since the appearance of the chapters mentioned
above.

The few thousand words in print of this projected trilogy
suggest that in design and scope it will be as grandiose as
The Silent Don. Though Sholokhov may ultimately intend this
work to meet a frequent criticism that in his fiction he has
limited himself to the Don region and Cossack characters, it
is noticeable that these early chapters open with a German
attack on Don villages, and the leading figures are again
Cossacks. However, the plan seems to call for a concentration

* The textual changes between the earlier Russian editions of *Virgin
Soil Upturned* and the 1953 edition have been indicated in some detail
in David H. Stewart's unpublished study already mentioned: "Sholokhov
and the Soviet Critics Since 1947." Fortunately the English translation
of *Virgin Soil Upturned* is a fairly faithful rendering of the early unchanged Soviet version of the novel.

on a variety of social types, drawn from the "new Soviet men,"
which are more or less alien to the types portrayed in Sholokhov's previous fiction. Thus the center of the stage is occupied in this beginning by three soldiers who have formed one
of those familiar, close, wartime friendships: a miner, Piotra
Lopakhin; a combine operator from a machine tractor station,
Ivan Zviagintsev; and an agronomist and intellectual, Nikolai
Streltsov. Out of the conversation, thoughts, and actions of
these friends, as well as of many other characters, Sholokhov
obviously plans to reveal the comprehensive pattern of pres-
ent-day Soviet life. The war is to be the crucible in which
these new Soviet men, whose qualities and values have been
formed and hardened by years of socialist existence in the
Soviet Union, receive their final testing. The many published
Soviet war novels have nothing comparable to the natural,
uninhibited soldier's dialogue (it was promptly criticized as
too frank and vulgar), the swift, sharp limning of characters
on their first appearance, or the realistic descriptions of military action which are to be found in this small sample of
"They Fought for Their Country." It is a most promising
beginning.

For two years after the end of the war Sholokhov published
nothing. When he broke his silence it was as an anti-Western
propagandist in a series of articles which appeared mostly in
Pravda. These pieces are filled with vicious attacks on American "war-mongering," big business, and on President Truman,
who was held responsible for the Korean war and international atomic bomb agitation. There was perhaps more reason
for the singular intemperateness of these attacks than a desire
to surpass his fellow propagandists. Unlike most Soviet writers,
Sholokhov has played hardly any part in the public expression of organized propaganda. However, the searing experience which his whole country underwent during the invasion
of the Germans, in the course of which his home was destroyed and his mother killed, undoubtedly intensified his

horror at the thought that this devastating experience might soon be repeated in his native land. In the postwar climate of fear it was perhaps natural that he should have been victimized by the Soviet propaganda line of another impending struggle, and that he should have manifested his revulsion in public statements of unusual virulence.

In 1904 Gorky wrote Leonid Andreev that "the Russian writer is an amazingly solitary, tragically solitary figure." The writer's individual struggle against society in prerevolutionary Russia intensified this sense of tragic loneliness and helped to inspire, in the novel, one of the great literatures of modern times. The tragedy of the Soviet writer in a collectivist society is that he has no claim to solitude and there is nothing vital within his individual experience that he is permitted to struggle against and give expression to in creative literature.

For years Sholokhov sought the isolation of his distant dwelling on the Don. Always remote and above the battle, he has abstained, until very recently, from participating in the endless ideological controversies which for years have been a prominent feature of Soviet literary life. In one of his rare, and always brief, public references to literature (1934), he lashed out in his blunt way at the clannishness of the critics, at "their liberal lisping and their patronizing, paternal attitude toward a writer." This behavior, as well as his artistic independence, which has led him to oppose the dictation of organized Party writers, has no doubt accounted over the years for much of the hostility of official critics. They have often pointedly and shamefully ignored him and, in their editorial capacities, have interfered with the publication of his works.

It is even possible that during periods before the war, and for one period directly after it, Sholokhov may have been out of favor with the leaders of the Party. His long silences have usually been attributed to the slowness with which he writes and his insistence upon endless polishing. There can be no question that he is a scrupulously careful writer, but the facts indicate that he completed the first two volumes of *The Silent Don* and the first volume of *Virgin Soil Upturned* in a very short time. As in the cases of Fedin and Leonov, one is tempted to explain his long lapses in publishing by his hostility to harsh political events and the extreme ideological regimentation in the middle thirties and in the postwar period before Stalin's death. If there has been any dissatisfaction with him among Party officials in the past, his huge popular national and even international fame has no doubt served to protect him, in his lonely eminence at Veshenskaya, from the public and official reprimand which has been so frequently inflicted upon Soviet artists in the press.

Most of the opposition to Sholokhov has centered in the literary politicians who run the Union of Soviet Writers. After Stalin's death, when the "thaw" in the arts, as in many other aspects of Soviet life, had set in, Sholokhov appeared in Moscow to deliver a stinging speech at the Second Congress of the Union of Soviet Writers in December, 1954. He spoke scornfully of "the dull stream of colorless, mediocre literature which in recent years has been pouring from the pages of our magazines and flooding the book market," and by implication he attacked the Soviet Writers' Union as the cause of this debacle, mentioning some of its prominent leaders by name, its review sheet, and the "cliques and factions" that control it. At the Twentieth Party Congress in February, 1956, Sholokhov was the only Soviet author, apart from A. Surkov, the head of the Union of Soviet Writers, who was invited to address this important gathering. The choice seemed deliberate and indicated not only a changed attitude toward Sholokhov among the new leaders of the Party, but also approval of his contention that the Union of Soviet Writers has been a demoralizing factor in the development of Soviet literature. In a characteristic, fearless talk, speckled with his pungent humor, he made an all-out attack on the union. It was filled with

"dead souls," he declared, and "in twenty years a thousand
authors' pens have produced about ten good books." He deplored the "love of power" of the union leaders and the
tendency to regard the organization as "a military unit" and
a "disciplinary barracks." And he concluded: "The entire
work of the Union of Writers must be decisively reorganized."

It should be understood that since 1934 the Union of Soviet
Writers has been the principal arm of the Party for regiment-
ing authors and implementing the Party line in literature. It
had the power to make or break a writer. Sholokhov's objection to it was based not only on the opposition of its leadership
to him, but on the conviction that its authoritarian adminis-
trative tactics thwarted the creation of good literature and
encouraged mediocre writers. As a faithful Communist, of
course, he condemned the instrument and not the hand that
wielded it. In fact, one of the significant points he made in
his speech was that the union tended to usurp the Party's
prerogative to guide the writer politically and ideologically.
The literary laurels which Soviet authors may have achieved,
he declared, "belong not so much to those who have written
as to that which has inspired the creation of great works—
our own Communist Party." Like other Soviet authors who
have matured in this conviction and are unwilling to believe
that the truly free artist must have a choice of many inspira-
tions, Sholokhov deeply resents the familiar foreign charge
that the Party dictates art. "Capitalism," he said in an interview in 1934, "domesticates writers and makes them merce-
nary; it destroys honest literature. The bourgeois writer is
placed in such financial circumstances that attributes of individualism are nurtured in him, pushing into the background
the significance of literary art." And in his speech to the
Second Congress of the Union of Soviet Writers, he declared:
"Malicious enemies abroad say of us Soviet writers that we
write according to the dictates of the Party. Matters are somewhat different. Each of us writes according to the dictates of

his own heart, but our hearts belong to the Party and to our people whom we serve with our art."

It is also in this spirit that Sholokhov has created his fiction. In over thirty years of writing, however, he has completed only one full-length novel. If his strange failure, during all this time, to finish *Virgin Soil Upturned* and "They Fought for Their Country" is in any way connected with a struggle of the artist with his environment, Sholokhov is unlikely to affirm it. His objectivity, which Western critics always emphasize as something miraculous in a land of politically controlled literature, is simply an artist's insistence upon the reality of his material and the truthfulness to life of his characters. The conflicts in the lives and souls of these characters, however, are interpreted by a stanch Communist.

Sholokhov is not a profoundly reflective novelist. The poetry and passion of philosophical debate, so distinctive a feature of the best nineteenth-century Russian fiction, is sacrificed to the certainties of human behavior. The characters he prefers to describe are essentially uncomplicated, natural men and women. Unlike Leonov, he never attempts by symbols or images to communicate the uncommunicable monologues of the mind. His characters live in action, in the pathos of discoverable feelings. There is no Proustian or Joycean involvement in the imponderables of human nature, which sometimes deludes Western critics into dismissing Sholokhov as a mere spinner of yarns. It is true that he is a superb storyteller, a talent uncommon among Russian writers but long familiar to the practitioners of English and American fiction before the advent of the contemporary novel.

It would be naive, however, to believe that Sholokhov is preoccupied solely with the art of telling a good story, an art which none of his Soviet colleagues of the pen possesses to an equal degree. All three of his novels, finished or unfinished, are concerned with vast themes of history—war, revolution, civil war, and national social change. The characters he portrays are caught up in the irresistible ebb and flow of these powerful, released forces. For the most part these simple peasants, whom Russian authors regarded as primitive children of nature, Sholokhov reveals with extraordinary fullness —all their folkways and traditions, their backwardness and aspirations, their generosity and meanness, and often their innate nobility which finds expression in the great moments of life and death.

But as a Marxist, Sholokhov believes that every action has its alternative and that history depends on the correct choice of action. His principal protagonists are faced with these choices and their striking individualities emerge from the give and take of this mortal struggle acted out against a background of broad social and historical change. However, like another distinguished Communist writer, the German Bertold Brecht, Sholokhov combines with his Marxism a certain belief in the individual and at the same time an awareness of the inevitability of the power over him compelling irrational moral choices. Out of such situations arises a profound human sympathy for the individual who, in opposition to the victorious, progressive path of the future, elects to follow the dead-end path of the past, adding a tragic dimension which is peculiarly Soviet and one which Sholokhov develops with conviction and psychological subtlety.

At the conclusion of *A Nest of Gentlefolk,* Turgenev avoids a discussion of the future fate of his hero by lamely asking: "Who knows? Who may say?" Circumstances compel one to take this same impotent way out in pronouncing on the future artistic fate of Sholokhov. As an artist Sholokhov, like his hero Gregor, has been caught in a quandary of irrational moral choices. If the literary mayhem he has perpetrated on the 1953 revised edition of his novels is any indication, he has made his choice and thus turned his back on that degree of artistic freedom which he had formerly allowed himself. Yet one cannot accurately prophesy what changes time and events may work on the fate of the artist in the Soviet Union. Without such beneficent, emancipating changes, however, it is unlikely that this most renowned of Soviet writers will ever complete his unfinished projected trilogy, "They Fought for Their Country," at least not in the spirit of artistic freedom with which he began his great masterpiece, *The Silent Don,* more than thirty years ago.

Works Discussed and Available English Translations

FEDIN

The Wasteland (*Pustyr*), Moscow, 1923. *Contains* "Anna Timo-fevna," "A Tale of One Morning" ("Rasskaz ob odnom utre"), "The Orchard" ("Sad").

Cities and Years (*Goroda i gody*), Leningrad, 1924.

Transvaal (*Transvaal*), Moscow-Leningrad, 1927. *Contains* "Trans-vaal," "The Peasants" ("Muzhiki"), "Morning in Viazhnoe" ("Utro v Viazhnom").

The Brothers (*Bratia*), Leningrad, 1928.

The Rape of Europe (*Pokhishchenie Evropy*), 2 vols., Leningrad, 1934–35.

Arctur Sanatorium (*Sanatorii Arktur*), Moscow, 1940.

Gorky Amongst Us (*Gorkii sredi nas*), 2 vols., Moscow, 1943–44.

Early Joys (*Pervye radosti*, literally "First Joys"), Moscow, 1946. Translated by Hilda Kazanina, Moscow, Foreign Languages Publishing House, 1948.

No Ordinary Summer (*Neobyknovennoe leto*), Saratov, 1948. Translated by Margaret Wettlen, Moscow, Foreign Languages Publishing House, 1950.

LEONOV

"The End of a Petty Man" ("Konets melkogo cheloveka"), *Krasnaia nov*, No. 3 (Moscow, 1924), pp. 30–96.

The Badgers (*Barsuki*), Leningrad, 1925. Translated by Hilda Kazanina, London, Hutchison, 1947.

The Thief (*Vor*), Moscow, 1928. Translated by Hubert Butler, New York, Dial Press, 1931.

Sot (*Sot*), Moscow, 1930. Translated by Ivor Montagu and Sergei Nolbandov, London, Putnam, 1931. Republished as *Soviet River*, New York, Dial Press, 1932.

Skutarevsky (*Skutarevskii*), Moscow, 1932. Translated by Alec Brown, London, Dickson and Thompson, 1936; New York, Harcourt Brace, 1936.

Road to the Ocean (*Doroga na okean*), Moscow, 1935. Translated by Norbert Guterman, New York, L. B. Fischer, 1944.

Chariot of Wrath (*Vziatie Velikoshumska*, literally "The Taking of Velikoshumsk"), Moscow, 1944. Translated by Norbert Guterman, New York, L. B. Fischer, 1946.

Russian Forest (*Russkii les*), Moscow, 1953. Four of seventeen chapters translated by Natalia Lukoshkova, *Soviet Literature*, No. 6 (Moscow, 1954), pp. 3–135.

SHOLOKHOV

The Azure Steppe: Tales (*Lazorevaia step: Rasskazy*), Moscow, 1926. Augmented edition, Moscow, 1931. Reissued as *Tales* (*Rasskazy*), Vol. I of *Collected Works* (*Sobranie sochinenii*), Moscow, 1956. *Contains* "Wormholes" ("Chervotochina"), "The Melon-Patch Worker" ("Bakhchevnik"), "The Mortal Enemy" ("Smertnyi vrag"), "The Foal" ("Zherebyonok"), "Alien Blood" ("Chuzhaia krov"), "The Impudent Brat" ("Nakhalyonok"), "The Chairman of the Revolutionary War Council of the Republic" ("Predsedatel revvoensoveta respubliki").

The Silent Don (*Tikhii Don*), 4 vols., Moscow, 1928–40. Complete edition in one volume, Moscow, 1941. Translated by Stephen Garry as *The Silent Don* (New York, Alfred A. Knopf, 1943), incorporating *And Quiet Flows the Don* (1934) and *The Don Flows Home to the Sea* (1940).

Virgin Soil Upturned (*Podniataia tselina*), Vol. I, Moscow, 1932. Translated by Stephen Garry as *Seeds of Tomorrow*, New York, Alfred A. Knopf, 1935. Reissued as an Alblabook edition, New York, Alfred A. Knopf, 1942. Translated by Stephen Garry as *Virgin Soil Upturned*, London, Putnam, 1935. Translated by Robert Daglish as *Virgin Soil Upturned*, Moscow, Foreign Languages Publishing House, n.d.

—— Vol. II, chaps. I–VIII, *Oktiabr* (Moscow, 1955), No. 5, pp. 3–48, and No. 6, pp. 3–30. Translated by Robert Daglish in *Soviet Literature* (Moscow, 1956), No. 1, pp. 3–92.

"They Fought for Their Country" ("Oni srazhalis za rodinu"). Fragments published in *Pravda*, May 5, 1943–February 15, 1944.

Index